AMERICA'S ALL-TIME FAVORITE SONGS

OVER 200 BEST-LOVED SONGS IN ONE VOLUME

FULL PIANO ARRANGEMENTS WITH COMPLETE LYRICS AND CHORD SYMBOLS.
ILLUSTRATED WITH HUNDREDS OF WOODCUTS, ENGRAVINGS, AND DRAWINGS.

COMPILED AND EDITED BY AMY APPLEBY ★ ARRANGED BY JERALD B. STONE
WITH A FOREWORD BY JEAN RITCHIE

W9-CBT-265

AMSCO PUBLICATIONS
NEW YORK/LONDON/SYDNEY

To Bryn Edwards, who knew a good song when he heard one

Cover photograph © Lightscapes
Music engraving by Music Pen, Inc.

This book Copyright © 1991 by Amsco Publications,
A Division of Music Sales Corporation, New York, NY.

Order No. AM 80052
US International Standard Book Number: 0.8256.1230.6
UK International Standard Book Number: 0.7119.2317.5

Exclusive Distributors:
Music Sales Corporation
257 Park Avenue South, New York, NY 10010 USA
Music Sales Limited
8/9 Frith Street, London W1V 5TZ England
Music Sales Pty. Limited
120 Rothschild Street, Rosebery, Sydney, NSW 2018, Australia

Printed in the United States of America by
Vicks Lithograph and Printing Corporation

TABLE OF CONTENTS

FOREWORD

Our country's rich musical tradition is certainly one of her most valuable cultural resources. As I think of the thousands of songs I have heard and sung over the years, I find it impossible to imagine what my life would have been like without them. In my younger times in the mountains of Eastern Kentucky, singing was an essential part of everyday life. A good song could lighten the load of a tedious job—or help express an emotion or a belief as mere words never could. Songs played and sung together at twilight brought a family together after work was done—and many a courting couple moved their engagement along with a romantic or humorous ditty. Even though the time was long past when ballads brought the latest news, the stories that they told of events far in the past never ceased to touch us in special ways—and a stranger who brought with him a new song was doubly welcome. He would either sing it over and over until we learned it, or would write out a "ballit"★ of it before he left. We had very few songbooks, counted among our most prized possessions. Nowadays, it is easy to make recordings, musical films, and video; put together song collections—but songs need to be sung to be most enjoyed. This collection is made for singing!

These songs are still around us—and they provide us with a tangible link to our shared past. There are old songs here that can take you back to the lives of the early settlers' who brought their precious music with them across an ocean to a new world. Here, you will also find songs that were (and could only have been) *created* in America—the joyous, heartfelt strains of blues, jazz, and rock.

Americans have always been proud of their musical tradition—and that tradition has never been healthier. American music may be said to combine the best of the musics of many cultures—just as our way of life has been influenced by the ideas and customs of many lands. Since the earliest Colonial times, our ears have been open to new sounds, and our musicians have always been willing to try new things. Over the years, American ingenuity has blended diverse musics with many surprising results. In the Colonies, music was originally that of the settlers' homelands—but as the new country was forged, and new countries sent settlers, a new music began to develop. On the frontier, new themes emerged to fit the new situations. Out of the close association of people from diverse backgrounds grew melodies and rhythms that had never been heard before. Such typically American musical forms as square-dance music, cowboy songs, and shape-note hymns are examples of the merging of the dance, ballad, and religious traditions of different cultures. The importance of the contributions of Africans brought here as slaves cannot be overestimated, for it is this melodic, harmonic, and rhythmic influence that made possible blues, jazz, gospel, country, and rock.

These kinds of cross-influences are still going on today at such a dizzying rate that it is a thankless task to try to pigeonhole much of today's music. Nevertheless, from the gentlest forms of new acoustic music to the most "far-out" modern jazz, you can often hear strains of what has gone before.

Through it all, homemade music has been an important part of this tradition, and it is always wonderful to me that people are still able to enjoy the profoundly simple pleasure of singing together, that some of the oldest songs are still "new" and treasured today. So, sing along! Many of the songs in this volume are so common as to be known by any little child; others may be completely new to you. Still others may be vaguely or partially remembered and deserving of a fresh acquaintance. They are all gathered here for you to discover (or rediscover) as you will.

Jean Ritchie

★ Probably from the French word *billet*.

INTRODUCTION

A true song classic lives forever in the heart of the public. It is reinterpreted, performed, and enjoyed across the tide of time and style—influencing generations of songwriters, performers, and listeners. Some songs are impressive hits in their time—but the classic favorite gains popularity with the passing of years. This collection of all-time favorite songs reflects three hundred years of American popular taste. Many of these song classics have found a place in the American way of life—and provide a living link to our treasured past. Others transcend their own period—and serve to inspire an altogether new musical style. This collection pays special tribute to those songs which have influenced the evolution of American popular music—from rock, pop, jazz, and rhythm and blues—to Broadway and the silver screen. Notes on each song may be found at the back of this volume, where the reader can trace each song's origin, history, and the performers and recording artists who made it famous.

America's favorite songs are as varied as her landscapes and peoples. The many faces of the American song reflect the musics of Europe, Latin America, and Africa—the legacy of colonists, immigrants, and slaves. From this background emerged the distinctly American song forms—folk, blues, bluegrass, country, ragtime, and jazz. These songs paint a portrait of the people who made America great: her pioneers, railroad workers, gold miners, farmers, travelling musicians, hoboes, soldiers, sailors, tradesmen, homesteaders, outlaws, patriots, lovers, churchmen, and slaves. America has long been the destination and crossroads for immigrants and travellers from across the globe. As a result, this collection naturally includes songs of other nations that have found their place among America's all-time favorite songs.

It's difficult to imagine that popular music has ever had more widespread appeal than it does today. However, Americans were as fanatical about music two hundred years ago as they are now. Long before television, radio, and studio recording—popular music was an important American industry. In fact, music-making has been a national pastime since early colony days. This volume of song favorites is offered in the spirit of this continuing tradition. You'll find hours of musical enjoyment exploring this collection on your own. The songs gathered here are also sure to be welcome wherever people are singing and playing music together—be it a party, club date, square dance, jam session, campfire singalong—or a church, school, or community concert.

COLONY TIMES &
BRITISH ROOTS

In Good Old Colony Times

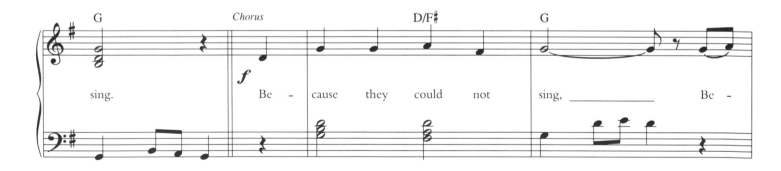

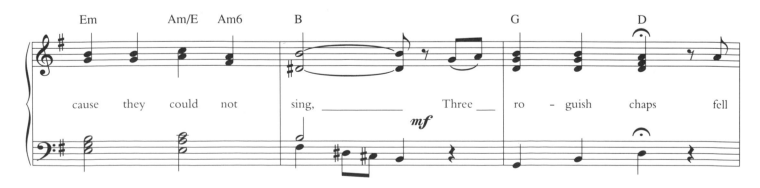

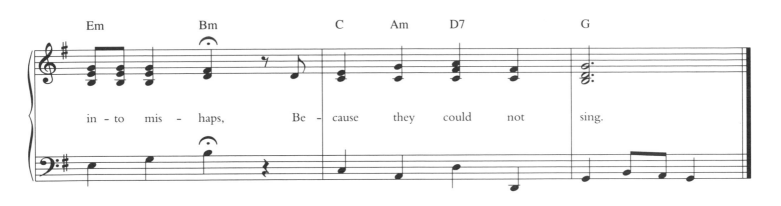

in - to   mis - haps,   Be - cause   they   could   not   sing.

2. The first he was a miller,
   And the second he was a weaver,
   And the third he was a little tailor,
   Three roguish chaps together.
      Three roguish chaps together,
      Three roguish chaps together,
      And the third he was a little tailor,
      Three roguish chaps together.

3. Now the miller he stole corn,
   And the weaver he stole yarn,
   And the little tailor he stole broadcloth,
   To keep these three rogues warm.
      To keep these three rogues warm,
      To keep these three rogues warm,
      And the little tailor he stole broadcloth,
      To keep these three rogues warm.

4. The miller got drowned in his dam,
   The weaver got hung in his yarn,
   And the devil clapped his claw on the little tailor,
   With the broadcloth under his arm.
      With the broadcloth under his arm,
      With the broadcloth under his arm,
      And the devil clapped his claw on the little tailor,
      With the broadcloth under his arm.

Yankee Doodle

Traditional

Brightly

Yan-kee Doo-dle went to town, A - rid-ing on a po - ny;

Stuck a feath - er in his cap, And called it mac - a - ro - ni.

Chorus

Yan - kee Doo - dle keep it up, Yan - kee Doo - dle dan - dy,

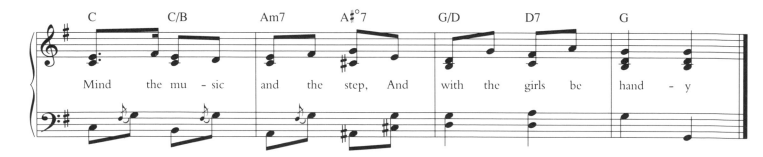

Mind the mu - sic and the step, And with the girls be hand - y

2. Father and I went down to camp,
   Along with Captain Gooding;
   There we saw the men and boys,
   As thick as hasty pudding.
   Chorus

3. And there we saw a thousand men,
   As rich as Squire David;
   And what they wasted ev'ry day,
   I wish it could be savèd.
   Chorus

4. And there was Captain Washington,
   Upon a slapping stallion,
   A-giving orders to his men;
   I guess there was a million.
   Chorus

5. But I can't tell you half I saw,
   They kept up such a smother;
   So I took my hat off, made a bow,
   And scampered home to mother.
   Chorus

Froggy Went A-Courtin'

Traditional

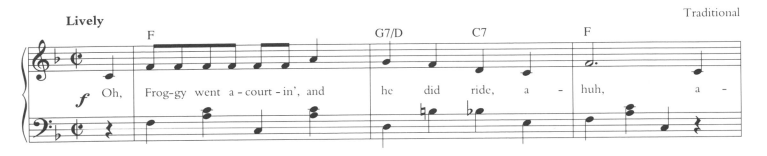

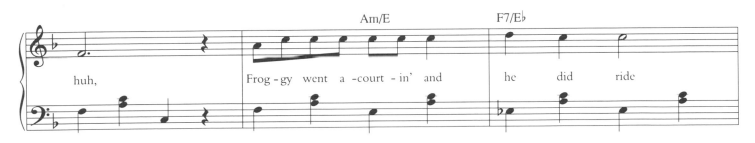

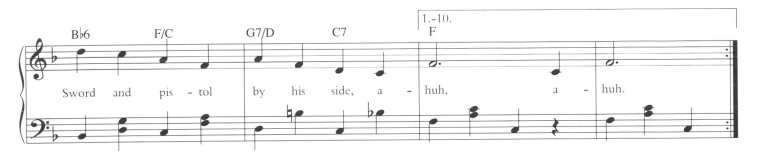

2. Well, he rode down to Miss Mouse's door, a-huh, a-huh,
   Well, he rode down to Miss Mouse's door,
   Where he had often been before, a-huh, a-huh.

3. He took Miss Mousie on his knee,*etc.*
   Said, "Miss Mousie will you marry me?"*etc.*

4. "I'll have to ask my Uncle Rat,"
   "See what he will say to that."

5. "Without my Uncle Rat's consent,"
   "I would not marry the President."

6. Well, Uncle Rat rode off to town,
   To buy his niece a wedding gown.

7. "Where will the wedding supper be?"
   "Way down yonder in a hollow tree."

8. "What will the wedding supper be?"
   "A fried mosquito and a roasted flea."

9. First to come in were two little ants,
   Fixing around to have a dance.

10. Next to come in was a bumblebee,
    Bouncing a fiddle on his knee.

11. And next to come was a big tomcat,
    He swallowed the frog and the mouse and the rat.

Greensleeves

Traditional

Mournfully

p A - las, my love, _____ you do me wrong, _____ To cast me

off so dis - cour - teous - ly; And I have loved _____

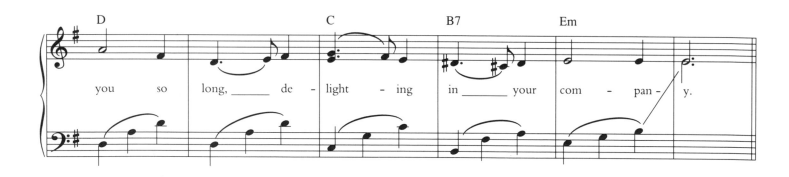

you so long, _____ de - light - ing in _____ your com - pan - y.

Chorus

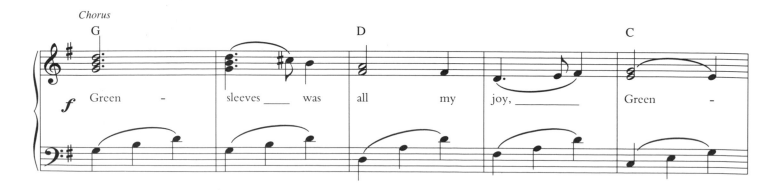

f Green - sleeves ___ was all my joy, _____ Green -

sleeves _____ was my de - light. Green - sleeves was my

mp   *f*

heart of gold _____ And who _____ but La - dy Green - sleeves

mf   *mp*

2. I have been ready at your hand,
   To grant whatever you would crave;
   I have both wagèd life and land,
   Your love and good will for to have.
   Chorus

3. I bought thee kerchiefs to thy head,
   That were wrought fine and gallantly;
   I kept thee both at board and bed,
   Which cost my purse well favour'dly.
   Chorus

4. I bought thee petticoats of the best,
   The cloth so fine as might be;
   I gave thee jewels for thy chest,
   And all this cost I spent on thee.
   Chorus

5. My men were clothèd all in green,
   And they did ever wait on thee;
   All this was gallant to be seen,
   And yet thou would'st not love me.
   Chorus

6. They set thee up, they took thee down,
   They served thee with humility;
   Thy foot might not once touch the ground,
   And yet thou would'st not love me.
   Chorus

7. Well I will pray to God on high,
   That thou my constancy may'st see;
   And that yet once before I die,
   Thou wilt vouchsafe to love me.
   Chorus

8. Greensleeves, now farewell, adieu,
   God I pray to prosper thee;
   For I am still thy lover true,
   Come once again and love me.
   Chorus

Barb'ra Allen

Traditional

Tenderly

mp In Scar-let town, where I was born, There was a fair maid dwel-lin', _____ made ev'-ry youth cry _____ "Well-a-day," Her name was Bar-b'ra Al-len. _____ bri-ar. _____

2. 'Twas in the merry month of May,
When green buds they were swellin';
Sweet William on his deathbed lay,
For love of Barb'ra Allen.

3. He sent his servant to the town,
The place where she was dwellin';
Cried, "Master bids you come to him,
If your name be Barb'ra Allen."

4. Well, slowly, slowly got she up,
And slowly went she nigh him;
But all she said as she passed his bed,
"Young man, I think you're dying."

5. She walked out in the green, green fields,
She heard his death bells knellin',
And every stroke it seemed to say,
"Hard-hearted Barb'ra Allen."

6. "Oh father, father, dig my grave,
Go dig it deep and narrow.
Sweet William died for me today;
I'll die for him tomorrow."

7. They buried her in the old churchyard,
Sweet William's grave was nigh her,
And from his heart grew a red, red rose,
And from her heart, a briar.

8. They grew and grew up the old church wall,
'Til they could grow no higher,
Until they tied a true-lovers' knot;
The red rose and the briar.

Chester

Words and Music by William Billings

Let ty - rants shake their i - ron ____ rod,

And slav - 'ry clank ___ her ____ gall - ing chains.

We fear them not, _____ we trust ___ in _____ God.

New _____ Eng - land's God _____ for - ev - er reigns.

2. The foe comes on with haughty stride,
   Our troops advance with martial noise,
   Their veterans flee before our youth,
   And gen'rals yield to beardless boys.

3. What grateful off'ring shall we bring?
   What shall we render to the Lord?
   Loud hallelujahs let us sing,
   And praise his name on ev'ry chord.

17

Danny Boy

(Londonderry Air)

Words by Frederick Edward Weatherly
Music traditional

With feeling

mp Oh Dan - ny boy, the pipes, the pipes are call - ing, From glen to

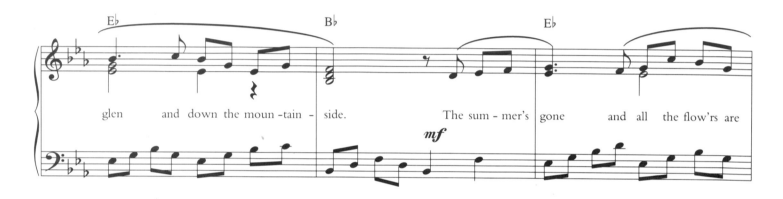

glen and down the moun - tain - side. The sum - mer's gone and all the flow'rs are

dy - ing, 'Tis you, 'tis you must go and I must bide. But come ye

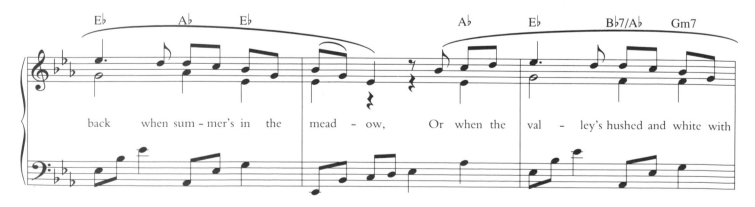

back when sum - mer's in the mead - ow, Or when the val - ley's hushed and white with

snow.   'Tis I'll be   there   in   sun-light or in   shad — ow,   Oh Dan-ny

mp

boy,   oh Dan-ny boy,   I   love   you   so. _____

rall.

2. And if you come when all the flowers are dying,
   And I am dead, as dead I well may be,
   You'll come and find the place where I am lying,
   And kneel and say an 'Ave' there for me.
   And I shall hear, though soft you tread above me,
   And all my dreams will warm and sweeter be.
   If you only tell me that you love me,
   Then I will sleep in peace until you come to me.

3. Oh Danny boy, the pipes, the pipes are calling,
   From glen to glen and down the mountainside.
   The summer's gone and all the flow'rs are dying,
   'Tis you, 'tis you must go and I must bide.
   But come ye back when summer's in the meadow,
   Or when the valley's hushed and white with snow.
   'Tis I'll be there in sunlight or in shadow,
   Oh Danny boy, oh Danny boy, I love you so.

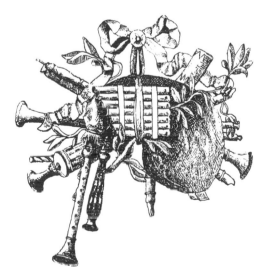

Black Is the Color of My True Love's Hair

Traditional

Tenderly

mp Black, black, black is the col - or ___ of my

true love's hair, Her lips ___ are some - thing

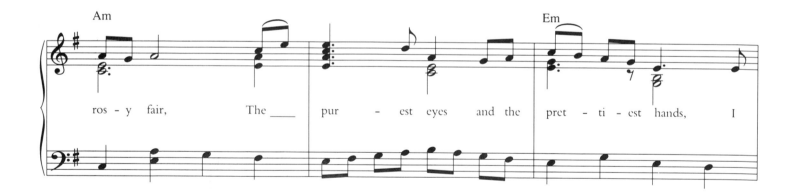

ros - y fair, The ___ pur - est eyes and the pret - ti - est hands, I

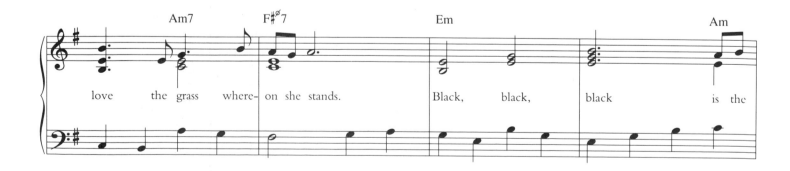

love the grass where- on she stands. Black, black, black is the

col - or ___ of my true love's hair. ___

2. Black, black, black is the color of my true love's hair,
   Her face is something truly rare.
   I know my love and well she knows,
   I love the grass whereon she goes.
   Black, black, black is the color of my true love's hair.

3. Black, black, black is the color of my true love's hair,
   Alone, my life would be so bare.
   If she on earth no more I see,
   My life would quickly fade away.
   Black, black, black is the color of my true love's hair.

Comin' Thro' the Rye

Words by Robert Burns
Music traditional

Liltingly

mf If a bod-y meet a bod-y, Com-in' thro' the rye;

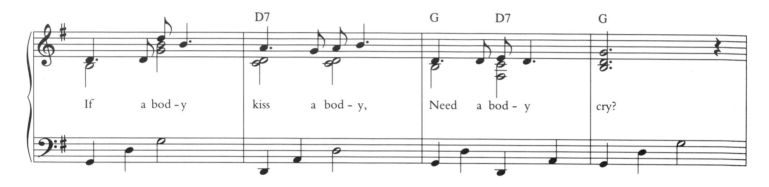

If a bod-y kiss a bod-y, Need a bod-y cry?

f Ev-'ry las-sie has her lad-die, None, they say have I; Yet

mf all the lads they smile on me, When com-in' thro' the rye.

Stewball

Traditional

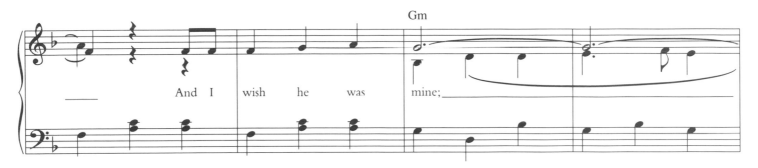

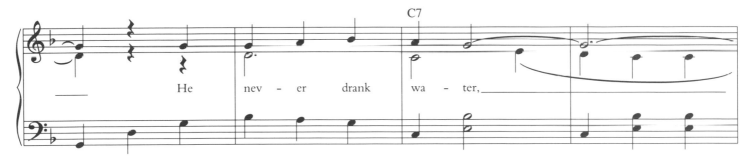

2. So come all of you gamblers,
   From near and from far,
   Don't bet your gold dollar
   On that little gray mare.

3. Most likely she'll stumble,
   Most likely she'll fall,
   But you never will lose, boys,
   On my noble Stewball.

4. As they were a-riding,
   About halfway 'round,
   That gray mare, she stumbled,
   And fell to the ground.

5. And away out yonder,
   Ahead of them all,
   Come a-dancing and a-prancing,
   My noble Stewball.

6. Oh, Stewball was a good horse,
   And he held a high head,
   And the mane on his foretop
   Was as fine as silk thread.

7. I rode him in England,
   And I rode him in Spain,
   And I never did lose, boys,
   I always did gain.

The Foggy, Foggy Dew

Traditional

Wistfully

mf When I was a bach – 'lor and lived all a – lone, I

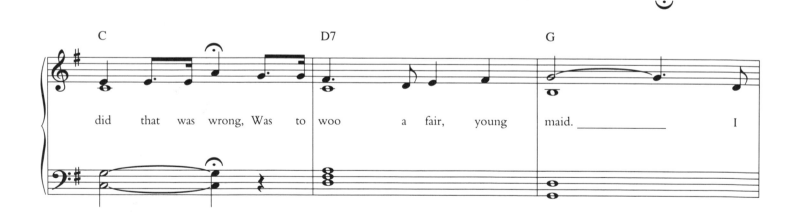

worked at the weav – er's trade; _____ And the on – ly, on – ly thing I

did that was wrong, Was to woo a fair, young maid. _____ I

wooed ____ her in the win – ter – time, _____ And part ____ of sum-mer

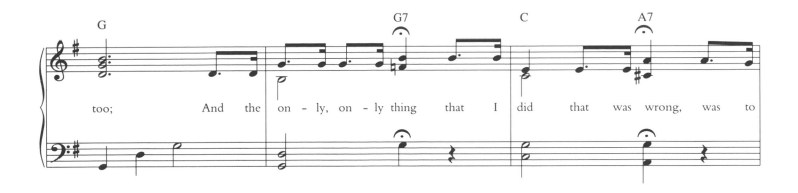

too;   And the on - ly, on - ly thing that I did that was wrong, was to

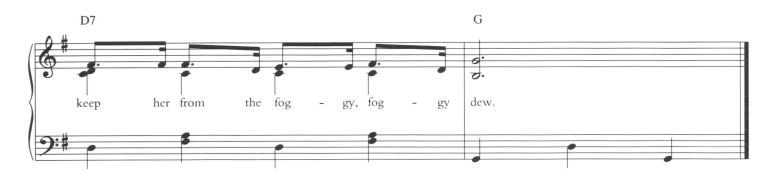

keep her from the fog - gy, fog - gy dew.

2. One night she knelt close by my side,
When I was fast asleep,
She threw her arms around my neck,
And then began to weep.
She wept, she cried, she tore her hair.
Ah me, what could I do?
So all night long I held her in my arms,
Just to keep her from the foggy, foggy dew.

3. Again I'm a bach'lor, I live with my son,
We work at the weaver's trade;
And ev'ry single time I look into his eyes,
He reminds me of the fair, young maid.
He reminds me of the wintertime,
And of the summer too,
And the many, many times that I held her in my arms,
Just to keep her from the foggy, foggy dew.

Sweet Molly Malone

Traditional

Moderately

In Dub-lin's fair cit-y, where girls are so pret-ty, I

first set my eyes on sweet Mol-ly Ma-lone, As she

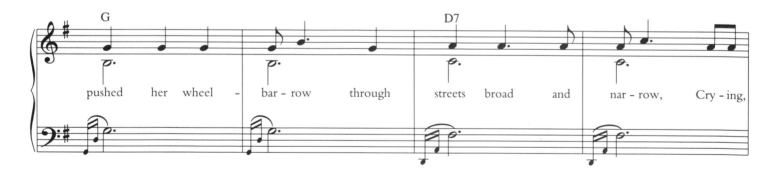

pushed her wheel-bar-row through streets broad and nar-row, Cry-ing,

"Cock-les and mus-sels, a-live, a-live-o!

A - live, a - live - o! ___ a - live, a - live - o!" ___ Cry - ing,

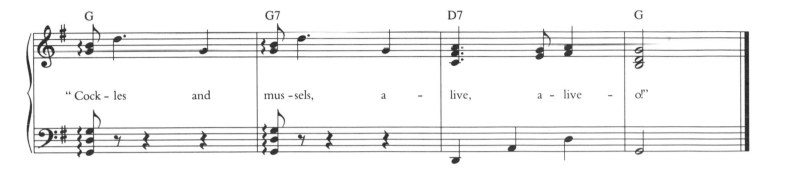

"Cock - les and mus - sels, a - live, a - live - o!"

2. She was a fishmonger, but sure 'twas no wonder,
   For so were her father and mother before,
   And they pushed their wheelbarrow,
   Through streets broad and narrow,
   Crying, "Cockles and mussels, alive, alive-o!"
   Chorus

3. She died of a fever, and no one could save her,
   And that was the end of sweet Molly Malone;
   Her ghost wheels her barrow,
   Through streets broad and narrow,
   Crying, "Cockles and mussels, alive, alive-o!"
   Chorus

Drink to Me Only With Thine Eyes

Words by Ben Jonson
Music traditional

With tenderness

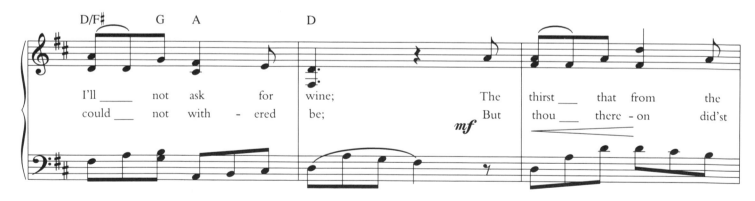

But might I of Jove's nec - tar sip, _____ I
Since when it of grows and smells, _____ I swear, _____ Not

would _____ not change for thine. _____
of _____ it - self, but thee. _____

ON THE WILD FRONTIER

Home on the Range

Traditional

Moderately

Oh, give me a home where the buf - fa - lo roam, Where the

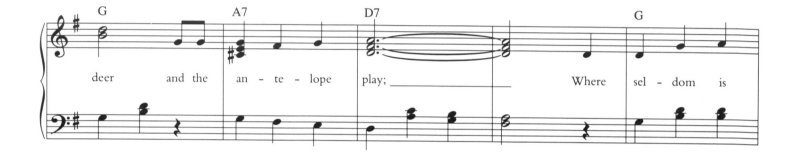

deer and the an - te - lope play; Where sel - dom is

heard a dis - cour - ag - ing word, And the skies are not cloud - y all

day. Home, home on the range,

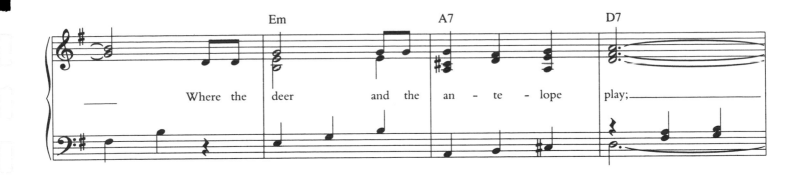

Where the deer and the an - te - lope play;

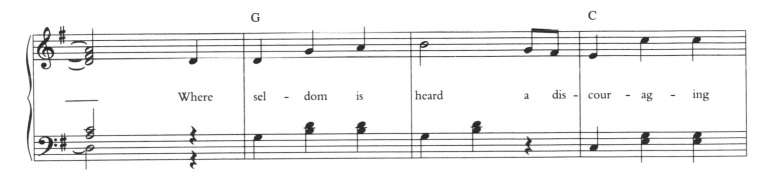

Where sel - dom is heard a dis - cour - ag - ing

word, And the skies are not cloud - y all day.

2. Oh, give me a land where the bright diamond sand,
Flows leisurely down the stream;
Where the graceful, white swan goes gliding along,
Like a maid in a heavenly dream.
Chorus

3. Where the air is so pure and the zephyrs so free,
The breezes so balmy and bright;
That I would not exchange my home on the range,
For all of the cities so bright.
Chorus

4. How often at night when the heavens are bright,
With the light of the glittering stars,
Have I stood there amazed and asked as I gazed,
If their glory exceeds that of ours.
Chorus

Sweet Betsy From Pike

Traditional

Lively

Oh, do you re - mem - ber sweet Bet - sy from Pike, Who

crossed the wide prai - rie with her lov - er Ike? With

two yoke of ox - en, a big yel - low dog, A ____

tall Shang - hai roost - er, and one spot - ted hog.

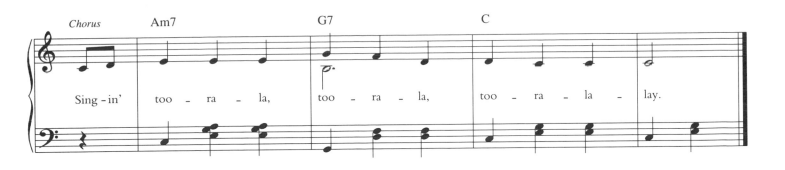

Chorus   Am7   G7   C

Sing - in' too – ra – la, too – ra – la, too – ra – la – lay.

2. One evening quite early they camped on the Platte,
   'Twas near by the road on a green shady flat,
   Where Betsy, sore-footed, lay down to repose,
   With wonder Ike gazed on that Pike County Rose.
   Chorus

3. The wagon broke down with a terrible crash,
   And out on the prairie rolled all kinds of trash;
   A few little baby clothes done up with care,
   'Twas rather suspicious, but all on the square.
   Chorus

4. The Shanghai ran off and their cattle all died,
   That morning the last piece of bacon was fried;
   Poor Ike was discouraged and Betsy got mad,
   The dog drooped his tail and looked wondrously sad.
   Chorus

5. They soon reached the desert, where Betsy gave out,
   And down in the sand she lay rolling about;
   While Ike, half distracted, looked on with surprise,
   Saying, "Betsy, get up, you'll get sand in your eyes."
   Chorus

6. Sweet Betsy got up in a great deal of pain,
   Declared she'd go back to Pike County again;
   But Ike gave a sigh, and they fondly embraced,
   And they travedled along with his arm 'round her waist.
   Chorus

7. They swam the wide rivers and crossed the tall peaks,
   And camped on the prairie for weeks upon weeks,
   Starvation and cholera and hard work and slaughter,
   They reached California spite of hell and high water.
   Chorus

8. Long Ike and sweet Betsy attended a dance,
   Where Ike wore a pair of his Pike County pants;
   Sweet Betsy was covered with ribbons and rings,
   Said Ike, "You're an angel, but where are your wings?"
   Chorus

9. A miner said, "Betsy, will you dance with me?"
   "I will that, old hoss, if you don't make too free,
   But don't dance me hard, do you want to know why?
   Doggone you, I'm chock-full of strong alkali."
   Chorus

10. The Pike County couple got married of course,
    But Ike became jealous, obtained a divorce;
    Sweet Betsy, well satisfied, said with a shout,
    "Good-bye, you big lummox, I'm glad you've backed out."
    Chorus

I Ride an Old Paint

Traditional

Moderately

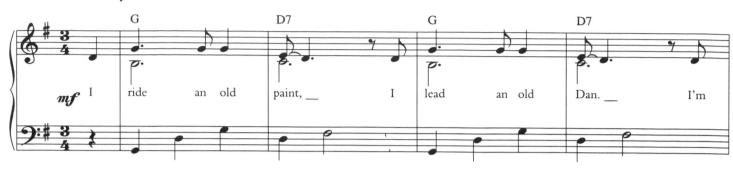

I ride an old paint, __ I lead an old Dan. __ I'm

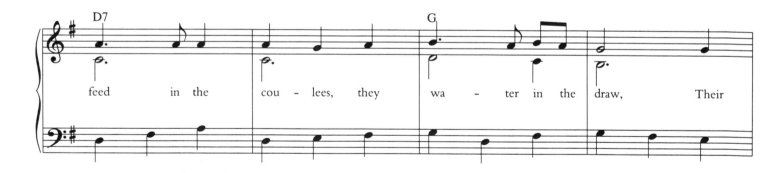

goin' to Mon - tan' just to throw the hool - i - han, They

feed in the cou - lees, they wa - ter in the draw, Their

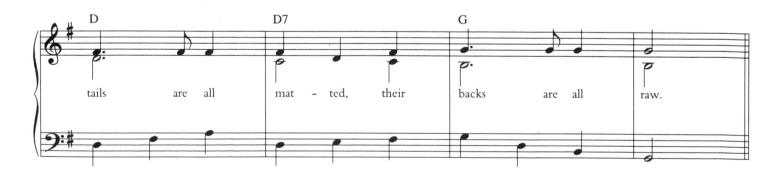

tails are all mat - ted, their backs are all raw.

Ride a - round lit - tle dog - gies, Ride a - round _____ them ___ slow, For the

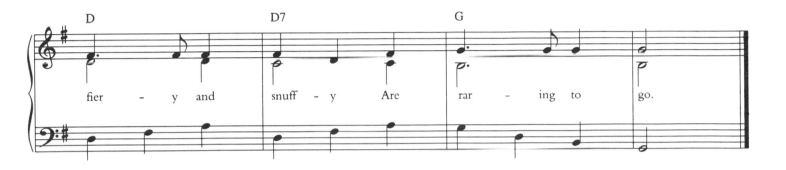

fier - y and snuff - y Are rar - ing to go.

2. Bill Jones had a daughter, Bill Jones had a son,
   The son went to college, the daughter went wrong,
   His wife she got killed in a poolroom fight,
   And still he keeps singing from morning till night.
   Chorus

3. Oh, when I die take my saddle from the wall,
   And put it on my pony, lead him out of his stall,
   Tie my bones to his back, turn our faces to the west,
   And we'll ride the prairie that we love the best.
   Chorus

I've Been Working on the Railroad

Vigorously

Traditional

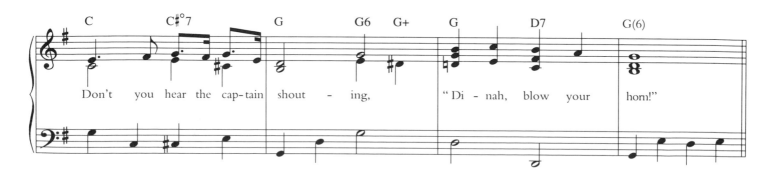

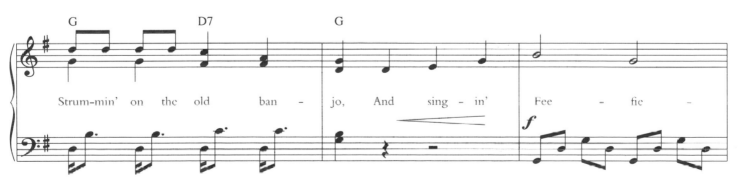

39

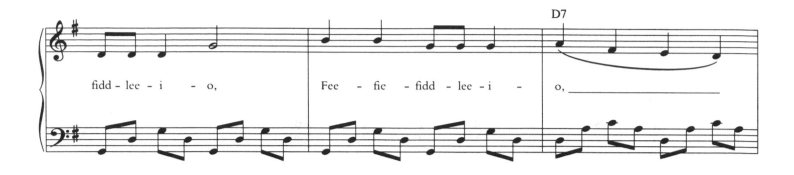

fidd – lee – i – o, Fee – fie – fidd – lee – i – o, _____

a tempo

G   G7   C   C#°7   G/D   D7   G

Fee – fie – fidd – lee – i – o, Strum-min' on the old ban – jo.

rit.

John Henry

With a driving beat

Traditional

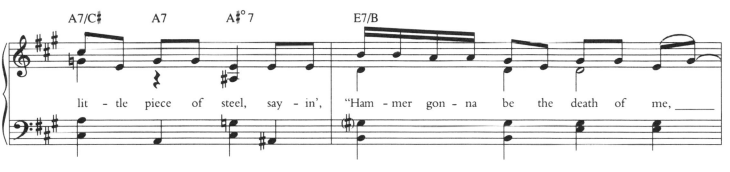

2. The captain said to John Henry,
   "I'm gonna bring that steam drill around,
   I'm gonna bring that steam drill out on the job,
   I'm gonna whup that steel on down, Lord, Lord,
   I'm gonna whup that steel on down."

3. John Henry said to his captain,
   "I know a man ain't nothing but a man,
   But before I'd let your steam drill beat me down,
   I'd die with a hammer in my hand, Lord, Lord,
   I'd die with a hammer in my hand."

4. Now John Henry said to his shaker,
   "Shaker, why don't you sing?
   Because I'm throwin' forty pounds from my hip on down,
   Listen to that cold steel ring, Lord, Lord,
   Listen to that cold steel ring."

5. Now the captain said to John Henry,
   "I believe that mountain's caving in."
   John Henry said right back to the captain,
   "Ain't nothing but my hammer sucking wind, Lord, Lord,
   Ain't nothing but my hammer sucking wind."

6. Now the man that invented the steam drill,
   He thought he was mighty fine,
   But John Henry drove fifteen feet,
   The steam drill only made nine, Lord, Lord,
   The steam drill only made nine.

7. John Henry hammered in the mountains,
   His hammer was a-strikin' fire,
   But he worked so hard, it broke his poor heart,
   And he laid down his hammer and he died, Lord, Lord,
   He laid down his hammer and he died.

The Streets of Laredo

Traditional

Sadly

Introduction

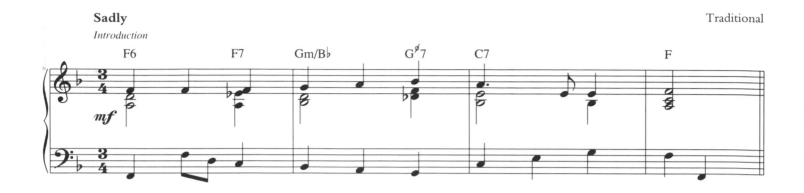

As I _____ walked out in the streets of La -

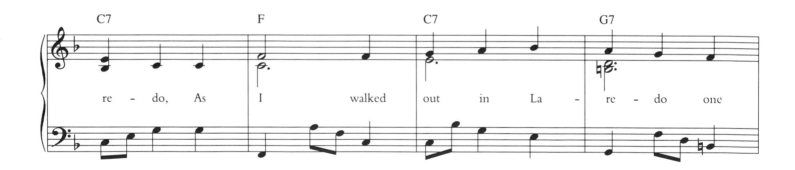

re - do, As I walked out in La - re - do one

day, I spied a poor cow - boy all wrapped in white

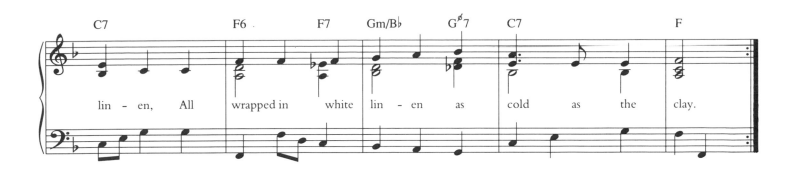

lin - en, All wrapped in white lin - en as cold as the clay.

2. "I see by your outfit that you are a cowboy,"
   These words he did say as I calmly went by,
   "Come sit down beside me and hear my sad story,
   I'm shot in the breast and I know I must die."

3. "'Twas once in the saddle I used to go dashing,
   With no one as quick on the trigger as I.
   I sat in a card game in back of the barroom,
   Got shot in the back and today I must die."

4. "Get six of my buddies to carry my coffin,
   Six pretty maidens to sing a sad song.
   Take me to the valley and lay the sod o'er me,
   For I'm a young cowboy who knows he's done wrong."

5. "Oh, beat the drum slowly and play the fife lowly,
   And play the dead march as they carry my pall.
   Put bunches of roses all over my coffin,
   The roses will deaden the clods as they fall."

6. "Go fetch me a cup, just a cup of cold water,
   To cool my parched lips," the cowboy then said.
   Before I returned, his brave spirit had left him,
   And, gone to his Maker, the cowboy was dead.

7. We beat the drum slowly and played the fife lowly,
   And bitterly wept as we carried him along,
   For we all loved our comrade, so brave, young, and handsome,
   We all loved our comrade although he done wrong.

Jesse James

Words and music by Billy Gashade

With a steady beat

Jes - se James was a lad who ___

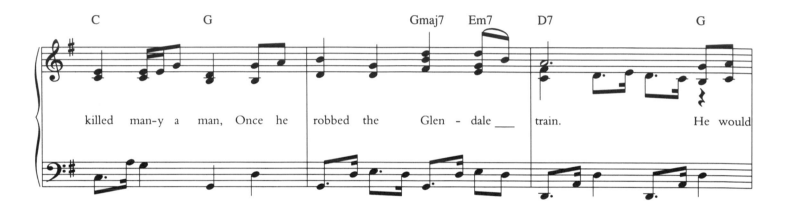

killed man-y a man, Once he robbed the Glen - dale ___ train. He would

steal from the rich, he would give to the poor, Had a hand and a heart and a

brain. ___ Poor Jes - se had a wife to ___ mourn for his life, Three

chil - dren, they were brave. _____ But the dirt -y lit - tle cow-ard ___ who

shot Jim-my How-ard ____ Has laid poor Jes - se in his grave. _____

2. Jesse James was a friend, and helped ev'ryone out,
   With the loot he stole from the bank,
   When a robbery occurred, no one had a doubt,
   It was he and his dear brother, Frank.
   Then, one day, Robert Ford, for the sake of a reward,
   His word to the Governor gave.
   Oh, the dirty little coward who shot Jimmy Howard,
   Has laid poor Jesse in his grave.

3. Jesse James took a name, "Jimmy Howard," and flew
   To where he wasn't known.
   But his friend, Robert Ford, neither faithful or true,
   Turned against him and caught him alone.
   Poor Jesse, he was mourned, and his killer was scorned,
   How can friendship so behave?
   Oh, the dirty little coward who shot Jimmy Howard,
   Has laid poor Jesse in his grave.

4. Jesse went to his rest with his hand on his breast,
   The devil will be upon his knee.
   He was born one day in the county of Clay,
   And came from a solitary race.
   This song was made by Billy Gashade,
   As soon as the news did arrive.
   He said there was no man with the law in his hand,
   Who could take Jesse James when alive.

The Banks of the Ohio

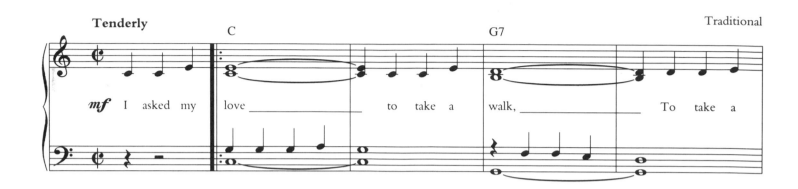

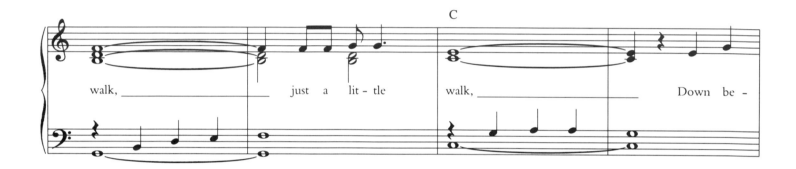

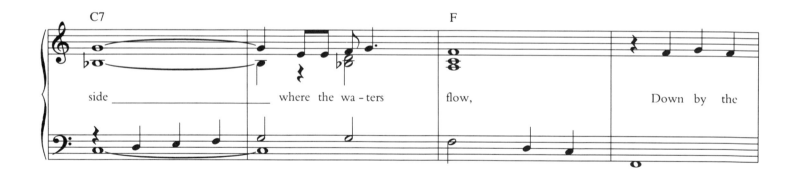

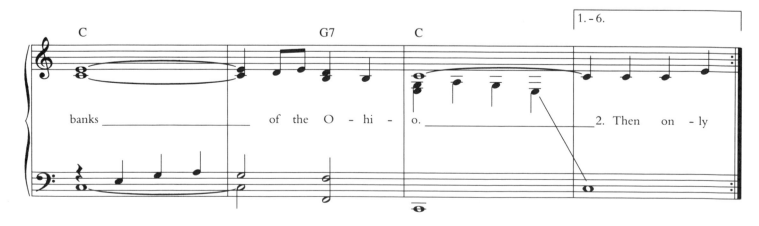

Down by the banks ___ of the O - hi - o. ___

2. Then only say that you'll be mine,
   And in no other arms entwine,
   Down beside where the waters flow,
   Down by the banks of the Ohio.

3. Said I to her, "Will you be mine?"
   Said she to me, "I must decline,
   My mother says, too young am I,
   To love one man till the day I die."

4. I held a knife against her breast,
   And gently in my arms she pressed,
   Crying, "Willie, don't you murder me,
   I'm unprepared for eternity."

5. I took her by her lily-white hand,
   And placed her gently on the sand,
   And when the tide was wide and deep,
   I pitched her in to rest in sleep.

6. I started back twixt twelve and one,
   I cried, "My God, what have I done?
   I've murdered the only woman I love,
   Because she would not be my bride."

7. Had she but said she will be mine,
   All would be well, all would be fine,
   And now she's there, way down below,
   Down by the banks of the Ohio.

Note: The second verse may be used as a chorus.

The Yellow Rose of Texas

Traditional

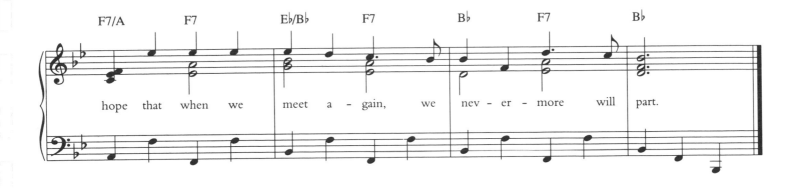

hope that when we meet a – gain, we nev – er – more will part.

2. She's the sweetest rose of color a fellow ever knew,
   Her eyes are bright as diamonds, they sparkle like the dew.
   You may talk about your dearest May, and sing of Rosa Lee,
   But the yellow rose of Texas beats the belles of Tennessee.

3. Down beside the Rio Grande, the stars were shining bright,
   We walked along together one quiet summer night.
   I hope that she remembers how we parted long ago,
   I'll keep my promise to return, and never let her go.

Drill, Ye Tarriers, Drill

With a marked tempo

Traditional

work all day for sug-ar in your tay, Down be -hind the

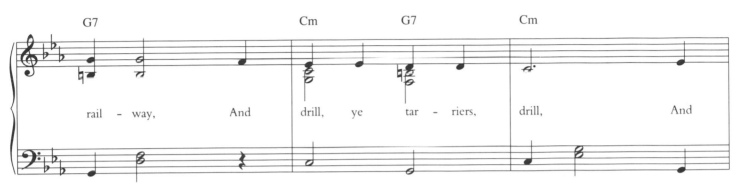

rail - way, And drill, ye tar - riers, drill, And

blast and fire! _____

2. Now our new foreman was Jim McGann,
   By golly, he was a blame mean man;
   Last week a premature blast went off,
   And a mile in the sky went Big Jim Goff.
   Chorus

3. Well, when next payday comes around,
   Jim Goff a dollar short was found;
   When asked the reason, came this reply,
   "You were docked for the time you were up in the sky."
   Chorus

4. Now, the boss was a fine man down to the ground,
   And he married a lady six feet round;
   She baked good bread and she baked it well,
   But she baked it hard as the holes in hell.
   Chorus

Bury Me Not on the Lone Prairie

Traditional

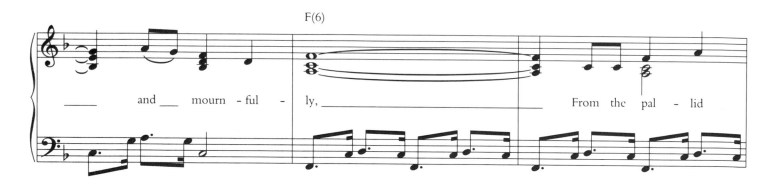

lay, _____ On his dy - ing bed _____

_____ at the close of day. _____

2. "Oh, bury me not on the lone prairie,
   Where the wild coyotes will howl o'er me,
   In a narrow grave just six by three.
   Oh, bury me not on the lone prairie."

3. "It matters not, I've oft been told,
   Where the body lies when the heart grows cold.
   Yet grant, oh grant, this wish to me:
   Oh, bury me not on the lone prairie."

4. "I've always wished to be laid when I died,
   In a little churchyard on the green hillside;
   By my father's grave, there let mine be,
   And bury me not on the lone prairie."

5. "Let my slumber be where my mother's prayer,
   And a sister's tear will mingle there;
   Where my friends can come and weep o'er me.
   Oh, bury me not on the lone prairie."

6. "Oh, bury me not"—and his voice failed there,
   But we took no heed of his dying prayer.
   In a narrow grave just six by three,
   We buried him on the lone prairie.

7. And the cowboys now as they roam the plain,
   (For they marked the spot where his bones were lain)
   Fling a handful of roses o'er the grave,
   With a prayer to Him who his soul will save.

8. "Oh, bury me not on the lone prairie,
   Where the wolves can howl and growl o'er me.
   Fling a handful of roses o'er my grave,
   With a prayer to Him who my soul will save."

Note. The second verse may be used as a chorus.

Casey Jones

Rhythmically

Traditional

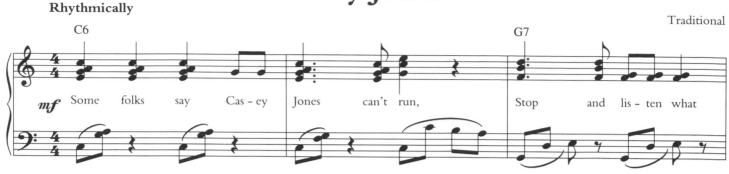

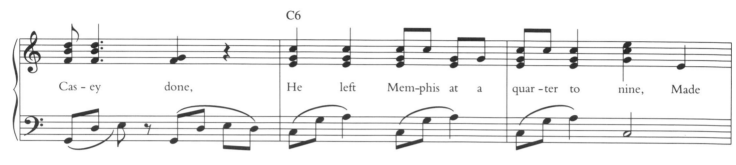

2. Casey Jones, before he died,
   Fixed the blinds so the bums couldn't ride.
   "If they ride, gotta ride the rod,
   And trust their life in the hands of God."
   In the hands of God, the hands of God,
   Trust their life in the hands of God.

3. There was a woman named Alice Fly,
   Said, "I'm gonna ride with Mr. Casey or die,
   I ain't good lookin' but I take my time,
   I'm a ramblin' woman with a ramblin' mind."
   With a ramblin' mind, *etc.*

4. Early one mornin', 'bout four o'clock,
   Told his fireman, "Get the boiler hot,
   All I need's a little water and coal,
   Look out my window, see the drivers roll."
   See the drivers roll,

5. He looked at his watch and his watch was slow,
   He looked at the water and the water was low,
   But the people all knew by the engine's moan,
   That the man at the throttle was Casey Jones.
   Was Casey Jones,

6. When he come within a mile of the place,
   Old Number Four stared him right in the face.
   Told his fireman, "Just keep your seat and ride,
   It's a double-track road, running side by side."
   Runnin' side by side,

7. You ought to have been there to see the sight,
   Screamin' an cryin', both colored and white,
   And I was a witness for the fact,
   They flagged Mr. Casey, but he never looked back.
   But he never looked back,

WAY DOWN SOUTH

Dixie

Words and music by Daniel Decatur Emmett

With spirit

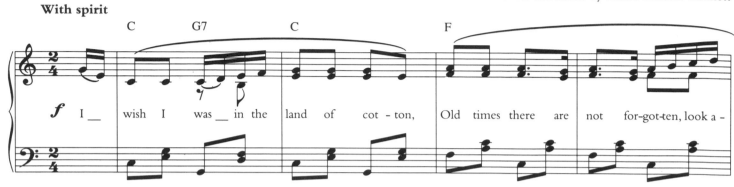

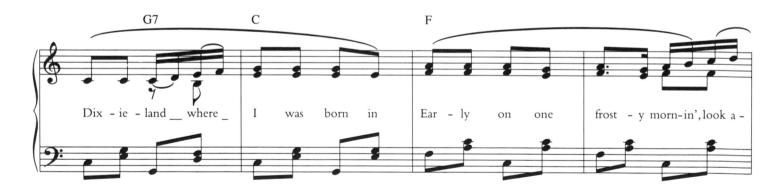

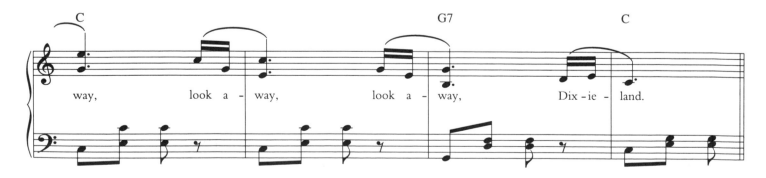

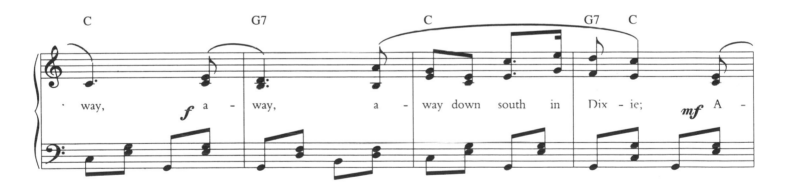

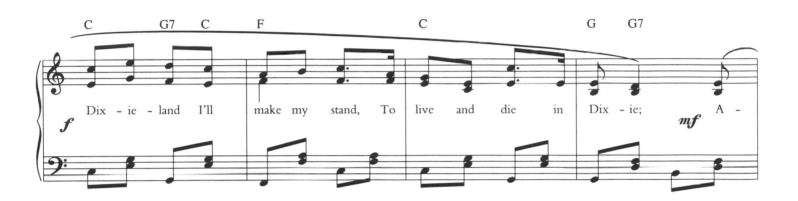

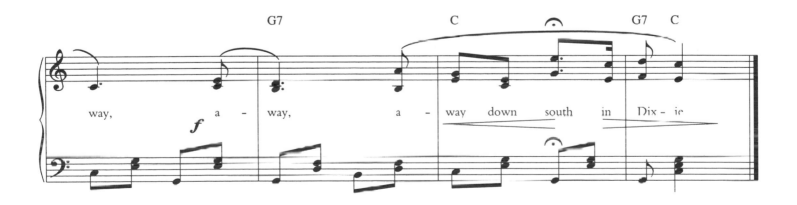

Old Folks at Home

Words and music by Stephen Foster

With feeling

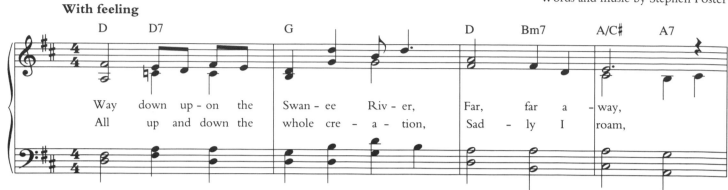

Way down up-on the Swan-ee Riv-er, Far, far a-way,
All up and down the whole cre-a-tion, Sad-ly I roam,

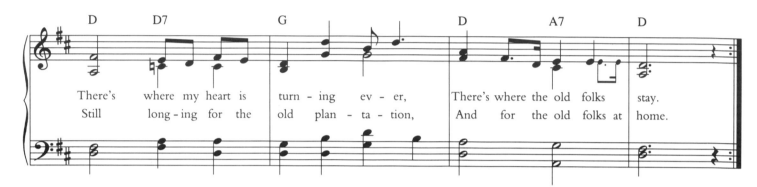

There's where my heart is turn-ing ev-er, There's where the old folks stay.
Still long-ing for the old plan-ta-tion, And for the old folks at home.

Chorus

All the world is sad and drear-y, Ev-'ry-where I roam.

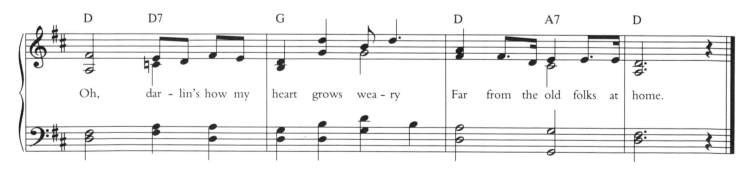

Oh, dar-lin's how my heart grows wea-ry Far from the old folks at home.

2. All 'round the little farm I wandered,
   When I was young,
   Then many happy days I squandered,
   Many the songs I sung.
   When I was playing with my brother,
   Happy was I.
   Oh! take me to my kind old mother,
   There let me live and die.
   Chorus

3. One little hut among the bushes,
   One that I love,
   Still sadly to my mem'ry rushes,
   No matter where I rove.
   When will I see the bees a-humming,
   All 'round the comb?
   When will I hear the banjo strumming,
   Down in my good old home?
   Chorus

The Blue Tail Fly

Traditional

2. And when he'd ride in the afternoon,
   I'd follow with a hickory broom;
   The pony being rather shy,
   When bitten by a blue tail fly.
   Chorus

3. One day he rode around the farm,
   The flies so numerous they did swarm;
   One chanced to bite him on the thigh,
   The devil take the blue tail fly.
   Chorus

4. The pony run, he jump, he pitch,
   He threw my master in the ditch;
   He died and the jury wondered why,
   The verdict was the blue tail fly.
   Chorus

5. They lay him under a 'simmon tree,
   His epitaph is there to see:
   "Beneath this stone I'm forced to lie,
   The victim of the blue tail fly."
   Chorus

Carry Me Back to Old Virginny

Words and music by James A. Bland

Longingly

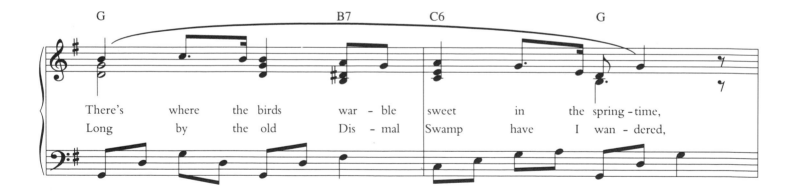

1. Car - ry me back to old Vir - gin - ny,
2. Car - ry me back to old Vir - gin - ny,

There's where the cot - ton and the corn and ta - ters grow;
There let me live till I with - er and de - cay.

There's where the birds war - ble sweet in the spring - time,
Long by the old Dis - mal Swamp have I wan - dered,

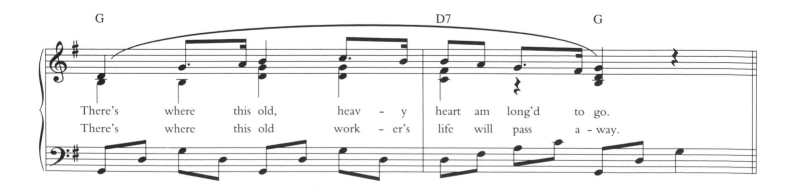

There's where this old, heav - y heart am long'd to go.
There's where this old work - er's life will pass a - way.

There's where I la-bored so hard for old mas-ter,
Mas-ter and Mis-sus have long gone be-fore me.

Day af-ter day in the field of yel-low corn.
Soon we will meet on that bright and gold-en shore.

No place on earth do I love more sin-cere-ly,
There we'll be hap-py and free from all sor-row;

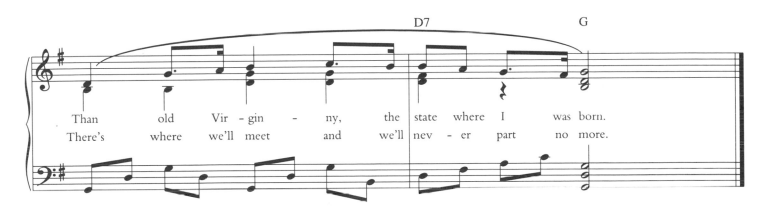

Than old Vir-gin-ny, the state where I was born.
There's where we'll meet and we'll nev-er part no more.

Turkey in the Straw

Traditional

Turkey in the hay, turkey in the straw, Roll 'em up, twist 'em up,

High tuck-a-haw, And ___ hit 'em up a tune ___ called ___ "Tur-key in the Straw."

2. Oh, I went out to milk and I didn't know how,
   I milked the goat instead of the cow.
   A monkey sittin' on a pile of straw,
   A-winkin' at his mother-in-law.
   Chorus

3. Well, I met Mister Catfish comin' downstream,
   Says Mister Catfish, "What do you mean?"
   I caught Mister Catfish by the snout,
   And turned that catfish wrong side out.
   Chorus

4. Then I came to the river and I couldn't get across,
   So, I paid five dollars for an old blind horse,
   Well, he wouldn't go ahead and he wouldn't stand still,
   So, he went up and down like an old saw mill.
   Chorus

5. As I came down the new cut road,
   I met Mister Bullfrog, I met Miss Toad,
   And every time Miss Toad would sing,
   Ole bullfrog cut a pigeon wing.
   Chorus

6. Oh, I jumped in the seat, and I gave a little yell,
   The horses run away, broke the wagon all to hell.
   Sugar in the gourd and honey in the horn,
   I never was so happy since the hour I was born.
   Chorus

Oh, Susanna

Words and music by Stephen Foster

Lively

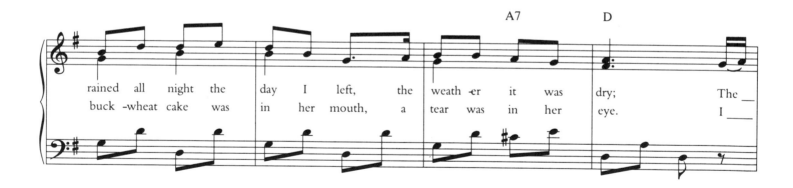

Chorus

Oh, Su - san - na, Oh, don't you cry for me. I ___

come from Al - a - bam - a with my ban - jo on my knee.

I Want to Be in Dixie

Words and music by Irving Berlin

Moderato

I want to be, _____ I want to be, _____ I want to be down home in

Dix - ie, Where the hens are dog - gone glad to lay, __ Scram-bled eggs in the

new-mown hay. __ You ought to see, _____ you ought to see, _____ You ought to

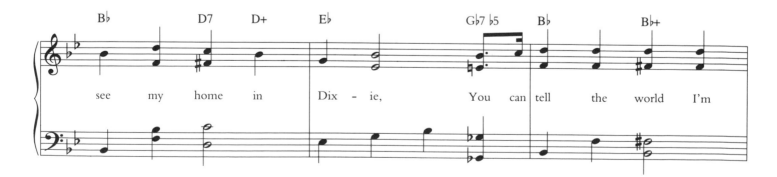

see my home in Dix - ie, You can tell the world I'm

go - ing to ___ D - I - X - I don't know how to spell it, But I'm

goin', _____ you bet I'm goin', To my home in Dix - ie - land.

Cindy

Traditional

Lively

mf You ought to see my Cin - dy, She lives a - way down South, And

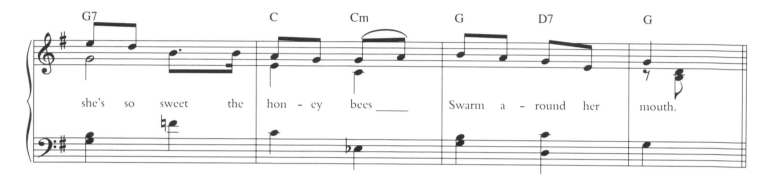

she's so sweet the hon - ey bees ____ Swarm a - round her mouth.

Chorus

Get a - long home, Cin - dy, Cin - dy, Get a - long home, Cin - dy,

Cin - dy, Get a - long home, Cin - dy, Cin - dy, I'll mar - ry you some - day.

2. I wish I was an apple,
A-hangin' on a tree,
And every time my Cindy passed,
She'd take a bite of me.
Chorus

3. I wish I had a needle,
As fine as I could sew,
I'd sew that gal to my coattail,
And down the road I'd go.
Chorus

4. I wish I had a nickel,
I wish I had a dime,
I wish I had my Cindy girl,
To love me all the time.
Chorus

5. Cindy in the springtime,
Cindy in the fall,
If I can't have my Cindy,
I'll have no girl at all.
Chorus

68

The Camptown Races

Words and music by Stephen Foster

Energetically

The Camp-town la-dies sing this song, Doo - dah! doo - dah! The
I come down there with my hat caved in, Doo - dah! doo - dah!

Camp-town race - track five miles long, Oh, the doo - dah - day!
Can't go home with a pock-et full of tin, Oh, the doo - dah - day!

Chorus

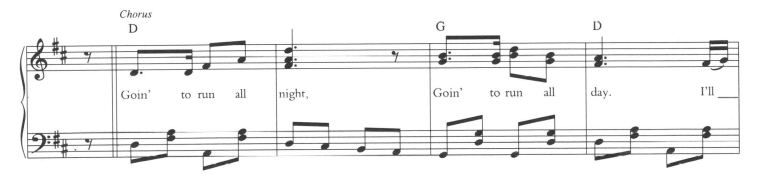

Goin' to run all night, Goin' to run all day. I'll ___

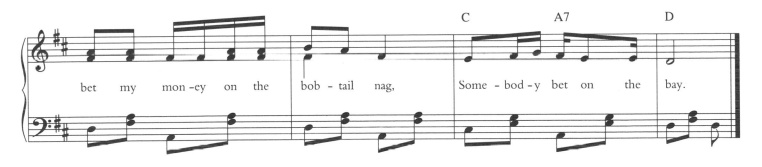

bet my mon-ey on the bob - tail nag, Some - bod-y bet on the bay.

2. The long-tail filly and the big black horse,
   Doodah! doodah!
   They fly the track and they both cut across,
   Oh, the doodah day!
   The blind horse stickin' in a big mud hole,
   Doodah! doodah!
   Can't touch bottom with a ten-foot pole,
   Oh, the doodah day!
   Chorus

3. Old muley cow comes onto the track,
   Doodah! doodah!
   The bobtail flinged her over his back,
   Oh, the doodah day!
   Then fly along like a railroad car,
   Doodah! doodah!
   Running a race with a shooting star.
   Oh, the doodah day!
   Chorus

4. See them flying on a ten-mile heat,
   Doodah! doodah!
   Round the racetrack, then repeat,
   Oh, the doodah day!
   I win my money on the bobtail nag,
   Doodah! doodah!
   I keep my money in an old tow-bag.
   Oh, the doodah day!
   Chorus

Kentucky Babe

Lazily

Words by Richard H. Buck
Music by Adam Geibel

1. Skeet - ers am a - hum - min' on the hon - ey - suck - le vine,
2. Dad - dy's in the cane - break with his lit - tle dog and gun,

Sleep, Ken - tuck - y babe.
Sleep, Ken - tuck - y babe.

Sand - man am a - com - in' to this
Pos - sum for your break - fast when your

lit - tle babe of mine, Sleep, Ken - tuck - y babe.
sleep - in' time is done, Sleep, Ken - tuck - y babe.

Sil - v'ry moon am shin - in' in the heav - ens up a - bove, Bob - o - link am pin - in' for his
Bog - ie man - 'll catch you sure un - less you close your eyes, Wait - in' just out - side your door to

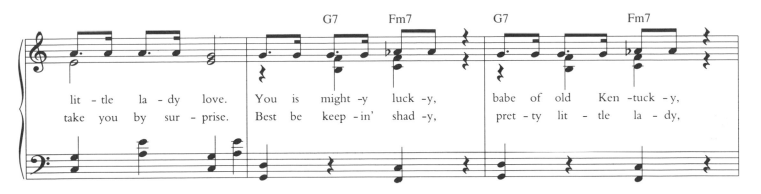

lit -- tle la -- dy love. You is might -- y luck -- y, babe of old Ken -- tuck -- y,
take you by sur -- prise. Best be keep -- in' shad -- y, pret -- ty lit -- tle la -- dy,

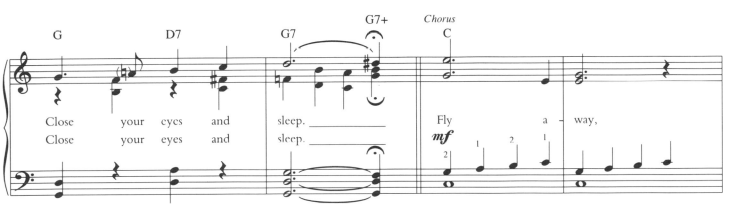

Close your eyes and sleep. Fly a -- way,
Close your eyes and sleep.

Fly a -- way Ken -- tuck -- y babe, fly a -- way to rest. Fly a -- way,

Lay your lit -- tle, sleep -- y head on your mam -- my's breast. Hm,

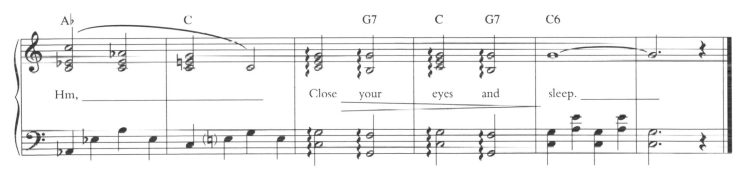

Hm, Close your eyes and sleep.

Listen to the Mockingbird

Words by Alice Hawthorne
(Pseudonym of Septimus Winner)
Music by Richard Milburn

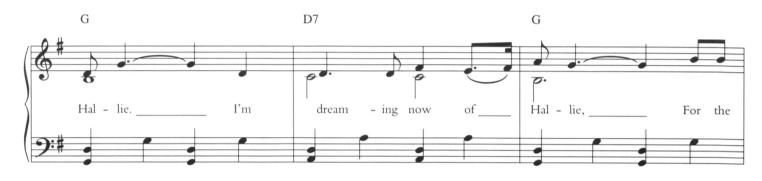

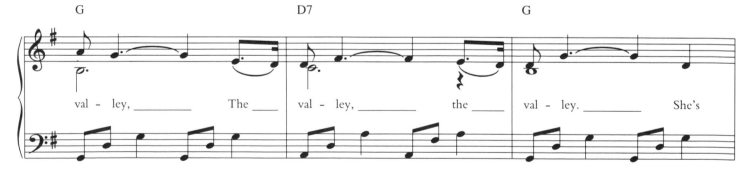

Chorus

lies. Lis – ten to the mock – ing – bird, lis – ten to the

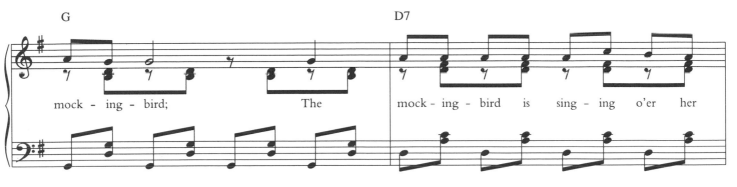

mock – ing – bird; The mock – ing – bird is sing – ing o'er her

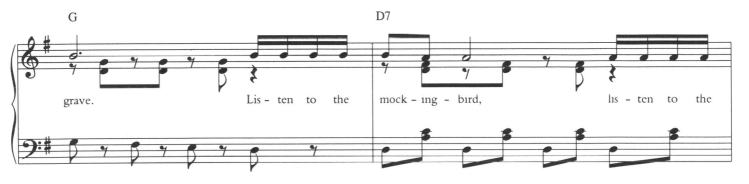

grave. Lis – ten to the mock – ing – bird, lis – ten to the

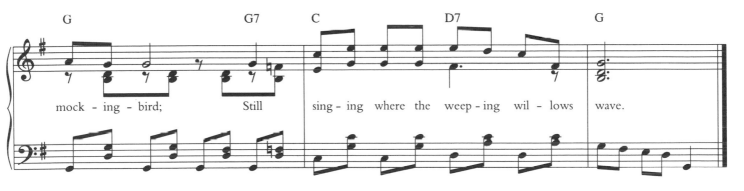

mock – ing – bird; Still sing – ing where the weep – ing wil – lows wave.

2. Ah! well I yet remember,
   Remember, remember,
   Ah! well I yet remember,
   When we gathered in the cotton side by side.
   'Twas in the mild September,
   September, September,
   'Twas in the mild September,
   And the mockingbird was singing far and wide.
   Chorus

3. When charms of spring are awaken,
   Are awaken, are awaken,
   When charms of spring are awaken,
   And the mockingbird is singing on the bough,
   I feel like one so forsaken,
   So forsaken, so forsaken,
   I feel like one so forsaken,
   Since my Hallie is no longer with me now.
   Chorus

My Old Kentucky Home

Words and music by Stephen Foster

la - dy, Oh, weep no more to - day. We will *mf*

sing one song for the old Ken - tuck - y home, For the

old Ken - tuck - y home, far a - way.

rit.

2. They hunt no more for the possum and the coon,
   On the meadow, the hill, and the shore.
   They sing no more by the glimmer of the moon,
   On the bench by the old cabin door.
   The day goes by like a shadow o'er the heart,
   With sorrow where all was delight;
   The time has come when the old folks have to part,
   Then my old Kentucky home, good-night.
   Chorus

3. The head must bow and the back will have to bend,
   Wherever the wanderer may go.
   A few more days, and the trouble all will end,
   In the field where the sugar canes grow.
   A few more days for to tote the weary load,
   No matter, 'twill never be light;
   A few more days will we totter on the road,
   Then my old Kentucky home, good-night.
   Chorus

When the Midnight Choo-Choo Leaves for Alabam'

Words and music by Irving Berlin

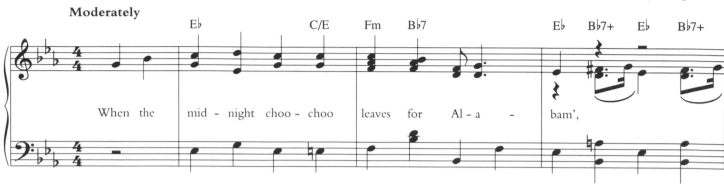

When the mid-night choo-choo leaves for Al-a-bam',

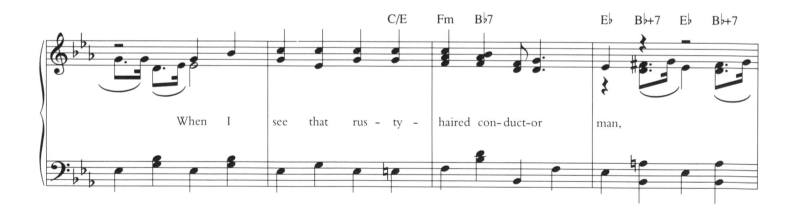

I'll be right there, _____ I've got my fare.

When I see that rus-ty-haired con-duct-or man,

I'll grab him by the col-lar, And I'll hol-ler, "Ala-a-bam', Al-a-bam'!"

That's where you stop your train,_____ That brings me

back a - gain,_____ Down home where I re - main,_____

____ Where my hon -ey - lamb am. I will be right

there with bells, __ When that old con - duct -or yells, ___ "All a -

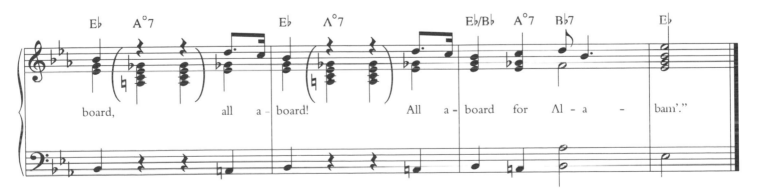

board, all a - board! All a - board for Al - a - bam'."

FROM THE
MOUNTAINS & VALLEYS

She'll Be Comin' Round the Mountain

Traditional

2. She'll be drivin' six white horses when she comes, *etc.*

3. Oh, we'll all go out to meet her when she comes, *etc.*

4. We will kill the old red rooster when she comes, *etc.*

5. We will all have chicken and dumplings when she comes, *etc.*

The Trail of the Lonesome Pine

Words by Ballard MacDonald
Music by Harry Carroll

Moderately

In the Blue Ridge Moun-tains of Vir - gin-ia, On the trail of the lone - some

pine, _____ In the pale moon - shine our hearts en - twine, Where she carved her name and

I carved mine. Oh, June, like the moun-tains I'm blue, __ like the pine, _____ I am

lone-some for you, _ In the Blue Ridge Moun-tains of Vir gin - ia, On the trail of the lone-some pine.

Cripple Creek

Moderately fast

Traditional

On Top of Old Smoky

Traditional

Moderately

On top of Old Smok - y, _____ All cov - ered with

snow, _____ I lost my true lov -

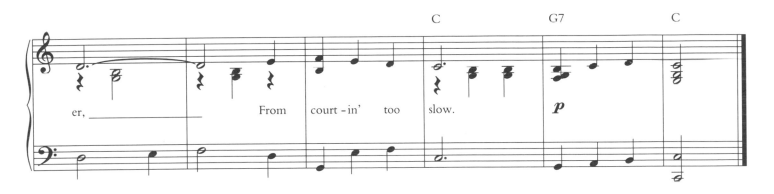

er, _____ From court -in' too slow. *p*

2. Now courtin's a pleasure,
   But partin' is grief,
   A false-hearted lover,
   Is worse than a thief.

3. A thief he will rob you,
   And take what you have,
   But a false-hearted lover,
   Will send you to your grave.

4. The grave will decay you,
   And turn you to dust,
   Not one boy in a hundred,
   A poor girl can trust.

5. They'll hug you and kiss you,
   And tell you more lies,
   Than cross-ties on the railroad,
   Or stars in the skies.

Sourwood Mountain

Traditional

Moderately

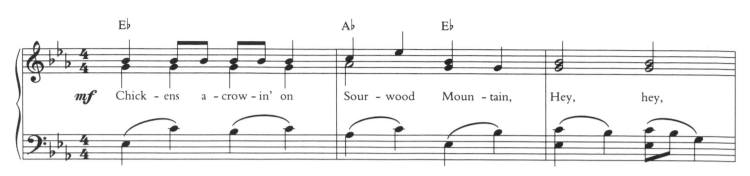

mf Chick - ens a - crow - in' on Sour - wood Moun - tain, Hey, hey,

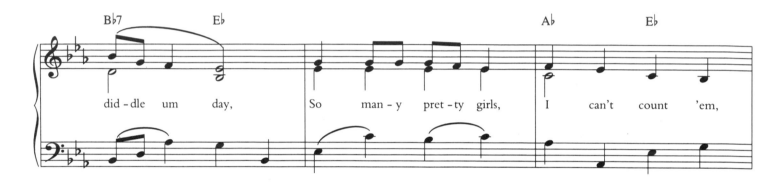

did - dle um day, So man - y pret - ty girls, I can't count 'em,

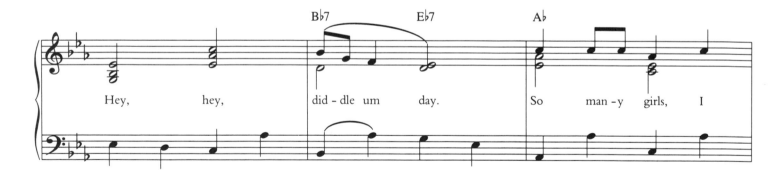

Hey, hey, did - dle um day. So man - y girls, I

just can't count 'em, So man - y girls on Sour - wood Moun - tain,

So man-y girls on Sour-wood Moun-tain, Hey, hey, did-dle um day.

2. I call my darling a blue-eyed daisy,
Hey, hey, diddle um day,
If she won't have me, I'll sure go crazy,
Hey, hey, diddle um day.
I got to have my blue-eyed daisy,
If she refuses, I'll go crazy,
I got to have my blue-eyed daisy,
Hey, hey, diddle um day.

3. Ducks go a-swimming across the river,
Hey, hey, diddle um day,
And in winter, we sure do shiver,
Hey, hey, diddle um day.
Ducks go a-swimming across the river,
And in winter, we sure do shiver,
I like the living on Sourwood Mountain,
Hey, hey, diddle um day.

4. My true love lives at the head of the holler,
Hey, hey, diddle um day,
She won't come and I won't foller,
Hey, hey, diddle um day.
My true love lives at the head of the holler,
She won't come and I won't foller,
My true love lives at the head of the holler,
Hey, hey, diddle um day.

5. My true love lives over the river,
Hey, hey, diddle um day,
A few more steps and I'll be with her,
Hey, hey, diddle um day.
My true love lives over the river,
A few more steps and I'll be with her,
My true love lives over the river,
Hey, hey, diddle um day.

Clementine

Words and music by Percy Montrose

With spirit

In a cav-ern, in a can-yon, Ex-ca-vat-ing for a mine, Lived a

min - er, for - ty - nin - er, And his daugh - ter, Clem - en - tine.

Chorus

Oh, my dar - ling, oh, my dar - ling, Oh, my dar - ling Clem-en - tine, You are

lost and gone for - ev - er, Dread - ful sor - ry, Clem - en - tine.

2. Light she was and like a fairy,
And her shoes were number nine,
Herring boxes without topses,
Sandals were for Clementine.
Chorus

3. Drove she ducklings to the water,
Ev'ry morning just at nine,
Stubbed her toe upon a splinter,
Fell into the foaming brine.
Chorus

4. Ruby lips above the water,
Blowing bubbles soft and fine,
But, alas, I was no swimmer,
So I lost my Clementine.
Chorus

5. How I missed her! How I missed her,
How I missed my Clementine,
But I kissed her little sister,
And forgot my Clementine.
Chorus

Down in the Valley

Traditional

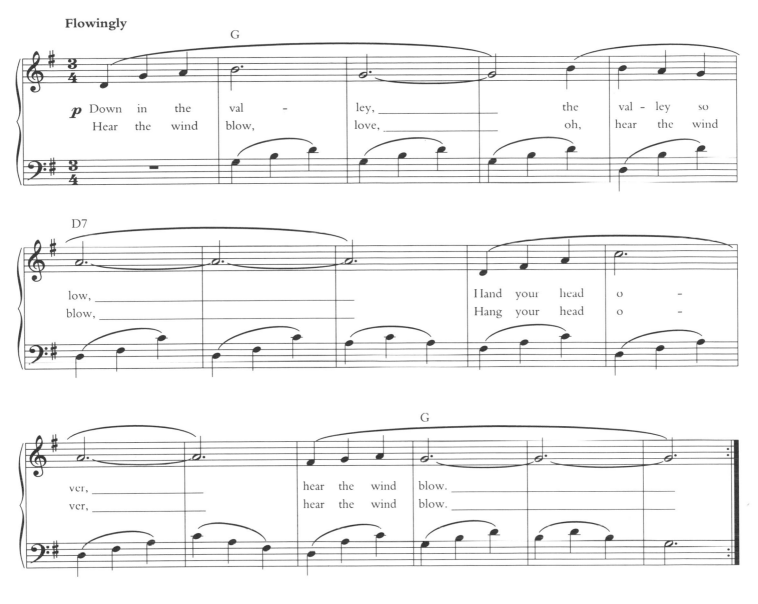

2. Roses love sunshine, violets love dew,
   Angels in heaven know I love you,
   Know I love you, dear, know I love you,
   Angels in heaven know I love you.

3. If you don't love me, love whom you please,
   Throw your arms 'round me, give my heart ease.
   Give my heart ease, love, give my heart ease,
   Throw your arms 'round me, give my heart ease.

4. Build me a castle forty feet high,
   So I can see him as he rides by.
   As he rides by, love, as he rides by,
   So I can see him as he rides by.

5. Write me a letter, send it by mail,
   Send it in care of the Birmingham jail.
   Birmingham jail, love, Birmingham jail,
   Send it in care of the Birmingham jail.

Cumberland Gap

With spirit

Traditional

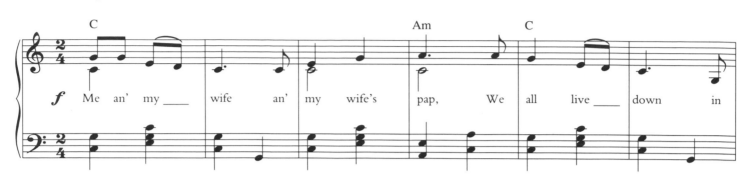

Me an' my ___ wife an' my wife's pap, We all live ___ down in

Chorus

Cum-ber-land Gap. Cum-ber-land Gap, Cum-ber-land Gap,

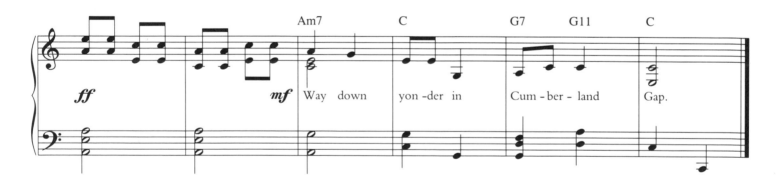

Way down yon-der in Cum-ber-land Gap.

2. I got a gal in Cumberland Gap,
   She's got a baby that calls me pap.
   Chorus

3. Cumberland Gap is a noted place,
   Three kinds of water to wash your face.
   Chorus

4. Cumberland Gap, it ain't very far,
   It's just three miles from Middlesboro.
   Chorus

5. Lay down, boys, and take a little nap,
   We're all goin' down to Cumberland Gap.
   Chorus

Springfield Mountain

Traditional

Flowingly

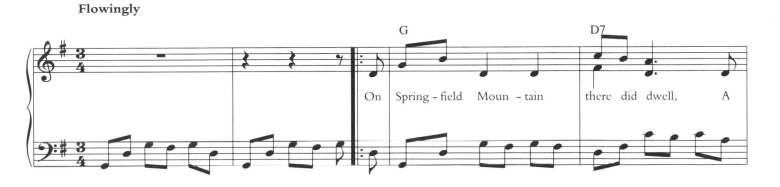

On Spring-field Moun-tain there did dwell, A

Chorus

love-ly youth, I knew him well. _____ Too - roo - di - noo, Too -

roo - di - nay, _ Too - roo - di - noo, Too - roo - di - nay. _____

2. One Monday morning, he did go,
   Down to the meadow for to mow.
   Chorus

3. He scarce had mowed half 'round the field,
   When a pesky serpent bit his heel.
   Chorus

4. They took him home to Molly dear,
   Which made her feel so very queer.
   Chorus

5. Now Molly had two ruby lips,
   With which the poison, she did sip.
   Chorus

6. Now Molly had a rotten tooth,
   And so the poison killed them both.
   Chorus

Red River Valley

Moderately

Traditional

mf From this val – ley they say you are go – ing, We will

miss your bright eyes and sweet smile, For they say you are tak – ing the

sun – shine, Which has bright – ened our path – ways a – while.

2. Come and sit by my side, if you love me,
Do not hasten to bid me adieu,
Just remember the Red River Valley
And the cowboy who loved you so true.

3. I've been thinking a long time, my darling,
Of the sweet words you never would say,
Now, alas, must my fond hopes all vanish?
For they say you are going away.

4. Do you think of the valley you're leaving?
Oh, how lonely and how dreary it will be.
Do you think of the kind hearts you're breaking,
And the pain you are causing to me?

5. They will bury me where you have wandered,
Near the hills where the daffodils grow,
When you're gone from the Red River Valley,
For I can't live without you I know.

Colorado Trail

Traditional

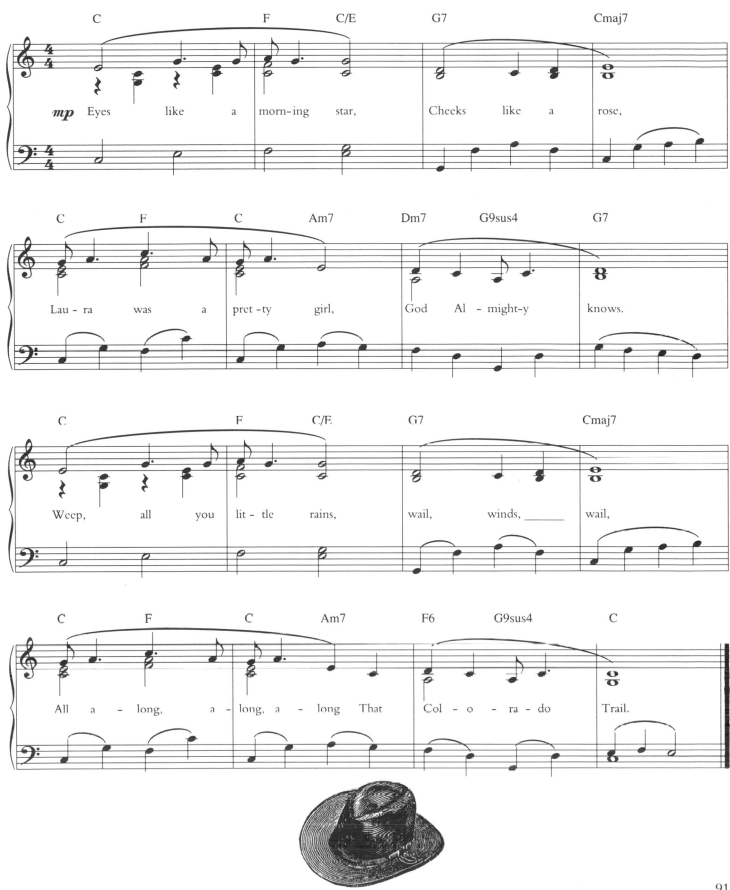

Expressively

mp Eyes like a morn-ing star, Cheeks like a rose,

Lau - ra was a pret -ty girl, God Al - might-y knows.

Weep, all you lit - tle rains, wail, winds, _____ wail,

All a - long, a - long, a - long That Col - o - ra - do Trail.

Big Rock Candy Mountain

With a steady rhythm

Traditional

sleet don't fall, And the wind don't blow, In the Big Rock Can - dy

Chorus

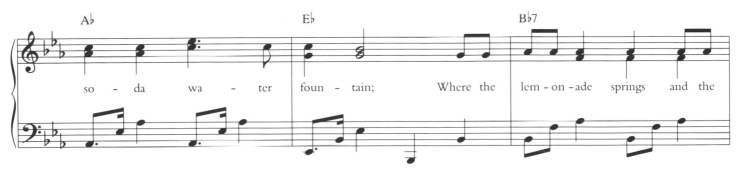

Moun - tain. Oh, the buz -zin' of the bees and the cig -a - rette trees, Near the

so - da wa — ter foun - tain; Where the lem -on -ade springs and the

blue - bird sings In the Big Rock Can - dy Moun - tain.

2. In the Big Rock Candy Mountain,
The cops have wooden legs;
The bulldogs all have rubber teeth,
And the hens lay soft-boiled eggs.
The farmers' trees are full of fruit,
And the barns are full of hay;
Yes, I want to go
Where there ain't no snow,
Where the sleet don't fall,
And the wind don't blow,
In the Big Rock Candy Mountain.
Chorus

3. In the Big Rock Candy Mountain,
The jails are made of tin;
And you can bust right out again,
As soon as you get in.
There ain't no hoes and shovels,
No axes, saws, nor picks;
Oh, I'm going to stay
Where you sleep all day,
Where they hung the jerk
Who invented work,
In the Big Rock Candy Mountain.
Chorus

BATTLE SONGS &
SEA SHANTIES

When Johnny Comes Marching Home

Words and music by Patrick S. Gilmore

With excitement

all   feel   gay   when   John -ny comes march – ing   home. _____

2. The old church bell will peal with joy,
   Hurrah! hurrah!
   To welcome home our darling boy,
   Hurrah! hurrah!
   The village lads and lassies say,
   With roses they will strew the way,
   And we'll all feel gay
   When Johnny comes marching home.

3. Get ready for the jubilee,
   Hurrah! hurrah!
   We'll give the hero three times three,
   Hurrah! hurrah!
   The laurel wreath is ready now,
   To place upon his loyal brow,
   And we'll all feel gay
   When Johnny comes marching home.

Blow the Man Down

With a lilt

Traditional

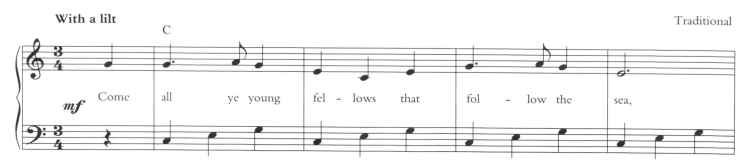

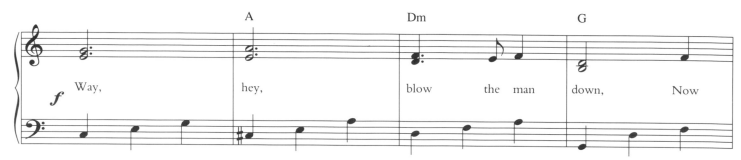

2. As I was a-walkin' down Paradise Street,
Way, hey, blow the man down,
A pretty young damsel I chanced for to meet,
Give me some time to blow the man down.

3. She hailed me with her flipper, I took her in tow,
Way, hey, blow the man down,
Yardarm to yardarm, away we did go,
Give me some time to blow the man down.

4. But as we were going she said unto me,
Way, hey, blow the man down,
"There's a spanking full-rigger just ready for sea."
Give me some time to blow the man down.

5. As soon as that packet was clear of the bar,
Way, hey, blow the man down,
The mate knocked me down with the end of a spar,
Give me some time to blow the man down.

6. As soon as that packet was out on the sea,
Way, hey, blow the man down,
'Twas devilish hard treatment of every degree,
Give me some time to blow the man down.

7. So I give you fair warning before we belay,
Way, hey, blow the man down,
Don't ever take heed of what pretty girls say,
Give me some time to blow the man down.

You're in the Army Now

Traditional

Tired march

Rally Round the Flag

Words and music by George F. Root

With a steady beat

_f_ Oh, we'll ral-ly round the flag, boys, ral-ly once a-gain,

Shout-ing the bat-tle cry of free - dom; We will

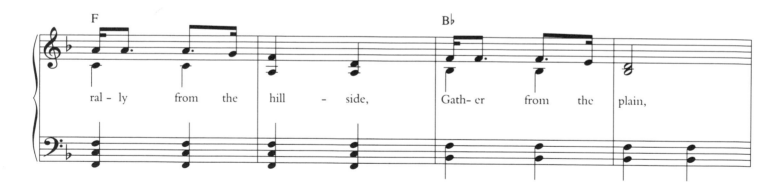

ral-ly from the hill-side, Gath-er from the plain,

Shout-ing the bat-tle cry of free - dom.

Chorus

The Un – ion for- ev - er, Hur - rah! boys, hur - rah!

Down with the trai - tor, And up with the star; While we

ral – ly round the flag, boys, Ral -ly once a - gain,

Shout – ing the bat - tle cry of free dom.

2. We are springing to the call
Of our brothers gone before,
Shouting the battle cry of freedom,
And we'll fill the vacant ranks
With a million freemen more,
Shouting the battle cry of freedom.
Chorus

3 We will welcome to our numbers
The loyal, true, and brave,
Shouting the battle cry of freedom,
And although they may be poor,
Not a man shall be a slave,
Shouting the battle cry of freedom
Chorus

4. So, we're springing to the call
From the East and from the West,
Shouting the battle cry of freedom,
And we'll hurl the rebel crew
From the land we love the best,
Shouting the battle cry of freedom.
Chorus

Shenandoah

Smoothly

Traditional

Oh, Shen-an-doah, I long to hear you, A - way, you roll-ing riv - er Oh, Shen-an-doah, I long to hear you, A - way, I'm bound-a way, 'Cross the wide Mis- sou - ri.

2. Oh, Shenandoah, I love your daughter,
Away, you rolling river,
For her I'd cross your roaming water,
Away, I'm bound away,
'Cross the wide Missouri.

3. Oh, Shenandoah, I'm bound to leave you,
Away, you rolling river,
Oh, Shenandoah, I'll not deceive you,
Away, I'm bound away,
'Cross the wide Missouri.

Sailing, Sailing

Words and music by Godfrey Marks

With movement

f Sail - ing, Sail - ing, o - ver the bound - ing main, _____ For

man -y a storm - y wind shall blow Ere Jack __ comes home a - gain. _____

Sail - ing, sail - ing, o - ver the bound - ing main, _____ For

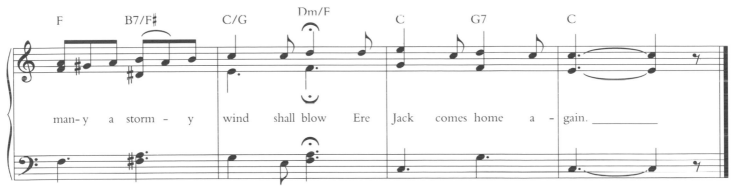

man -y a storm - y wind shall blow Ere Jack comes home a - gain. _____

103

Tenting Tonight

Words and music by Walter Kittredge

We're tent - ing to - night on the old camp ground,

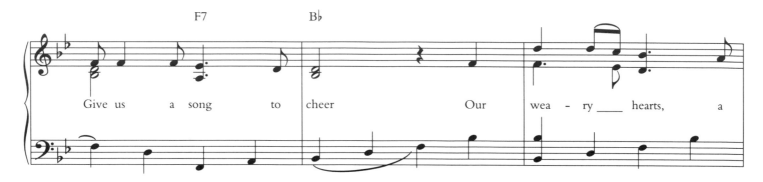

Give us a song to cheer Our wea - ry ___ hearts, a

song of home, And friends we love so dear.

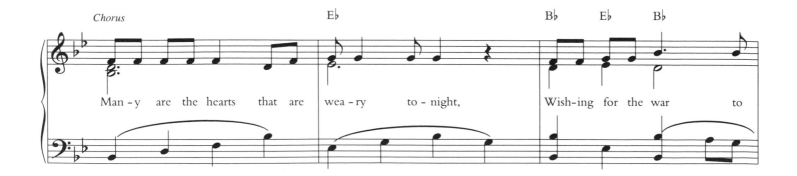

Chorus

Man - y are the hearts that are wea - ry to - night, Wish - ing for the war to

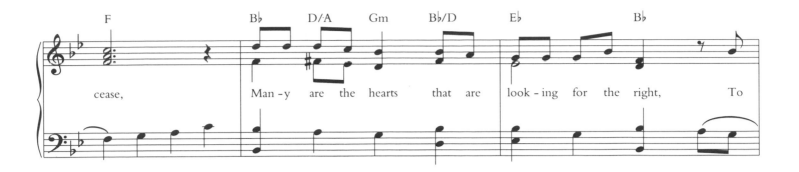

cease,   Man-y are the hearts that are   look-ing for the right,   To

see   the   dawn   of   peace.   Tent-ing   to - night,

tent - ing   to - night,   Tent - ing on the old   camp   ground.

2. We've been tenting tonight on the old camp ground,
   Thinking of days gone by,
   Of the loved ones at home that gave us the hand,
   And the tear that said, "Goodbye."
   Chorus

3. We are tired of war on the old camp ground,
   Many are dead and gone,
   Of the brave and true who've left their home,
   Others been wounded long.
   Chorus

4. We've been fighting tonight on the old camp ground,
   Many are lying near;
   Some are dead and some are dying,
   Many are in tears.
   Chorus

The Erie Canal

Words and music by Thomas S. Allen

With a steady beat

I've got a mule, ___ her name is Sal,

Fif - teen miles ___ on the E - rie Ca - nal. ___ She's a

good old work - er and a good old pal, Fif - teen miles ___ on the

E - rie Ca - nal. ___ We've hauled some barg — es in our day,

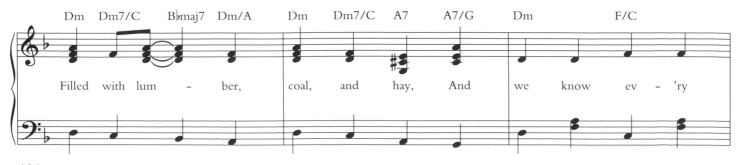

Filled with lum - ber, coal, and hay, And we know ev - 'ry

inch of the way, From Al – ban – y _____ to _____ Buf – fa – lo. _____

Chorus

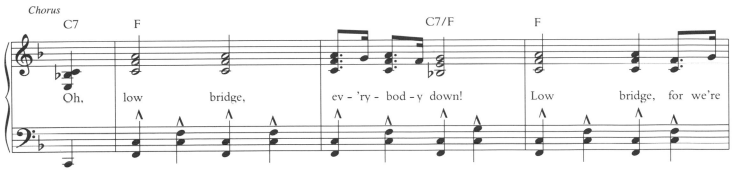

Oh, low bridge, ev – 'ry – bod – y down! Low bridge, for we're

com – ing to a town! And you'll al – ways know your neigh – bor, you'll

al – ways know your pal, If you've ev – er nav – i – gat – ed on the E – rie Can – al.

2. We'd better look around for a job, old gal,
   Fifteen miles on the Erie Canal.
   'Cause you bet your life I'd never part with Sal,
   Fifteen miles on the Erie Canal.
   Get up there, mule, here comes a lock,
   We'll make Rome 'bout six o'clock,
   One more trip and back we'll go,
   Right back home to Buffalo.
   Chorus

3. Oh, where would I be if I lost my pal?
   Fifteen miles on the Erie Canal.
   Oh, I'd like to see a mule as good as Sal,
   Fifteen miles on the Erie Canal.
   A friend of mine once got her sore,
   Now he's got a broken jaw,
   'Cause she let fly with her iron toe,
   And kicked him into Buffalo.
   Chorus

Just Before the Battle, Mother

Words and busic by George F. Root

Slowly

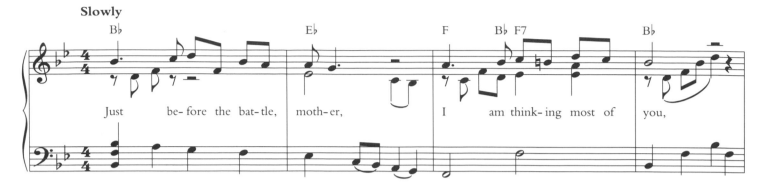

Just be-fore the bat-tle, moth-er, I am think-ing most of you,

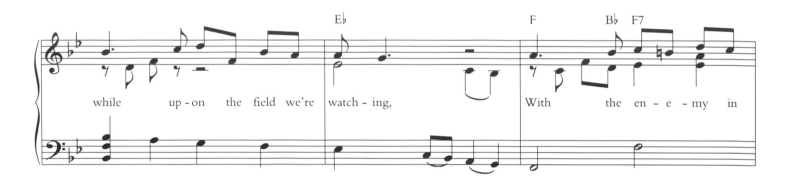

while up-on the field we're watch-ing, With the en-e-my in

view. Com - rades brave are 'round me ly - ing,

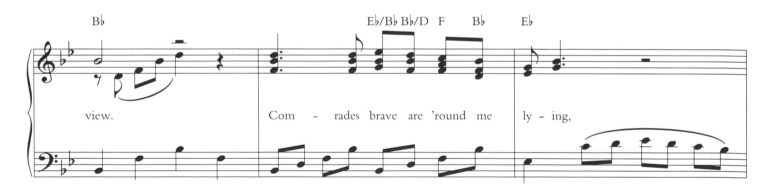

Filled with thought of home and God; For well they know that on the

mor -row, Some will sleep be- neath the sod.

Chorus

Fare - well, moth -er, you may nev -er Press me to your breast a -

gain; But, oh, you'll not for -get me, moth -er,

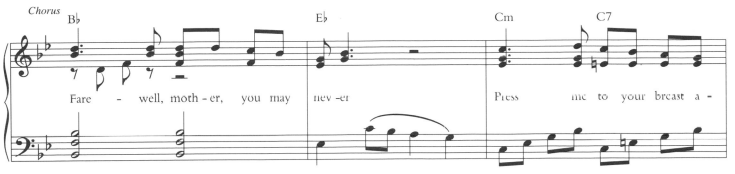

If I'm num -bered with the slain.

2. Oh, I long to see you, mother,
And the loving ones at home,
But I'll never leave the banner,
Till in honor I can come.
Tell the traitors all around you
That cruel words we know,
In every battle kill our soldiers
By the help they give the foe.
Chorus

3. Hark! I hear the bugles sounding,
'Tis the signal for the fight,
Now may God protect us, mother,
As He ever does the right.
Hear the "Battle Cry of Freedom,"
How it swells upon the air,
Oh, yes, we'll rally 'round the standard,
Or we'll perish nobly there.
Chorus

The Eddystone Light

Traditional

Jauntily

1. My fa - ther was the keep - er of the Ed - dy - stone Light, He courted a mer - maid one fine night. From this un - i - on

there came three; A por - poise and a por - gy and the oth - er was me.

Chorus

Yo, ho, ho! the wind blows free, Oh, for the life on the

roll   -   ing   sea.   2. One

sea.

2. One night while I was trimmin' of the glim,
   Singing a verse of the evening hymn,
   A voice from the starboard shouted, "Ahoy!"
   And there was my mother a-sittin' on a buoy.
   Chorus

3. "Oh, what has become of my children three?"
   My mother then she asked of me.
   "One was exhibited as a talking fish,
   And the other was served on a chafing dish."
   Chorus

4. Then the phosphorus flashed in her seaweed hair,
   I looked again, my mother wasn't there.
   A voice came echoing out of the night,
   "To the devil with the keeper of the Eddystone Light!"
   Chorus

Johnny Has Gone for a Soldier

Traditional

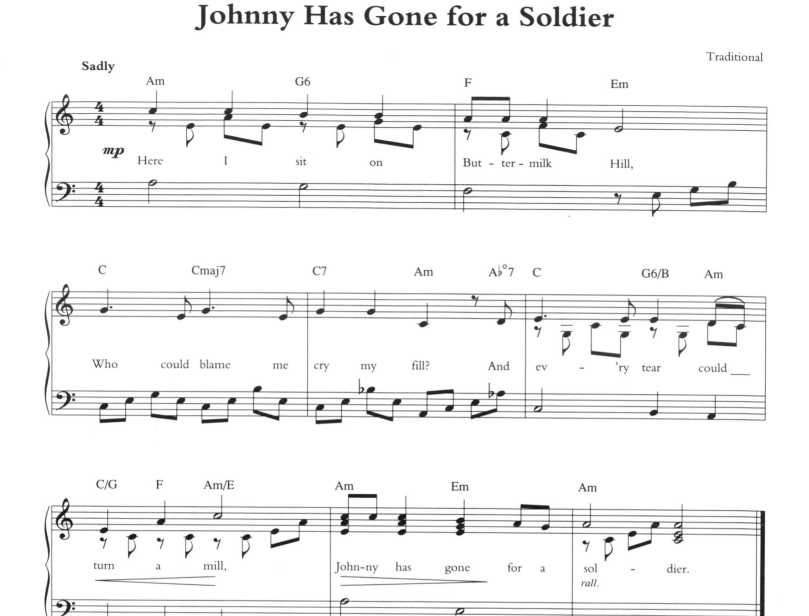

2. I'll sell my clock, I'll sell my reel,
   Likewise I'll sell my spinning wheel,
   To buy my love a sword of steel,
   Johnny has gone for a soldier.

3. Me, oh my, I love him so,
   Broke my heart to see him go,
   And only time can heal my woe,
   Johnny has gone for a soldier.

HYMNS & SPIRITUALS

Amazing Grace

Fervently

Traditional

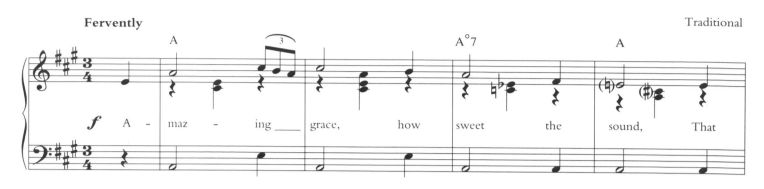

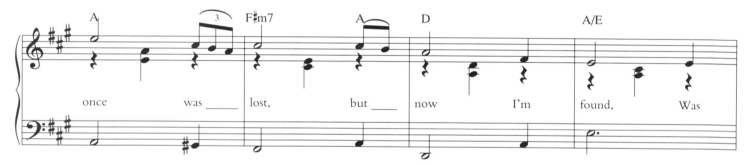

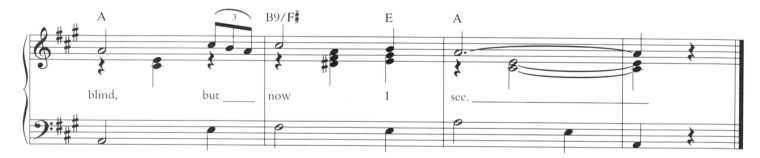

2. 'Twas grace that taught my heart to fear,
   And grace my fears relieved.
   How precious did that grace appear,
   The hour I first believed.

3. Through many dangers, toils, and snares,
   I have already come.
   'Tis grace that brought me safe thus far,
   And grace will lead me home.

4. How sweet the name of Jesus sounds,
   In a believer's ear.
   It soothes his sorrow, heals his wounds,
   And drives away his fear.

5. When we've been there ten thousand years,
   Bright shining as the sun,
   We've no less days to sing God's praise,
   Then when we first begun.

Swing Low, Sweet Chariot

Traditional

2. If you get there before I do,
    Comin' for to carry me home,
    Tell all of my friends I'm coming after you,
    Comin' for to carry me home.

3. I'm sometimes up and sometimes down,
    Comin' for to carry me home,
    But still my soul feels heaven-bound,
    Comin' for to carry me home.

Rock-a My Soul

Traditional

Rhythmically

soul   got   hap -py   and   I   stayed   all   day,   Oh,   rock -a   my   soul. _____

2. When I came home from the valley at night,
   Oh, rock–a my soul,
   I knew that ev'rything would be all right,
   Oh, rock–a my soul.
   Chorus

3. I felt so sad on the morning before,
   Oh, rock–a my soul,
   I found the peace that I was looking for,
   Oh, rock–a my soul.
   Chorus

4. The sun shines bright on the cloudiest day,
   Oh, rock–a my soul,
   A pray'r is all you need to light your way,
   Oh, rock–a my soul.
   Chorus

A Mighty Fortress Is Our God

Words and music by Martin Luther

Fervently

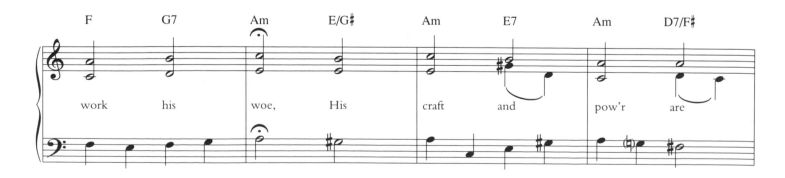

great,   And   armed   with   cru   -   el   hate,   On

earth   is   not   his _____   e   -   qual.

2. Did we in our own strength confide,
   Our striving would be losing,
   Were not the right man on our side,
   The man of God's own choosing.
   Dost ask who that may be?
   Christ Jesus, it is He,
   Lord Sabaoth His name,
   From age to age the same,
   And He must win the battle.

4. That word above all earthly pow'rs,
   No thanks to them, abideth;
   The Spirit and the gifts are ours,
   Through Him who with us sideth.
   Let goods and kindred go,
   This mortal life also;
   The body they may kill,
   God's truth abideth still;
   His kingdom is forever.

3. And though this world, with devils filled,
   Should threaten to undo us,
   We will not fear, for God hath willed,
   His truth to triumph through us.
   The prince of darkness grim,
   We tremble not for him,
   His rage we can endure,
   For lo! his doom is sure,
   One little word shall fell him.

Sometimes I Feel Like a Motherless Child

Traditional

Sadly

Some - times I feel like a moth - er - less child, Some - times I feel like a moth- er - less child, Some - times I feel like a moth-er - less child, A long, long way ___ from home, ___ A long, long way ___ from home, true be - liev - er, I'm a long, long way ___ from home, ___ A long, long way ___ from home.

2. Sometimes I feel like I'm almost gone,
Sometimes I feel like I'm almost gone,
Sometimes I feel like I'm almost gone,
Way up in the heavenly land,
Way up in the heavenly land, true believer,
Way up in the heavenly land,
Way up in the heavenly land.

3. Sometimes I feel like a feather in the air,
Sometimes I feel like a feather in the air,
Sometimes I feel like a feather in the air,
A long, long way from home,
A long, long way from home, true believer,
A long, long way from home,
A long, long way from home.

This Train

Traditional

Moderate tempo

f This train is bound for glo - ry, this train.

This train is bound for glo - ry, this train. This train is

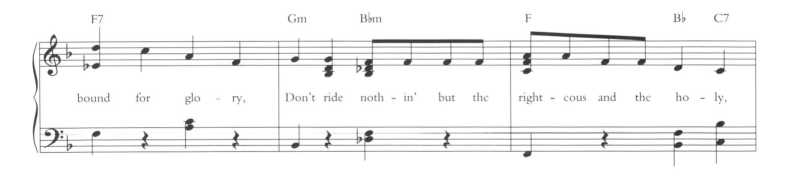

bound for glo - ry, Don't ride noth - in' but the right - eous and the ho - ly,

This train is bound for glo - ry, this train. _____

2. This train don't carry no gamblers, this train.
This train don't carry no gamblers, this train.
This train don't carry no gamblers,
No hypocrites, no midnight ramblers,
This train is bound for glory, this train.

3. This train don't carry no liars, this train.
This train don't carry no liars, this train.
This train don't carry no liars,
The truth is what the Lord desires,
This train is bound for glory, this train.

Wondrous Love

Words by Alex Means
Music traditional

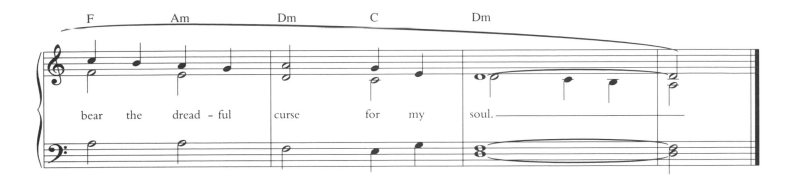

bear the dread – ful curse for my soul. _____

2. When I was sinking down, sinking down, sinking down,
   When I was sinking down, sinking down;
   When I was sinking down, beneath God's righteous frown,
   Christ laid aside his crown for my soul, for my soul,
   Christ laid aside his crown for my soul.

3. And when from death I'm free, I'll sing on, I'll sing on,
   And when from death I'm free, I'll sing on;
   And when from death I'm free, I'll sing and joyful be,
   And through eternity, I'll sing on, I'll sing on,
   And through eternity, I'll sing on.

Nobody Knows the Trouble I've Seen

Traditional

2. Now, you may think that I don't know, oh yes, Lord.
But I've had troubles here below, oh yes, Lord.
Chorus

3. One day when I was walkin' along, oh yes, Lord,
The sky opened up and love came down, oh yes, Lord.
Chorus

4. What made old Satan hate me so? oh yes, Lord,
He had me once and let me go, oh yes, Lord.
Chorus

5. I never shall forget that day, oh yes, Lord,
When Jesus washed my sins away, oh yes, Lord.
Chorus

Old Hundredth
(The Doxology)

Music by Louis Bourgeois
Words by Thomas Ken

Joyously

Praise God from Whom all bless - ings flow, Praise

Him all crea - tures here be - low. Praise Him a - bove the

heav'n - ly host; Praise Fa - ther, Son, and Ho - ly Ghost.

Poor Wayfaring Stranger

Traditional

Roam, _____ I'm just a - go — ing o - ver _____

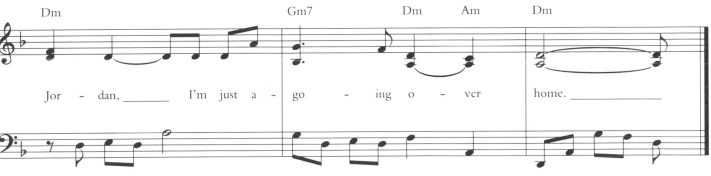

Jor - dan, _____ I'm just a - go — ing o — ver home. _____

2. I know dark clouds will gather 'round me,
   I know my way is steep and rough,
   But beauteous fields lie just beyond me,
   Where souls redeemed their vigil keep.
   I'm going there to meet my mother,
   She said she'd meet me when I come,
   I'm only going over Jordan,
   I'm only going over home.

3. I want to wear a crown of glory,
   When I get home to that bright land,
   I want to shout salvation's story,
   In concert with that bloodwashed band.
   I'm going there to meet my Savior,
   To sing His praises evermore,
   I'm only going over Jordan,
   I'm only going over home.

He's Got the Whole World in His Hands

Traditional

With a steady beat

He's got the whole world ___ in His hands, ___ He's got the

whole wide world ___ in His hands, ___ He's got the whole world ___

in His hands, ___ He's got the whole world in His hands. _____

2. He's got the earth and sky in His hands, *etc.*
    He's got the whole world in His hands.

3. He's got the land and sea in His hands, *etc.*
    He's got the whole world in His hands.

4. He's got the little bitty baby in His hands, *etc.*
    He's got the whole world in His hands.

5. He's got you and me brother in His hands, *etc.*
    He's got the whole world in His hands.

6. He's got the gamblin' man in His hands, *etc.*
    He's got the whole world in His hands.

7. He's got the whole world in His hands, *etc.*
    He's got the whole world in His hands.

Patriotic Anthems

America, the Beautiful

Words by Katherine Lee Bates
Music by Samuel A. Ward

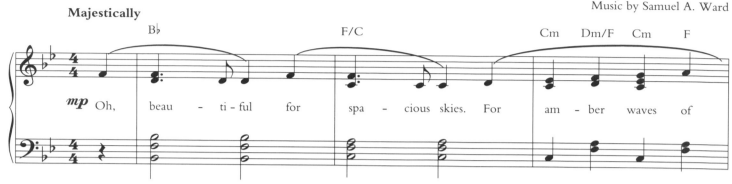

Oh, beau - ti - ful for spa - cious skies. For am - ber waves of

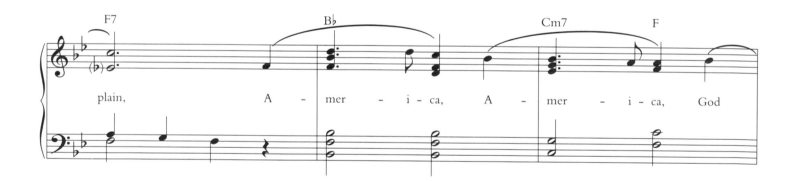

grain, For pur - ple moun - tain maj - es - ties, A - bove the fruit - ed

plain, A - mer - i - ca, A - mer - i - ca, God

shed His grace on thee, And crown thy good with

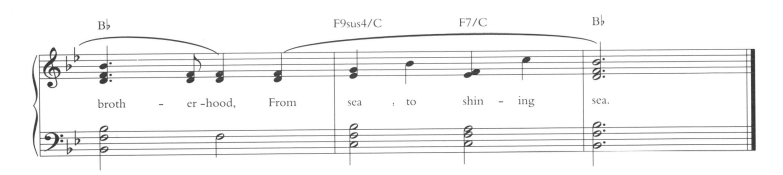

broth - er -hood, From sea to shin - ing sea.

2. Oh, beautiful for pilgrim feet,
   Whose stern impassioned stress,
   A thoroughfare for freedom beat,
   Across the wilderness.
   America, America,
   God mend thine ev'ry flaw,
   Confirm thy soul in self-control,
   Thy liberty in law.

3. Oh, beautiful for heroes proved,
   In liberating strife,
   Who more than self their country loved,
   And mercy more than life.
   America, America,
   May God thy gold refine,
   Till all success be nobleness,
   And ev'ry gain divine.

4. Oh, beautiful for patriot dream,
   That sees beyond the years,
   Thine alabaster cities gleam,
   Undimmed by human tears.
   America, America,
   God shed His grace on thee,
   And crown thy good with brotherhood,
   From sea to shining sea.

Anchors Aweigh

Words by Alfred Hart Miles and R. Lovell
Music by Charles A Zimmerman

Brightly

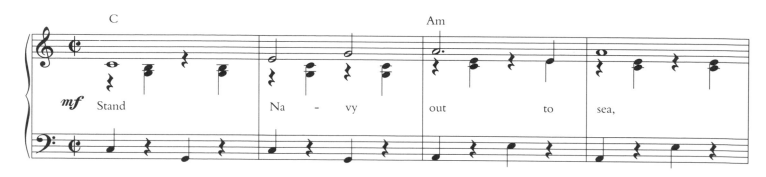

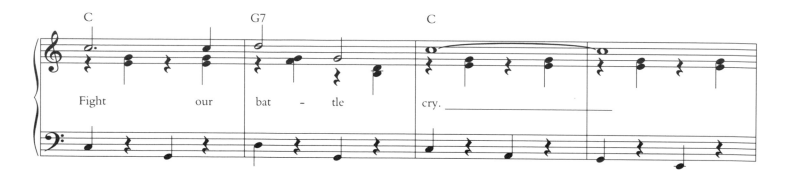

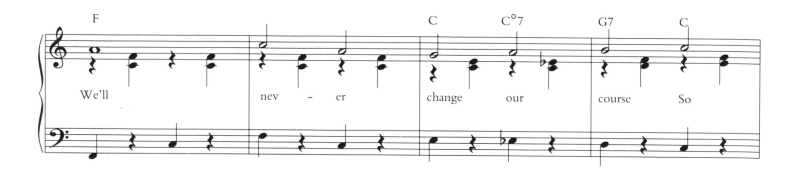

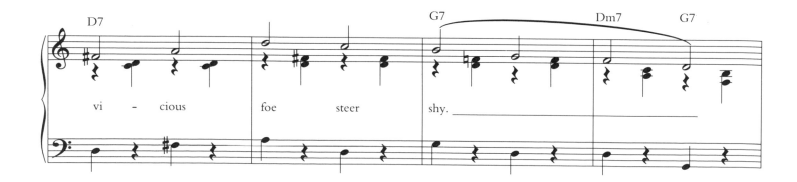

Roll out the T. N. T.,

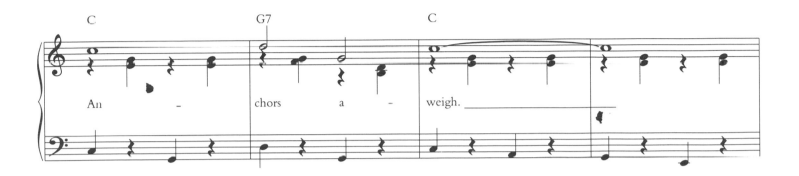

An - chors a - weigh. _____

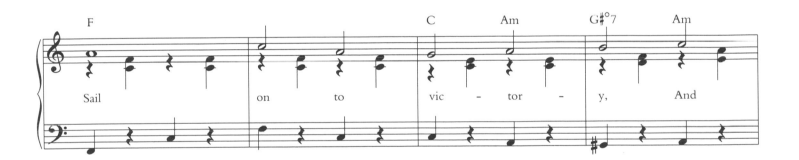

Sail on to vic - tor - y, And

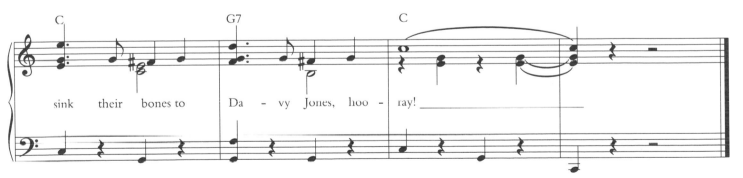

sink their bones to Da - vy Jones, hoo - ray! _____

College Version

1. Anchors aweigh, my boys,
   Anchors aweigh.
   Farewell to college joys,
   We sail at break of day.
   Through our last night on shore,
   Drink to the foam;
   Until we meet once more,
   Here's wishing you a happy voyage home.

2. Stand, Navy, down the field,
   Sail to the sky.
   We'll never change our course,
   So, Army, you steer shy.
   Roll up the score, Navy,
   Anchors aweigh.
   Sail, Navy, down the field,
   And sink the Army, sink the Army Grey.

You're a Grand Old Flag

Words and music by George M. Cohan

With spirit

You're a grand old flag you're a high fly - ing flag, And for -

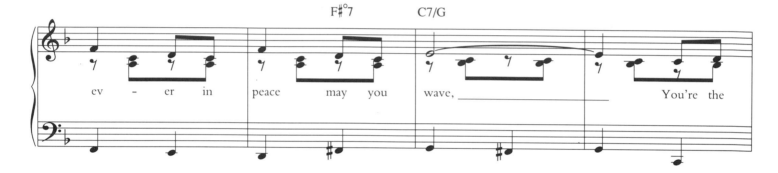

ev - er in peace may you wave, _____ You're the

em - blem of the land I love, The

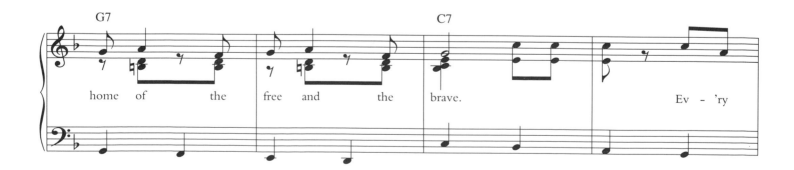

home of the free and the brave. Ev - 'ry

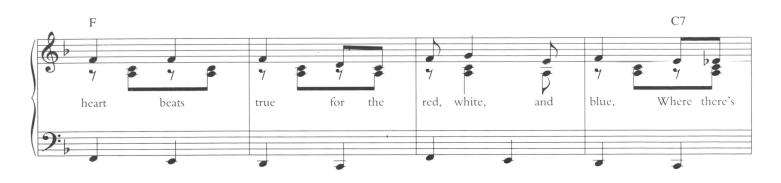

heart beats true for the red, white, and blue, Where there's

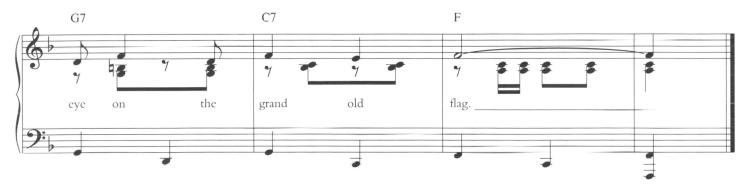

nev — er a boast or brag, _____ But should

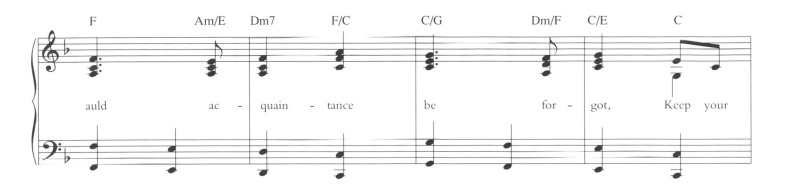

auld ac - quain - tance be for - got, Keep your

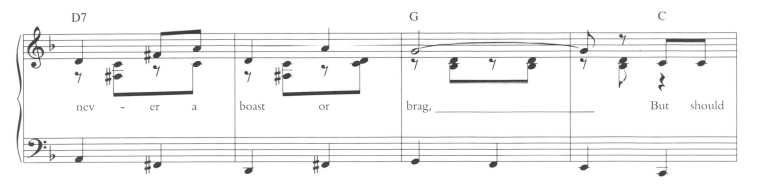

eye on the grand old flag. _____

The Marines' Hymn

Music from Jacques Offenbach's *Geneviève de Brabant*
Words anonymous

Courageously

From the Halls of Mon - te - zu - ma, To the

shores of Tri - po - li, _____ We ____

fight our coun - try's bat - tles, On the

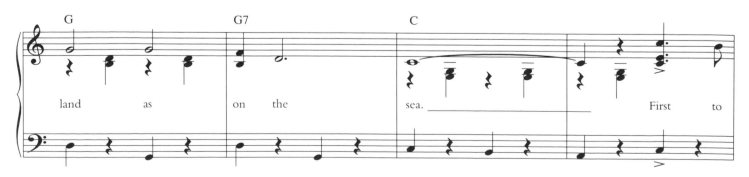

land as on the sea. _____ First to

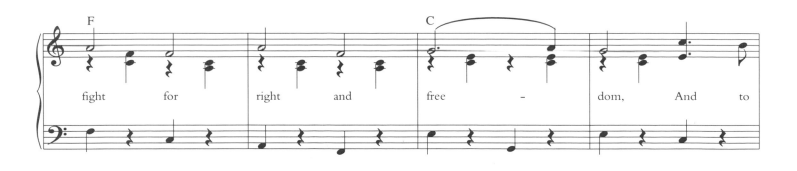

fight   for   right   and   free   -   dom,   And   to

keep   our   hon - or   clean, _____   We   are

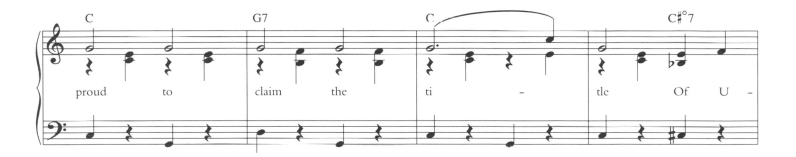

proud   to   claim   the   ti - tle   Of   U -

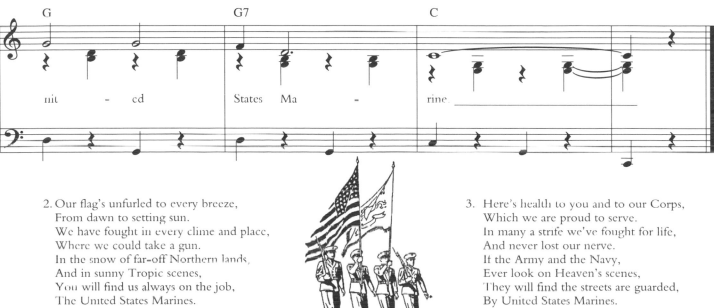

nit - ed   States   Ma - rine. _____

2. Our flag's unfurled to every breeze,
From dawn to setting sun.
We have fought in every clime and place,
Where we could take a gun.
In the snow of far-off Northern lands,
And in sunny Tropic scenes,
You will find us always on the job,
The United States Marines.

3. Here's health to you and to our Corps,
Which we are proud to serve.
In many a strife we've fought for life,
And never lost our nerve.
If the Army and the Navy,
Ever look on Heaven's scenes,
They will find the streets are guarded,
By United States Marines.

The Star-Spangled Banner

Words by Francis Scott Key
Music by John Stafford Smith

With vigor

Oh, ___ say can you see by the dawn's ear - ly light, What so

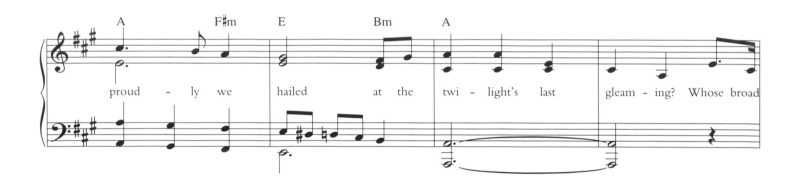

proud - ly we hailed at the twi - light's last gleam - ing? Whose broad

stripes and bright stars, through the per - i - lous fight, O'er the

ram - parts we watched were so gal - lant - ly stream - ing? And the

rock - ets red glare, the bombs burst - ing in air, Gave

proof through the night that our flag was still there. Oh,

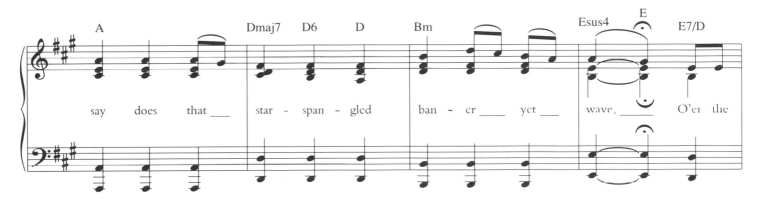

say does that ___ star - span - gled ban - er ___ yet ___ wave, ___ O'er the

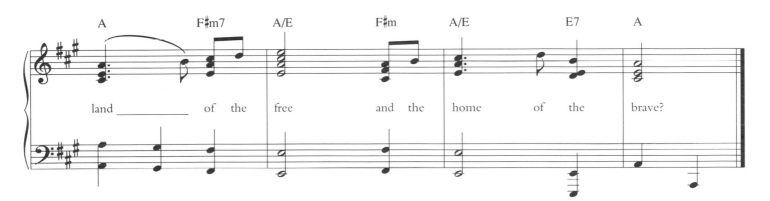

land ___ of the free and the home of the brave?

2. On the shore, dimly seen through the mists of the deep,
Where the foe's haughty host in dread silence reposes,
What is that which the breeze, o'er the towering steep,
As it fitfully blows half conceals, half discloses?
Now it catches the gleam of the morning's first beam,
In full glory reflected now shines on the stream;
'Tis the Star-Spangled Banner, oh long may it wave,
O'er the land of the free and the home of the brave.

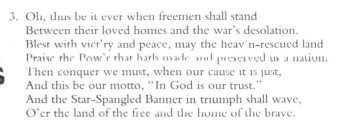

3. Oh, thus be it ever when freemen shall stand
Between their loved homes and the war's desolation.
Blest with vict'ry and peace, may the heav'n-rescued land
Praise the Pow'r that hath made and preserved us a nation.
Then conquer we must, when our cause it is just,
And this be our motto, "In God is our trust."
And the Star-Spangled Banner in triumph shall wave,
O'er the land of the free and the home of the brave.

The Caissons Go Rolling Along

Words and music by Edmund L. Gruber

With movement

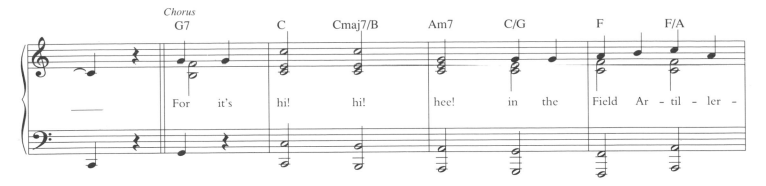

Chorus

For it's hi! hi! hee! in the Field Ar - til - ler -

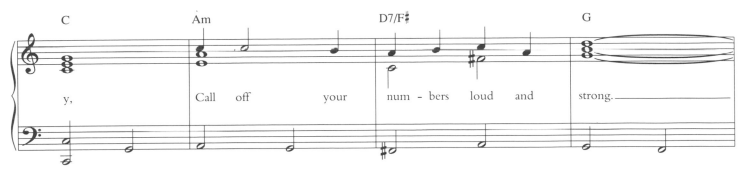

y, Call off your num - bers loud and strong.

And where - e'er, we go, You will al - ways

know, That those cais - sons go roll - ing a - long.

Yes, those cais - sons go roll - ing a - long.

Columbia, the Gem of the Ocean

Words and music by Thomas A. Becket and David T. Shaw

With majesty

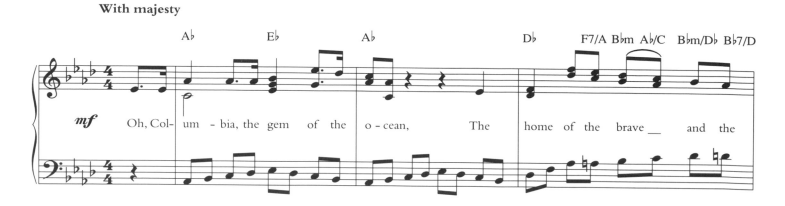

mf Oh, Col- um - bia, the gem of the o - cean, The home of the brave __ and the

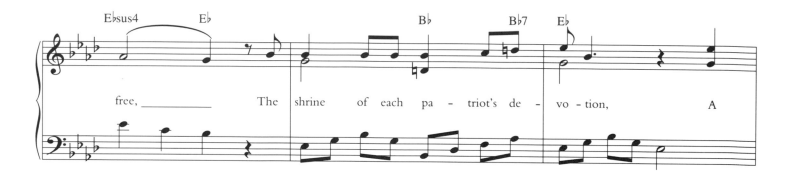

free, _____ The shrine of each pa - triot's de - vo - tion, A

world __ of - fers hom - age to thee. Thy __ man - dates make he - roes as -

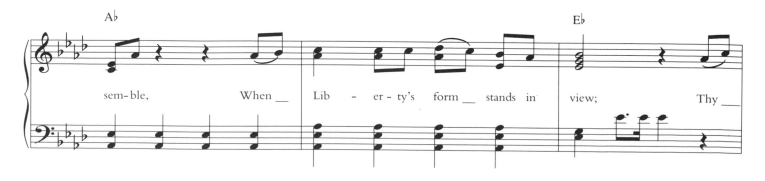

sem - ble, When __ Lib - er - ty's form __ stands in view; Thy __

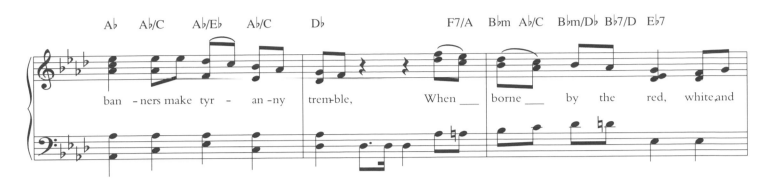

ban - ners make tyr - an - ny trem-ble, When borne by the red, white, and

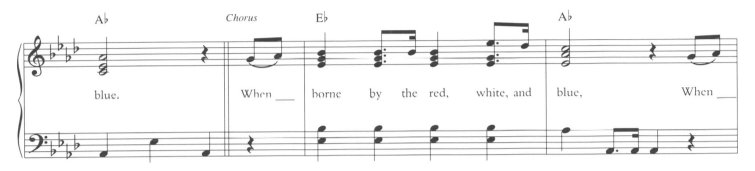

blue. When borne by the red, white, and blue, When

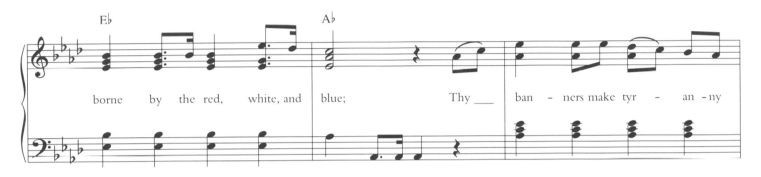

borne by the red, white, and blue; Thy ban - ners make tyr - an - ny

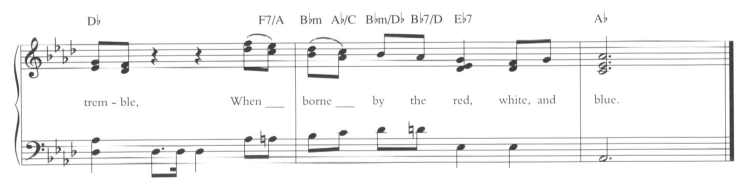

trem - ble, When borne by the red, white, and blue.

2. When war winged its wide desolation,
   And threatened the land to deform,
   The ark then of freedom's foundation,
   Columbia rode safe through the storm:
   With her garlands of vict'ry around her,
   When so proudly she bore her brave crew,
   With her flag proudly floating before her,
   The boast of the red, white, and blue
   The boast of the red, white, and **blue,** *etc.*

3. The star-spangled banner bring hither,
   O'er Columbia's true sons let it wave;
   May the wreaths they have won never wither,
   Nor its stars cease to shine on the brave:
   May thy service, united ne'er sever,
   But hold to their colors so true;
   The army and navy forever,
   Three cheers for the red, white, and blue.
   Three cheers for the red, white, and **blue,** *etc.*

Hail to the Chief

Words by Sir Walter Scott
Music by James Sanderson

Majestically

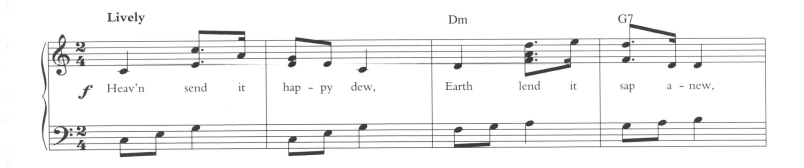

Lively   Dm   G7

f Heav'n send it hap-py dew, Earth lend it sap a-new,

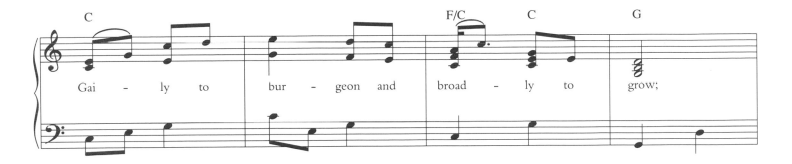

C   F/C   C   G

Gai - ly to bur - geon and broad - ly to grow;

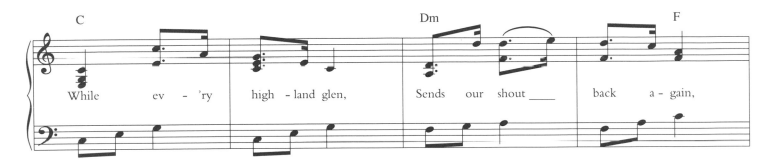

C   Dm   F

While ev - 'ry high - land glen, Sends our shout ____ back a - gain,

C

"Rod - er - igh Vich Al - pine dhu, ho! i - e - roe!"

2. Ours is no sapling, chance-sown by the fountain,
    Blooming at Beltane, in winter to fade;
    When the whirlwind has stripp'd ev'ry leaf on the mountain,
    The more shall Clan-Alpine exult in her shade.
    Ours is no sapling, chance-sown by the fountain,
    Blooming at Beltane, in winter to fade;
    When the whirlwind has stripp'd ev'ry leaf on the mountain,
    The more shall Clan-Alpine exult in her shade.
    Moor'd in the rifted rock, proof to the tempest shock,
    Firmer he roots him, the ruder it blow;
    Menteith and Breadalbane, then, echo his praise again,
    "Roderigh Vich Alpine dhu, ho! ieroe!"

3. Row, vassals, row for the pride of the Highlands!
    Stretch to your oars for the evergreen pine!
    Oh, that the rosebud that graces yon islands,
    Were wreath'd in a garland around him to twine!
    Row, vassals, row, for the pride of the Highlands!
    Stretch to your oars for the evergreen pine!
    Oh, that the rosebud that graces yon islands,
    Were wreath'd in a garland around him to twine!
    O, that some seedling gem, worthy such noble stem,
    Honor'd and bless'd in their shadow might grow!
    Loud should Clan-Alpine then, ring from her deepmost glen,
    "Roderigh Vich Alpine dhu, ho! ieroe!"

The Battle Hymn of the Republic

Words by Julia Ward Howe
Music traditional

Majestically

Glo - ry, glo - ry hal - le - lu - jah! His truth is march - ing on!

2. I have seen Him in the watchfires of a hundred circling camps,
   They have builded Him an altar in the evening dews and damps,
   I can read His righteous sentence by the dim and flaring lamps,
   His day is marching on.
   Chorus

3. I have read a fiery gospel writ in burnished rows of steel.
   "As ye deal with My contemners, so with you My grace shall deal."
   Let the Hero, born of woman, crush the serpent with His heel,
   Since God is marching on.
   Chorus

4. He has sounded forth the trumpet that shall never call retreat,
   He is sifting out the hearts of men before His judgment seat.
   Oh, be swift, my soul, to answer Him, be jubilant, my feet!
   Our God is marching on.
   Chorus

5. In the beauty of the lilies, Christ was born across the sea,
   With a glory in His bosom that transfigures you and me,
   As He died to make men holy, let us die to make men free,
   While God is marching on.
   Chorus

America
(My Country 'Tis of Thee)

Words by Samuel Francis Smith
Music traditional

Proudly

My coun - try, 'tis of thee, Sweet land of

lib - er - ty, Of thee I sing. Land where my

fa - thers died, Land of the pil - grim's pride,

From ev - 'ry___ moun - tain - side, let___ free - dom ___ ring.

2. My native country, thee,
Land of the noble free,
Thy name I love.
I love thy rocks and rills,
Thy woods and templed hills;
My heart with rapture thrills
Like that above.

3. Let music swell the breeze,
And ring from all the trees,
Sweet freedom's song.
Let mortal tongues awake,
Let all that breathe partake,
Let rocks their silence break,
The sound prolong.

4. Our fathers' God, to Thee,
Author of liberty,
To Thee we sing.
Long may our land be bright
With freedom's holy light,
Protect us by Thy might,
Great God, our King.

Good Old Fashioned
School Days

School Days

Words by Will D. Cobb
Music by Gus Edwards

School days, school days, Dear old gold - en rule days;

Read - in' and writ - in' and 'rith - ma - tic, Taught to the tune of the

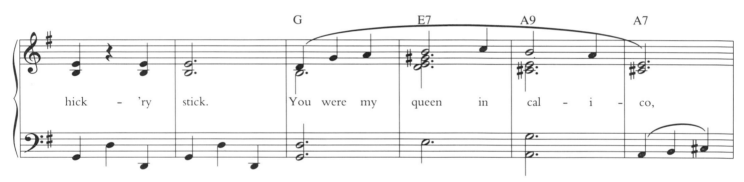

hick - 'ry stick. You were my queen in cal - i - co,

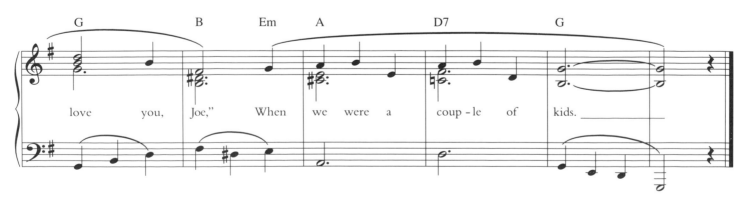

I was your bash - ful, bare - foot beau, And you wrote on my slate, "I

love you, Joe," When we were a coup - le of kids.

Hail! Hail! the Gang's All Here

Words by Theodore and Theodora Morse
Music by Theodore Morse

Energetically

f Hail! Hail! _____ the gang's all here;

What the heck do we care, what the heck do we care.

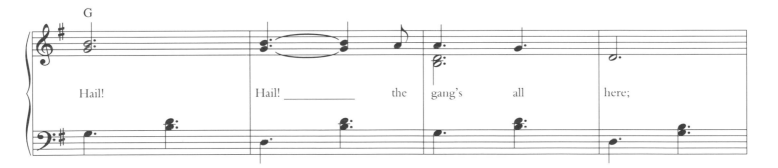

Hail! Hail! _____ the gang's all here;

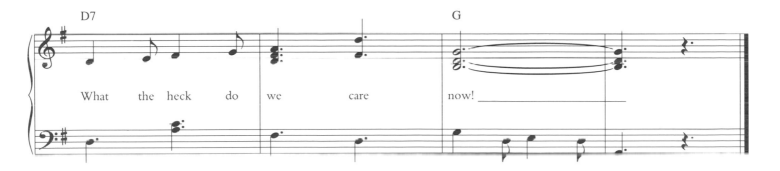

What the heck do we care now! _____

151

Bright College Years

Words by H.S. Durand
Music by Carl Wilhelm

With movement

1. Bright col – lege years, with pleas – ure rife, The short – est, glad – dest
2. In af – ter years, should troub – les rise To cloud the blue of

years of life; How swift – ly are ye glid – ing by! Oh,
sun – ny skies; How bright – ly seen through mem –'ry's haze, Those

why doth time so quick – ly fly? The sea – sons come, the
hap – py, gold – en, by – gone days. Oh, let us strive that

sea – sons go, The earth is green, or white with snow;
ev – er we May let these words our watch – cry be;

A♭6/F	A♭+	D♭		A♭	Fm	B♭m	C

But   time and   change _____ shall   naught   a -   vail

Wher - e'er up -   on _____ life's   sea   we   sail:

Fm	A♭7/G♭	A♭°7	A♭/C		E♭	E♭7/G	A♭/E♭	E♭7	A♭

To   break the   friend -   ships   formed   at   Yale. _____

"For   God, for   Coun -   try,   and   for   Yale." _____

Goodnight, Ladies

Words and music by E.P. Christy

Brightly

Good- night, la - dies! good - night, la - dies!

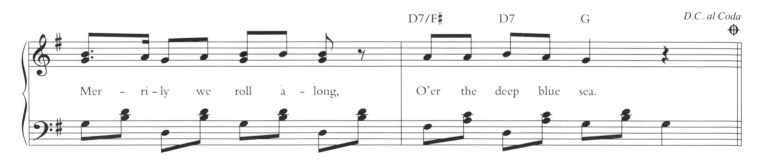

Good - night, la - dies! we're going to leave you now.

Chorus

Mer - ri-ly we roll a - long, Roll a - long, roll a - long,

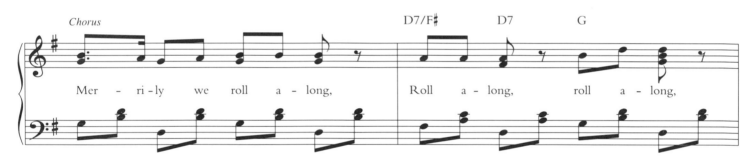

Mer - ri-ly we roll a - long, O'er the deep blue sea.

Coda

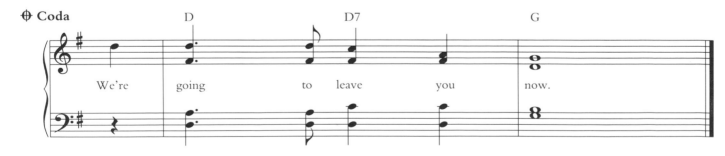

We're going to leave you now.

2. Farewell, ladies! farewell, ladies!
   Farewell, ladies! we're going to leave you now.
   Chorus

3. Sweet dreams, ladies! sweet dreams, ladies!
   Sweet dreams, ladies! we're going to leave you now.
   Chorus

Whiffenpoof Song

Words by Meade Minnegirode and George S. Pomeroy
Music by Tod B. Galloway

With feeling

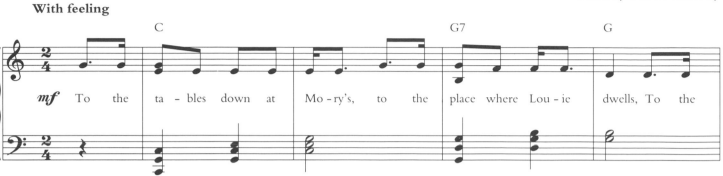

mf To the ta - bles down at Mo - ry's, to the place where Lou - ie dwells, To the

dear old Tem - ple Bar we love so well, ___ Sing the Whif - fen - poofs as -

sem - bled with their glass - es raised on high, And the ma - gic of their sing - ing casts a

spell. ___ Yes, the ma - gic of their sing - ing of the songs we love so

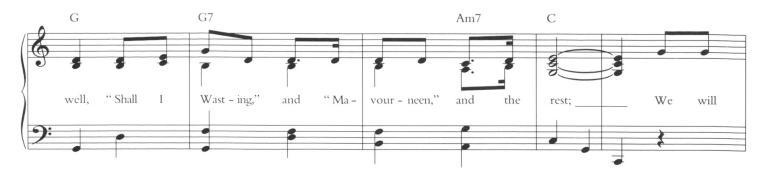

well, "Shall I Wast – ing," and "Ma – vour – neen," and the rest; We will

ser – e – nade our Lou – ie _____ while life and voice shall last, Then we'll

pass and be for – got – ten with the rest. _____ We're poor lit – tle

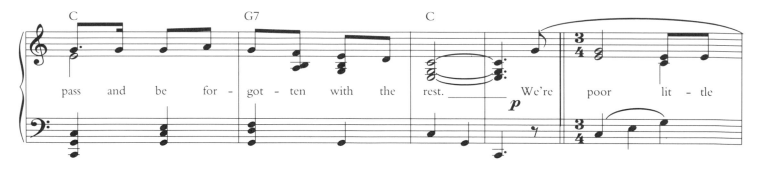

lambs who have lost their way: Baa, baa, baa. _____

_____ We're lit – tle black sheep who have gone a – stray; Baa,

baa, baa. _____ Gen - tle -men song - sters

_ff_

off on a spree, Damned from here to e -

ter - ni - ty; God have mer - cy on such as

_pp_

we: Baa, baa, baa. _____

Gaudeamus Igitur

Stately

Traditional

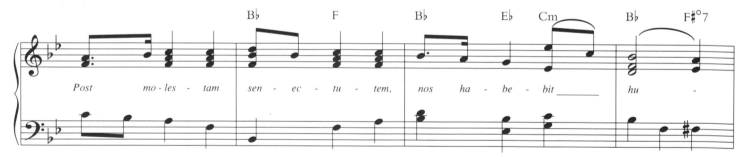

2. *Ubi sunt, qui antenos,*
   In mundo fuere?
   Ubi sunt, qui antenos,
   In mundo fuere?
   Transeas ad superos,
   Abeus ad inferos,
   Quos si vis videre,
   Quos si vis videre.

3. *Vivat academia,*
   Vivat professores,
   Vivat academia,
   Vivat professores,
   Vivat membrum quodlibet,
   Vivant membra quaelibet,
   Semper sint in flore,
   Semper sint in flore.

For He's a Jolly Good Fellow

Traditional

Brightly

For he's a jol - ly good fel - low, For he's a jol - ly good

fel - low, For he's a jol - ly good fel - low, Which

no - bod - y can de - ny. _____ Which no - bod - y can de - ny, _____ Which

no - bod - y can de - ny, _____ For he's a jol - ly good

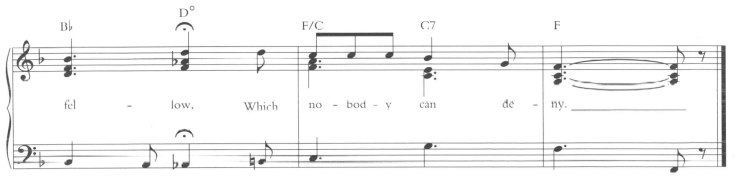

fel - low, Which no - bod - y can de - ny. _____

There Is a Tavern in the Town

Traditional

Raucously

There is a tav - ern in the town, in the town, And
there my dear love sits him down, sits him down, __ And __ drinks his wine 'mid
laugh - ter ___ free, And nev - er, nev - er thinks of me. _____

Chorus

Fare thee well, for I must leave thee, Do not let the part - ing grieve thee, Just re -

mem - ber that the best of friends must part, must part. A -

dieu, a - dieu my friends, a - dieu, yes a - dieu. I can no long - er stay with

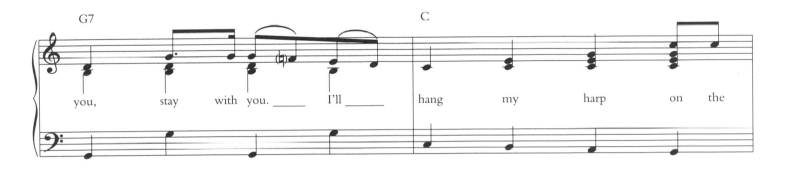

you, stay with you. _____ I'll _____ hang my harp on the

weep - ing wil - low tree, And nev - er, nev - er think of thee.

2. He left me for a damsel dark, damsel dark,
   Each Friday night they used to spark, used to spark,
   And now my love, who once was true to me,
   Takes that dark damsel on his knee.
   Chorus

3. Oh, dig my grave both wide and deep, wide and deep,
   Put tombstones at my head and feet, head and feet,
   And on my breast carve a turtledove,
   To signify I died of love
   Chorus

The Sweetheart of Sigma Chi

Words by Byron D. Stokes
Music by F. Dudleigh Vernor

Romantically

The girl of my dreams is the sweet — est girl Of

all the girls I know._____ Each sweet co-

ed, like a rain — bow trail, Fades in the

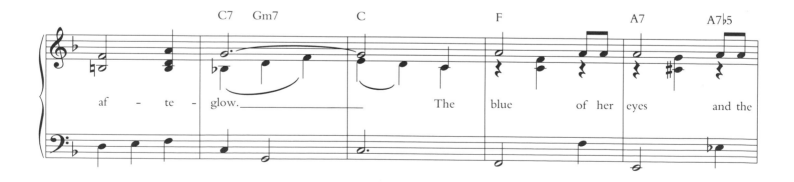

af — te — glow._____ The blue of her eyes and the

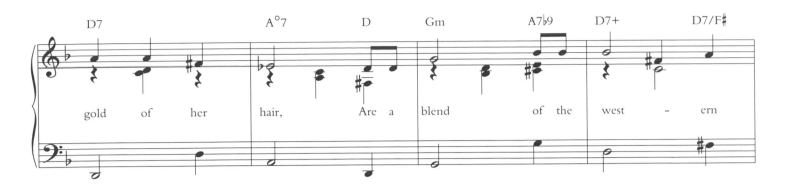

gold   of   her   hair,   Are   a   blend   of   the   west —   ern

sky, _____   And   the   moon —   light   beams _____   on   the

girl   of   my   dreams;   She's   the   sweet - heart   of   Sig —   ma

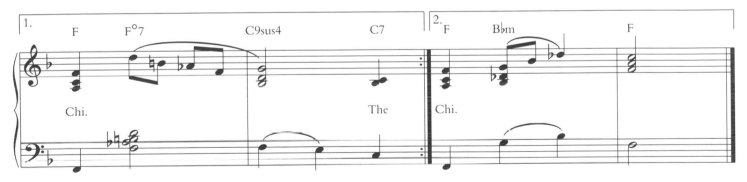

Chi.   The   Chi.

HOME FOR
THE HOLIDAYS

Home, Sweet Home

Words by John Howard Payne
Music by Henry R. Bishop

Gently moving

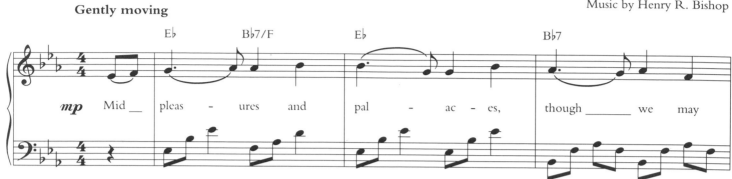

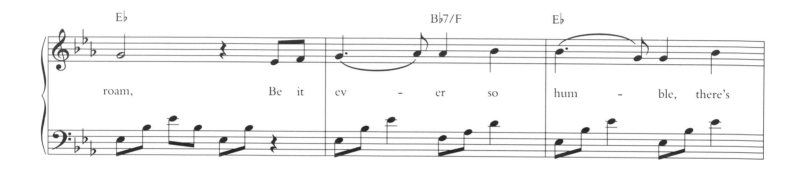

Mid __ pleas - ures and pal - ac - es, though _____ we may

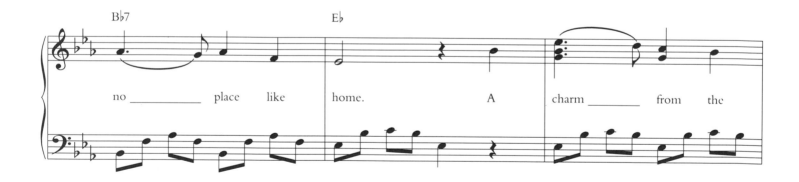

roam, Be it ev - er so hum - ble, there's

no _____ place like home. A charm _____ from the

skies seems to hal - low us there, Which,

seek _____ through the world, is ne'er met _____ with else - where.

Chorus

Home, home, _____ sweet, sweet home, There's no _____ place like

home, There's no _____ place like home.

rall.

2. I gaze on the moon as I tread the drear wild,
   And feel that my mother now thinks of her child,
   As she looks on that moon from our own cottage door,
   Through the woodbine whose fragrance shall cheer me no more.
   Chorus

3. An exile from home, splendor dazzles in vain;
   Oh, give me a lowly thatched cottage again;
   The birds singing gaily, that came at my call,
   Give me them, and that peace of mind, dearer than all.
   Chorus

Over the River and Through the Wood

Traditional

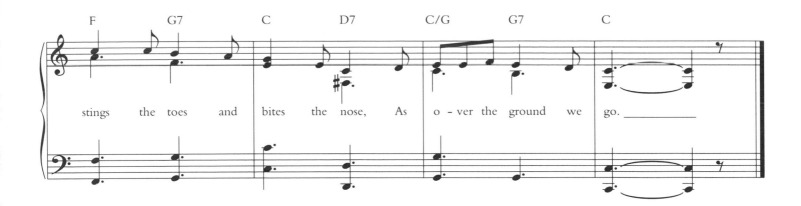

stings   the toes   and   bites   the nose,   As   o - ver the ground   we   go. _____

2. Over the river and through the wood,
   To have a full day of play.
   Oh, hear the bells ringing "ting-a-ling ling,"
   For it's Thanksgiving Day.
   Over the river and through the wood,
   Trot fast, my dapple gray.
   Spring o'er the ground just like a hound.
   Hurrah for Thanksgiving Day!

3. Over the river and through the wood,
   And straight through the barnyard gate.
   It seems that we go so dreadfully slow,
   It is so hard to wait.
   Over the river and through the wood,
   Now grandma's cap I spy.
   Hurrah for fun, the pudding's done,
   Hurrah for the pumpkin pie!

Prayer of Thanksgiving

Traditional

With reverence

We gath - er to - geth - er, To ask the Lord's bless - ing; He

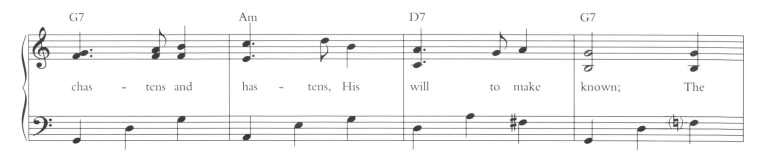

chas - tens and has - tens, His will to make known; The

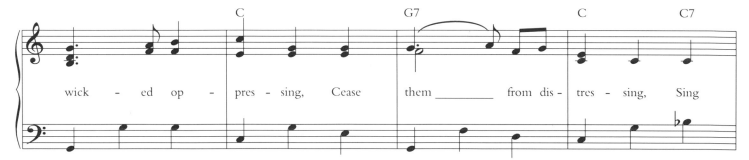

wick - ed op - pres - sing, Cease them _____ from dis - tres - sing, Sing

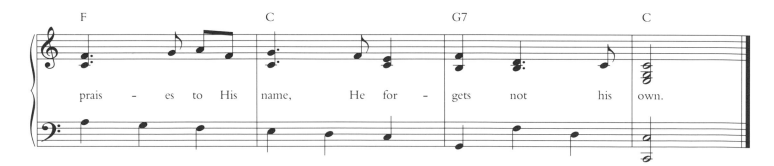

prais - es to His name, He for - gets not his own.

2. Beside us to guide us,
   Our God with us joining,
   Ordaining, maintaining
   His kingdom divine;
   So from the beginning,
   The fight we were winning,
   Thou, Lord, wast at our side,
   Let the glory be Thine.

3. We all do extol Thee,
   Thou leader in battle,
   And pray that Thou still
   Our defender will be.
   Let Thy congregation
   Escape tribulation.
   Thy name be ever praised,
   And Thy people be free.

Joy to the World

Words by Isaac Watts
Music by Lowell Mason

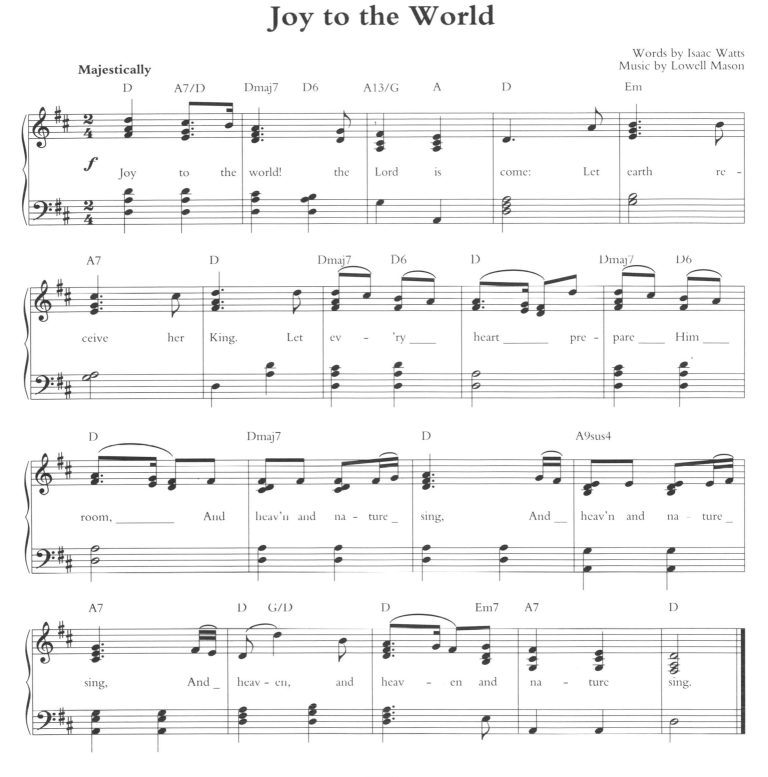

2. Joy to the world! the Savior reigns.
Let men their songs employ,
While fields and floods,
Rocks, hills, and plains,
Repeat the sounding joy,
Repeat the sounding joy,
Repeat, repeat the sounding joy.

3. He rules the world with truth and grace,
And makes the nations prove,
The glories of
His righteousness,
And wonders of His love,
And wonders of His love,
And wonders, wonders of His love.

Havah Nagilah

Traditional

Vigorous hora

Somewhat faster

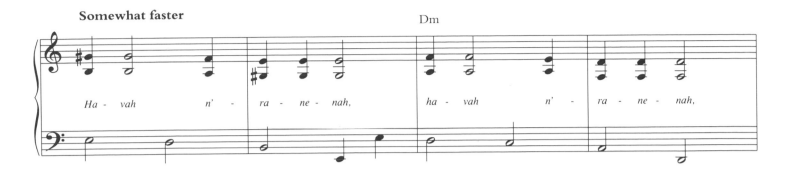

Ha - vah n' - ra - ne - nah, ha - vah n' - ra - ne - nah,

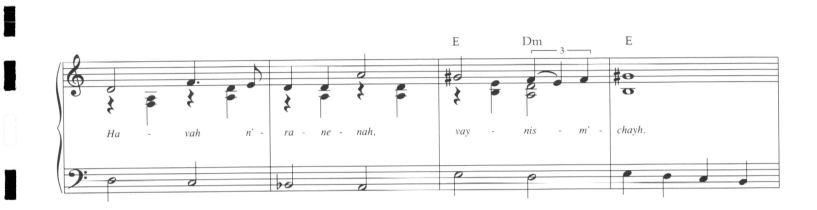

Ha - vah n' - ra - ne - nah, vay - nis - m' - chayh.

Ha - vah n' - ra - ne - nah, ha - vah n' - ra - ne - nah,

Ha - vah n' - ra - ne - nah, vay - nis - m' - chayh.

octaves optional to end

Silent Night

Words by Joseph Mohr
Music by Franz Gruber

Quietly

Si - lent night, ho - ly night, All is calm,

all is bright, 'Round yon vir - gin moth - er and Child,

Ho - ly In - fant, so ten - der and mild, Sleep in heav - en - ly

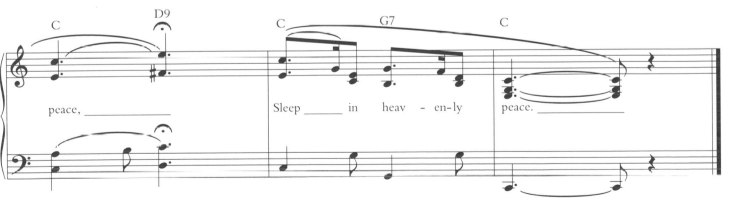

peace, _____ Sleep _____ in heav - en - ly peace. _____

2. Silent night, holy night,
   Shepherds quake at the sight,
   Glories stream from heaven afar,
   Heav'nly hosts sing alleluia,
   Christ, the Savior, is born,
   Christ, the Savior, is born.

3. Silent night, holy night,
   Son of God, love's pure light,
   Radiant beams from Thy holy face,
   With the dawn of redeeming grace,
   Jesus, Lord at Thy birth,
   Jesus, Lord at Thy birth.

Jingle Bells

Words and music by J. S. Pierpont

Cheerfully

Dash – ing through the snow, In a one horse o – pen sleigh,

O'er the fields we go, Laugh–ing all the way,

Bells on bob – tail ring, Mak – ing spir – its bright, What

fun it is to ride and sing A sleigh–ing song to – night. Oh,

Chorus

jin - gle bells, jin - gle bells, jin - gle all the way.

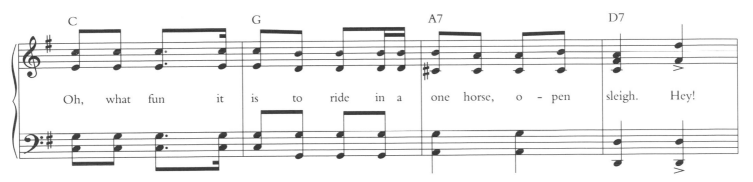

Oh, what fun it is to ride in a one horse, o - pen sleigh. Hey!

Jin - gle bells, jin - gle bells, jin - gle all the way,

Oh, what fun it is to ride in a one horse, o - pen sleigh.

2. A day or two ago,
   I though I'd take a ride,
   And soon Miss Fannie Bright,
   Was seated by my side.
   The horse was lean and lank,
   Misfortune seemed his lot,
   He got into a drifted bank,
   And we, we got upsot.
   Chorus

3. Now the ground is white,
   Go it while you're young,
   Take the girls tonight,
   And sing this sleighing song.
   Just get a bob-tailed nag,
   Two-forty for his speed,
   Then hitch him to an open sleigh,
   And crack! you'll take the lead.
   Chorus

The First Noel

Traditional

Chorus

No - el, _____ No - el, No - el, No -

el, Born is the King _____ of Is - ra - el.

2. They looked up and saw a star,
   Shining in the East, beyond them far,
   And to the earth, it gave great light,
   And so it continued both day and night.
   Chorus

3. This star drew nigh to the Northwest,
   O'er Bethlehem it took its rest,
   And there it did both stop and stay,
   Right over the place where Jesus lay.
   Chorus

We Wish You a Merry Christmas

Traditional

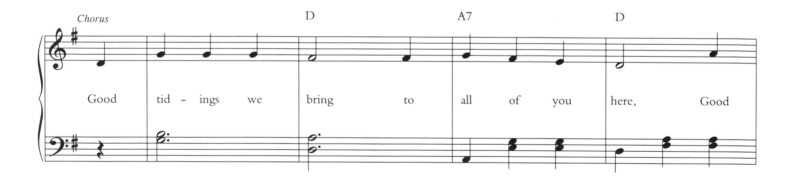

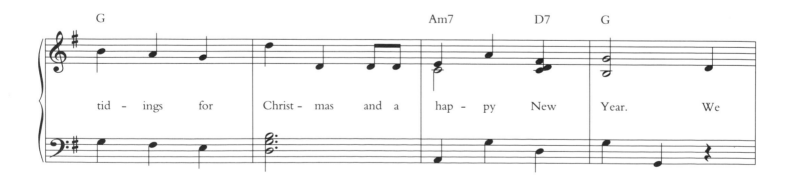

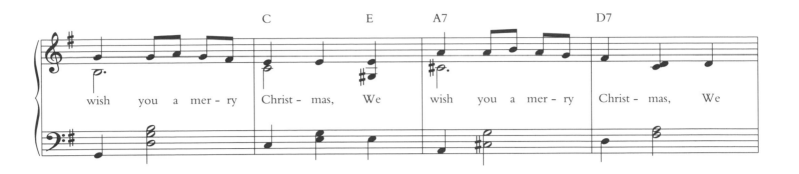

wish you a mer – ry Christ – mas, We wish you a mer – ry Christ – mas, We

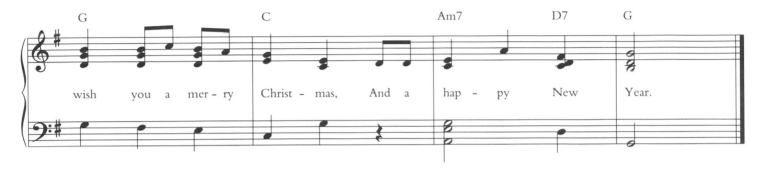

wish you a mer – ry Christ – mas, And a hap – py New Year.

2. Oh, bring us some figgy pudding,
   Oh, bring us some figgy pudding,
   Oh, bring us some figgy pudding,
   And a cup of good cheer.
   Chorus

3. We won't go until we get some,
   We won't go until we get some,
   We won't go until we get some,
   So bring it right here.
   Chorus

Hanukkah Song

Traditional

Oh, Ha - nuk - kah, oh, Ha - nuk - kah, come light the me - no - rah,

Let's have a par - ty, we'll all dance the *ho - ra.* Gath-er 'round the ta - ble, we'll

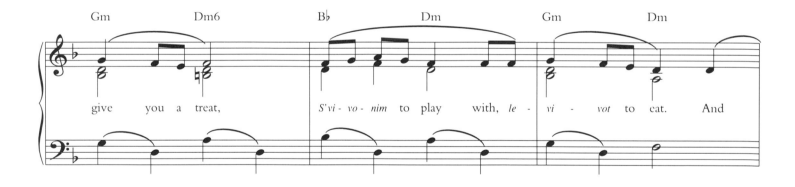

give you a treat, *S'vi - vo - nim* to play with, *le - vi - vot* to eat. And

while we are play- ing, The can - dles are burn - ing ____ low;

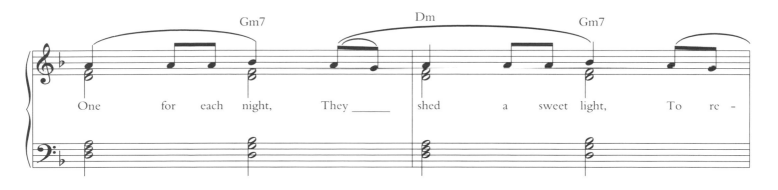

One   for   each   night,   They _____ shed   a   sweet   light,   To   re -

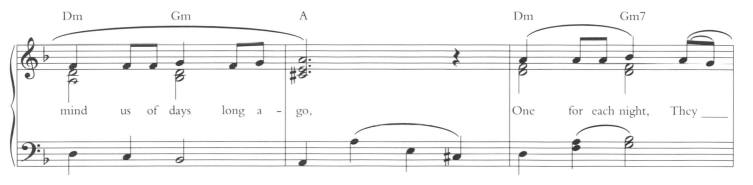

mind   us   of   days   long   a - go,   One   for   each night,   They ____

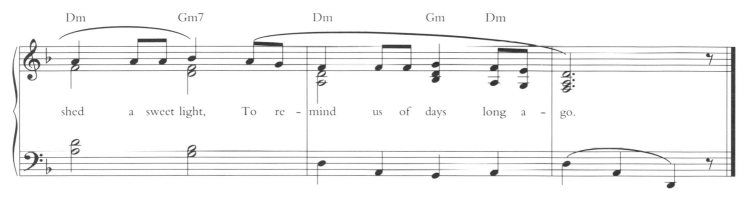

shed   a   sweet light,   To   re - mind   us   of   days   long   a - go.

Auld Lang Syne

Words by Robert Burns
Music traditional

With fervor

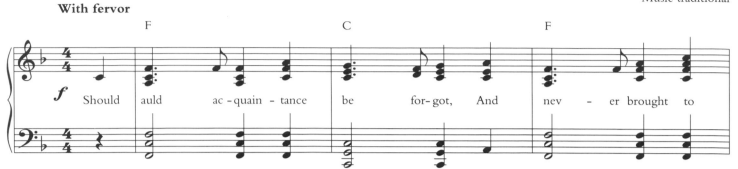

Should auld ac-quain-tance be for-got, And nev — er brought to

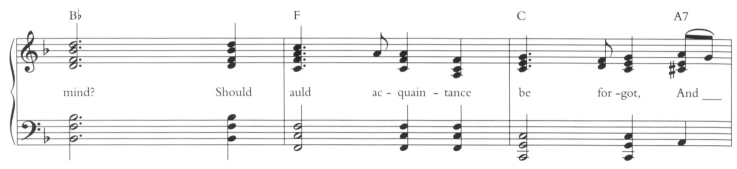

mind? Should auld ac-quain-tance be for-got, And ___

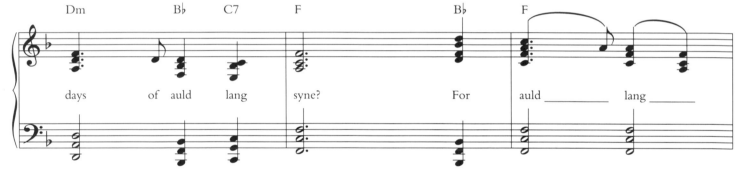

days of auld lang syne? For auld _____ lang _____

syne, my dear For auld _____ lang _____ syne, We'll

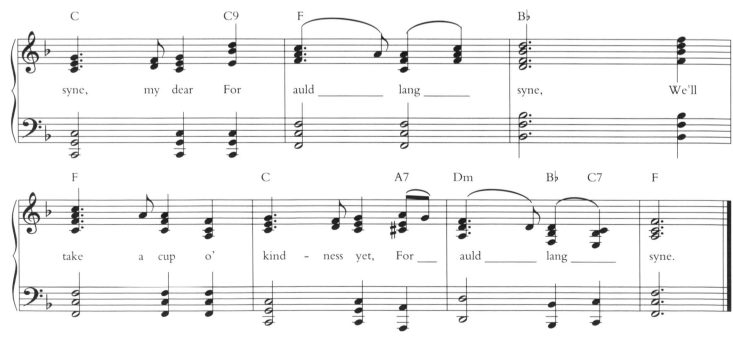

take a cup o' kind — ness yet, For ___ auld _____ lang _____ syne.

2. We twa ha'e ran aboot the braes,
   And pu'd the gowans fine,
   We've wandered many a weary foot,
   Sin auld lang syne.

3. We twa ha'e sported i' the burn,
   Frae mornin' sun till dine,
   But seas between us braid ha'e roared,
   Sin auld lang syne.

4. And here's a hand my trusty frien',
   And gie's a hand o' thine,
   We'll take a cup o' kindness yet,
   For auld lang syne.

SONGS OF THE HEART

Love's Old Sweet Song

Words and music by G. Clifton Bingham
and James Lyman Molloy

Sweetly

1. Once in the dear, dead days be - yond re - call, When on the world the
2. E - ven to - day we hear love's song of yore, Deep in our hearts it

mists be - gan to fall; Out of the dreams that rose in hap - py throng,
dwells for - ev - er - more; Foot - steps may fal - ter, wea - ry grow the way,

Low to our hearts love sang an old sweet song; And in the dusk, where
Still we can hear it at the close of day; So till the end, when

fell the fire - light gleam, Soft - ly it wove it - self in - to our dream.
life's dim sha - dows fall, Love will be found the sweet- est song of all.

186

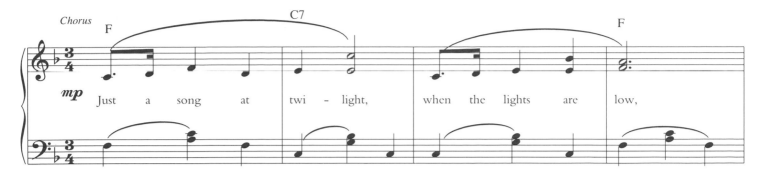

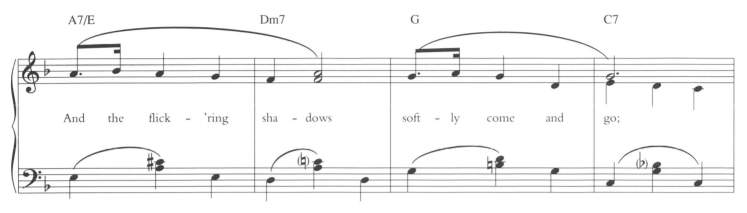

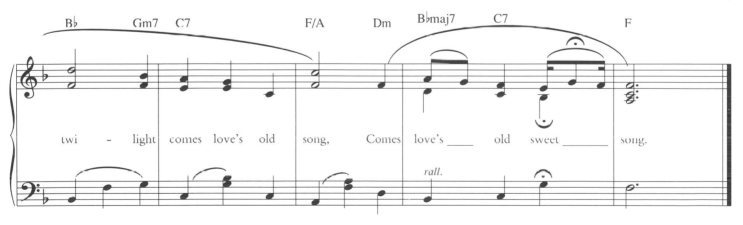

Long, Long Ago

Words and music by Thomas H. Bayly

With movement

Tell me the tales that to me were so dear, Long, long a-go,

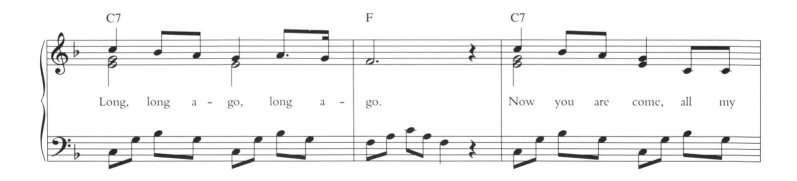

long, long a-go. Sing me the songs I de-light-ed to hear,

Long, long a-go, long a-go. Now you are come, all my

grief is re-moved, Let me for-get that so long you have roved.

Let me be - lieve that you love as you loved,

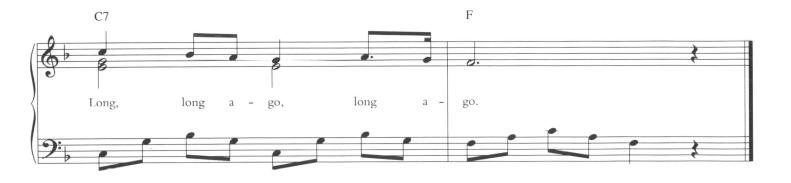

C7   F

Long, long a - go, long a - go.

2. Do you remember the path where we met,
   Long, long ago, long, long ago?
   Ah, yes, you told me you ne'er would forget,
   Long, long ago, long ago.
   Then to all others my smile you preferred,
   Love, when you spoke, gave a charm to each word,
   Still my heart treasures the praises I heard,
   Long, long ago, long ago.

3. Tho' by your kindness my fond hopes were raised,
   Long, long ago, long, long ago,
   You by more eloquent lips have been praised,
   Long, long ago, long ago.
   But, by long absence your truth has been tried,
   Still to your accents I listen with pride,
   Blessed as I was when I sat by your side,
   Long, long ago, long ago.

Beautiful Dreamer

With feeling

Words and music by Stephen Foster

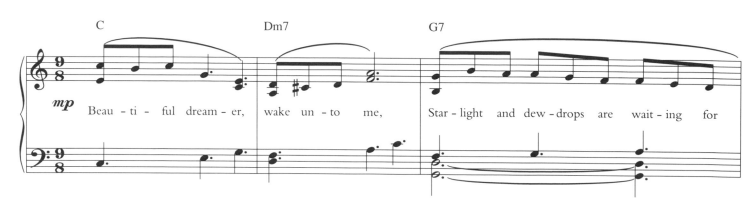

mp Beau - ti - ful dream - er, wake un - to me, Star - light and dew - drops are wait - ing for

thee. _____ Sound of the rude world heard in the day,

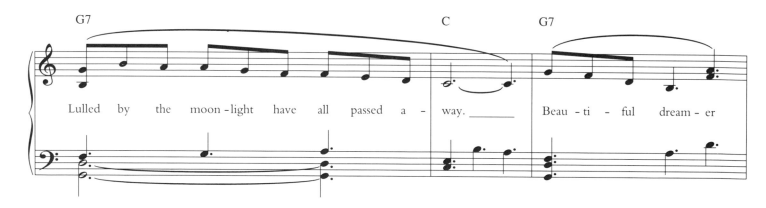

Lulled by the moon - light have all passed a - way. _____ Beau - ti - ful dream - er

queen of my song, List while I woo thee with soft mel - o - dy.

Gone are the cares of life's bus-y throng, Beau-ti-ful dream-er a-wake un-to

Broaden

me. _____ Beau-ti-ful dream-er a-wake un-to me. _____

2. Beautiful dreamer, out on the sea,
   Mermaids are chanting the wild lorelie;
   Over the streamlet vapors are borne,
   Waiting to fade at the bright coming morn.
   Beautiful dreamer, beam in my heart,
   E'en as the morn on the streamlet and sea;
   Then will all clouds of sorrow depart,
   Beautiful dreamer, awake unto me!
   Beautiful dreamer, awake unto me!

3. Beautiful dreamer, wake unto me,
   Starlight and dewdrops are waiting for thee.
   Sound of the rude world heard in the day,
   Lulled by the moonlight have all passed away.
   Beautiful dreamer, queen of my song,
   List while I woo thee with soft melody.
   Gone are the cares of life's busy throng,
   Beautiful dreamer, awake unto me.
   Beautiful dreamer, awake unto me.

Aura Lee

Words by W.W. Fosdick
Music by George R. Poulton

As the black-bird in the Spring, 'Neath the wil-low tree,

Sat and piped, I heard him sing, Sing of Aur-a Lee.

Chorus

Aur-a Lee, Aur-a Lee, Maid with gold-en hair,

Sun-shine came a-long with thee, And swal-lows in the air.

2. Take my heart and take my ring,
I give my all to thee,
Take me for eternity,
Dearest Aura Lee.
Chorus

3. In thy blush the rose was born;
Music when you spake;
Through thine azure eye, the morn,
Sparkling, seemed to break.
Chorus

4. Aura Lee, the bird may flee
The willow's golden hair,
Then the wintry winds may be
Blowing ev'rywhere,

Final Chorus
Yet if thy blue eyes I see,
Gloom will soon depart,
For to me, sweet Aura Lee
Is sunshine to the heart.

192

I Love You Truly

Words and music by Carrie Jacobs-Bond

With movement

I'll Take You Home Again, Kathleen

Words and music by Thomas P. Westendorf

Fondly

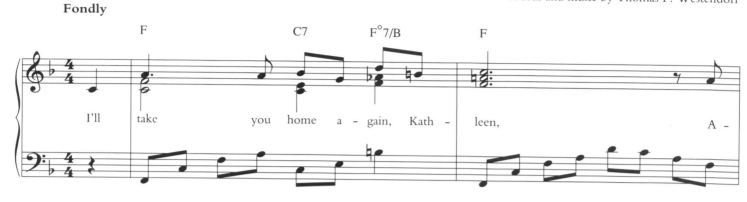

I'll take you home a - gain, Kath - leen, A -

cross the o - cean wild and wide, To where your heart has ev - er

been, Since first you were my bon - ny bride. The

ros — es all have left your cheek, I've watched them fade a - way and

die; Your voice is sad when-e'er you speak, And

tears be-dim your lov-ing eyes. *Chorus* Oh, I will take you back, Kath-

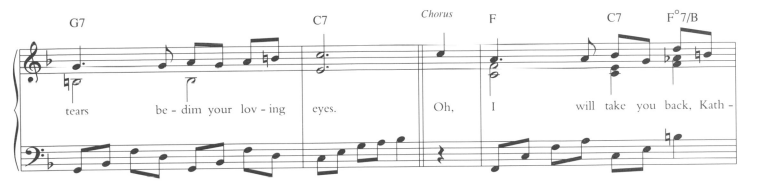

leen, To where your heart will feel no pain, And

when the fields are fresh and green, I will take you to your home a - gain.

2. I know you love me, Kathleen dear,
   Your heart was ever fond and true,
   I always feel when you are near,
   That life holds nothing dear, but you.
   The smiles that once you gave to me,
   I scarcely ever see them now;
   The many, many times I see,
   A dark'ning shadow on your brow.
   Chorus

3. To that dear home beyond the sea,
   My Kathleen shall again return,
   And when thy old friends welcome thee,
   Thy loving heart will cease to yearn.
   Where laughs the little silver stream,
   Beside your mother's humble cot,
   And brightest rays of sunshine gleam,
   There all your grief will be forgot.
   Chorus

(Around Her Neck)
She Wore a Yellow Ribbon

Traditional

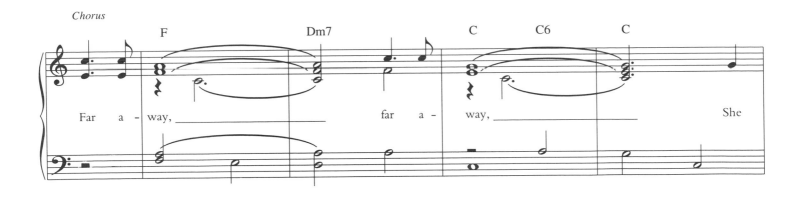

Chorus

Far a - way, _____ far a - way, _____ She

wore it for her lov - er who was far, far a - way.

The Riddle Song

Traditional

Smoothly

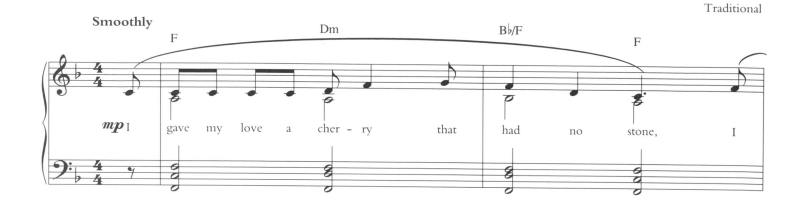

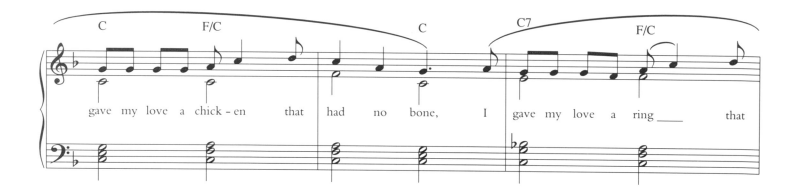

2. How can there be a cherry that has no stone?
   How can there be a chicken that has no bone?
   How can there be a ring that has no end?
   How can there be a baby with no cryin'?

3. A cherry when it's bloomin' it has no stone,
   A chicken when it's pippin', it has no bone,
   A ring when it's rollin', it has no end,
   A baby when it's sleepin' has no cryin'.

Annie Laurie

Words by William Doublas
Music by Lady John Scott

With movement

Max – wel – ton's braes are bon – nie, Where ear – ly falls the ___

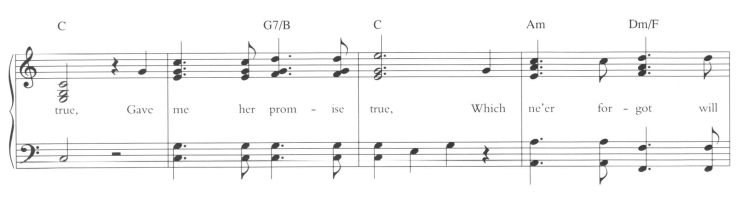

dew, And 'twas there that An – nie Lau – rie Gave me her prom – ise

true, Gave me her prom – ise true, Which ne'er for – got will

be, And for bon – nie An – nie ___ Lau – rie, I'd ___ lay ___ me doon and dee.

2. Her brow is like a snowdrift,
Her throat is like the swan,
Her face it is the fairest,
That e'er the sun shone on,
That e'er the sun shone on,
And dark blue is her e'e,
And for bonnie Annie Laurie,
I'd lay me doon and dee.

3. Like dew on th'gowan lying,
Is the fall of her fairy feet,
And like winds in summer sighing,
Her voice is low and sweet,
Her voice is low and sweet,
And she's all the world to me,
And for bonnie Annie Laurie,
I'd lay me doon and dee.

Silver Threads Among the Gold

Words by Eben E. Rexford
Music by Hart P. Danks

Tenderly

Dar - ling, I am grow - ing old, _____ Sil - ver threads a - mong the

gold, Shine up - on my brow to - day, _____

Life is fad - ing fast a - way. But, my dar - ling, you will

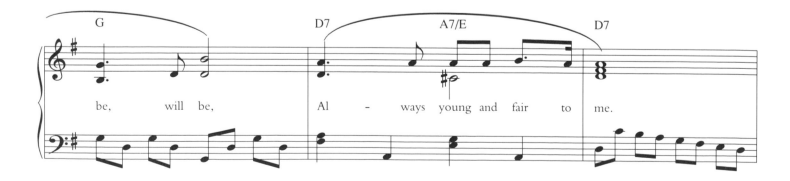

be, will be, Al - ways young and fair to me.

Yes, my dar-ling, you will be _____ Al - ways young and fair to

Chorus

me. Dar - ling, I am grow - ing, grow - ing old,

Sil - ver threads a - mong the gold, Shine up - on my brow to -

day, _____ life is fad - ing fast a - way.

2. When your hair is silver white,
And your cheeks no longer bright,
With the roses of the May,
I will kiss your lips and say:
"Oh, my darling, mine alone, alone,
You have never older grown,
Yes, my darling, mine alone,
You have never older grown."
Chorus

3. Love can never more grow old,
Locks may lose their brown and gold,
Cheeks may fade and hollow grow,
But the hearts that love will know:
Never, never winter's frost and chill,
Summer warmth is in them still,
Never winter's frost and chill,
Summer warmth is in them still.
Chorus

4. Love is always young and fair:
What to us is silver hair,
Faded cheeks or steps grown slow,
To the heart that beats below?
Since I kissed you, mine alone, alone,
You have never older grown,
Since I kissed you, mine alone,
You have never older grown.

A Boy's Best Friend Is His Mother

Words and music by J.P. Skelly

Fondly

While __ plod – ding on our way, the toil – some road of life, How

few the friends that dai – ly there we meet. Not __ man – y will stand by in

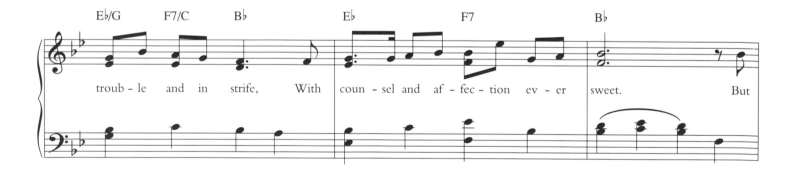

troub – le and in strife, With coun – sel and af – fec – tion ev – er sweet. But

there is one whose smile will ev – er on us beam, Whose love is dear – er far than an – y

oth - er, _____ And wher - ev - er we may turn, This les - son we will learn, A

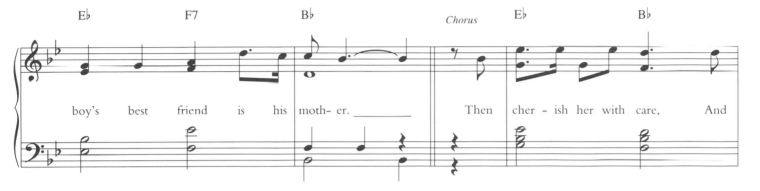

Chorus

boy's best friend is his moth- er. _____ Then cher - ish her with care, And

smooth her sil - v'ry hair, When gone, you will nev - er get an - oth - er; _____ And wher-

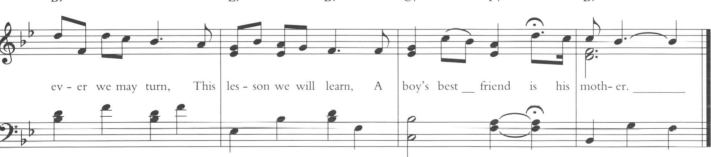

ev - er we may turn, This les - son we will learn, A boy's best __ friend is his moth- er. _____

2. Though all the world may frown, and ev'ry friend depart,
   She never will forsake us in our need.
   Our refuge evermore, is still within her heart,
   For us her loving sympathy will plead.
   Her pure and gentle smile, forever cheers our way,
   'Tis sweeter and 'tis purer than all other.
   When she goes from earth away,
   We'll find out while we stray,
   A boy's best friend is his mother.
   Chorus

3. Her fond and gentle face, not long may greet us here,
   Then cheer her with our kindness and our love.
   Remember at her knee in childhood bright and dear,
   We heard her voice like angel's from above
   Though after years may bring their gladness or their woe,
   Her love is sweeter far than any other.
   And our longing heart will learn,
   Wherever we may turn,
   A boy's best friend is his mother.
   Chorus

After the Ball

Words and music by Charles K. Harris

A lit – tle maid – en climbed an old man's

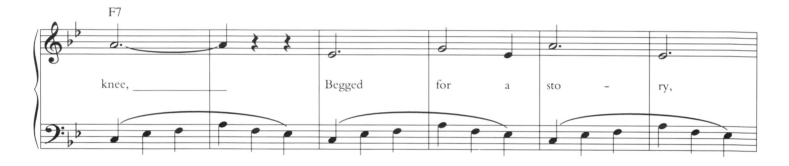

knee, Begged for a sto – ry,

"Do Un – cle, please." "Why are you

sin – gle; why live a – lone?

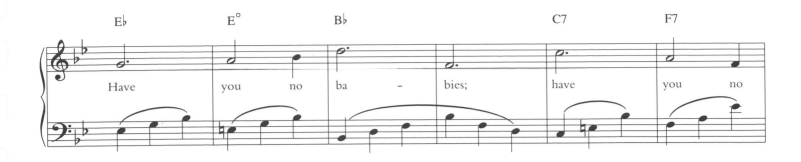

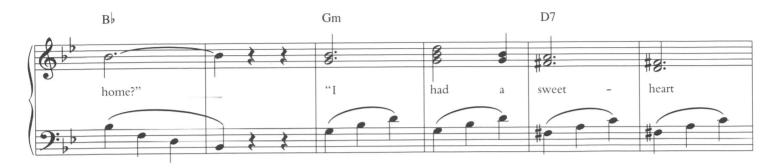

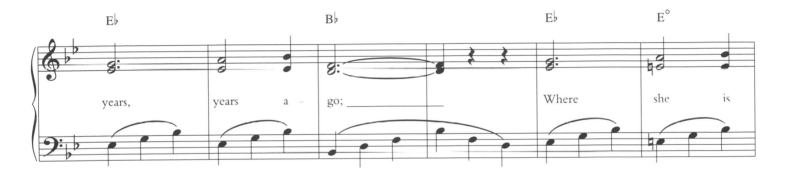

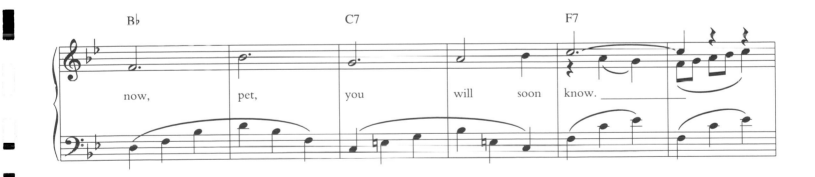

205

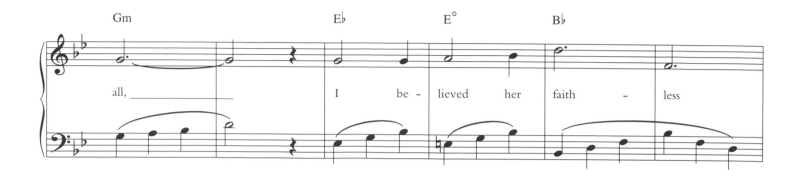

all, _____ I be - lieved her faith - less

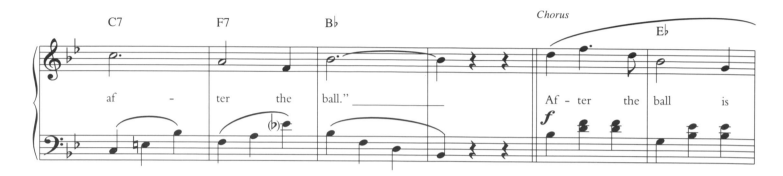

af - ter the ball." _____ Af - ter the ball is

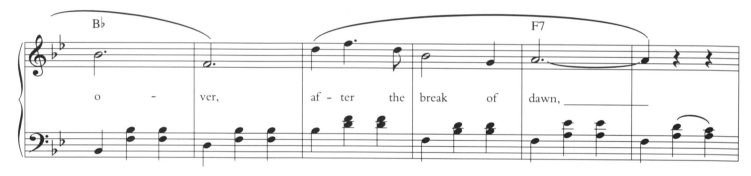

o - ver, af - ter the break of dawn, _____

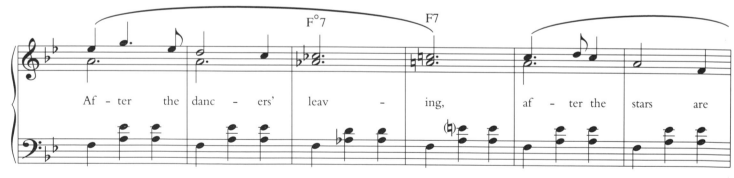

Af - ter the danc - ers' leav - ing, af - ter the stars are

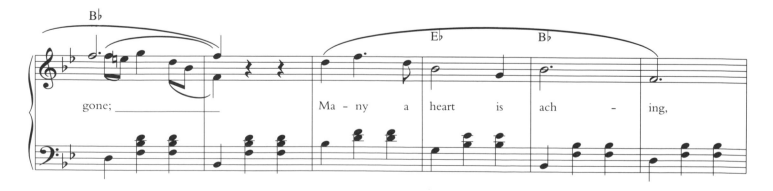

gone; _____ Ma - ny a heart is ach - ing,

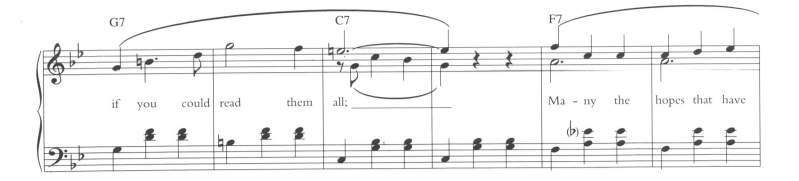

if you could read them all;_____ Ma - ny the hopes that have

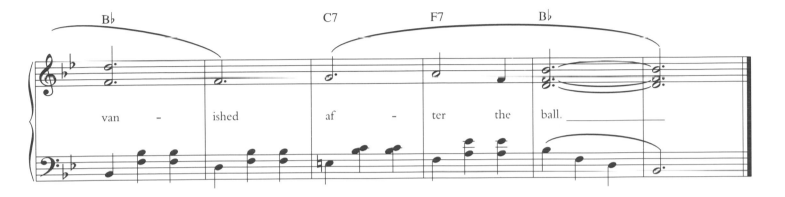

van - ished af - ter the ball._____

2. Bright lights were flashing in the grand ballroom,
   Softly the music, playing sweet tunes.
   There came my sweetheart, my love, my own;
   "I wish some water, leave me alone."
   When I returned, dear, there stood a man,
   Kissing my sweetheart, as lovers can;
   Down fell the glass, pet, broken, that's all;
   Just as my heart was after the ball.
   Chorus

3. Long years have passed, child, I've never wed;
   True to my lost love, though she is dead.
   She tried to tell me, tried to explain;
   I would not listen, pleadings were vain.
   One day a letter came from that man;
   He was her brother, the letter ran.
   That's why I'm lonely, no home at all;
   I broke her heart, pet, after the ball.
   Chorus

NOVELTIES & MEMORIES

Daisy Bell

Words and music by Harry Dacre

Moderately

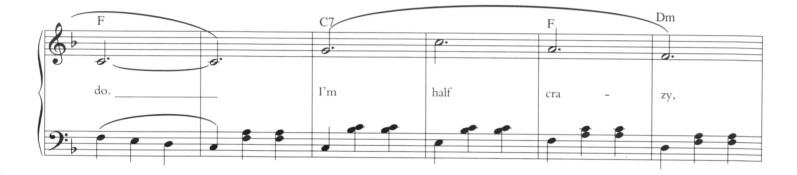

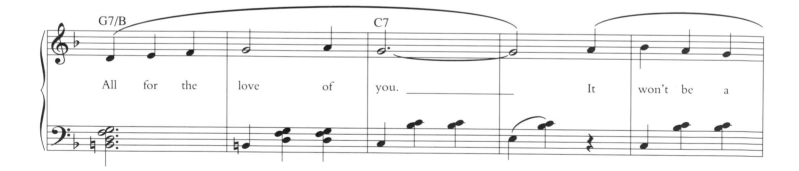

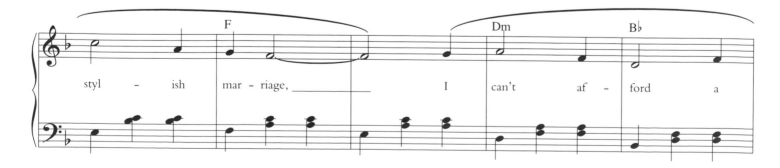

car - riage, _____ But you'd look sweet Up - on the

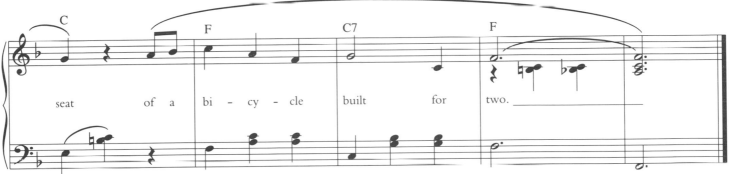

seat of a bi - cy - cle built for two. _____

The Daring Young Man
(On the Flying Trapeze)

Words by George Leybourne
Music by Alfred Lee

Brightly

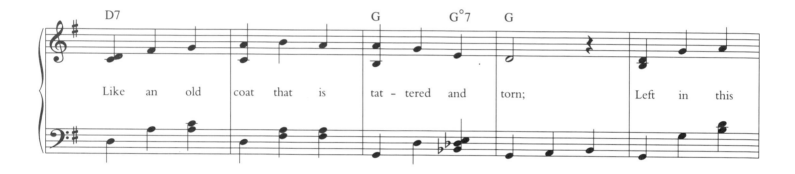

Oh, once I was hap-py, but now I'm for-lorn, Like an old coat that is tat-tered and torn;

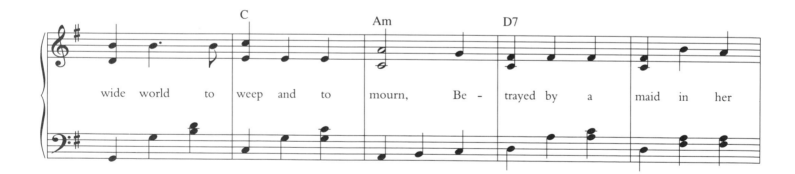

Left in this wide world to weep and to mourn, Be-trayed by a maid in her teens.

Oh, this maid that I loved, she was hand-some

And I tried all I knew, her to please, _____ But I

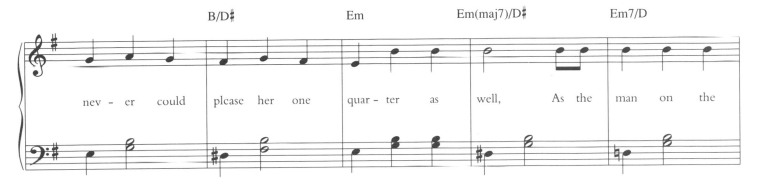

nev - er could please her one quar - ter as well, As the man on the

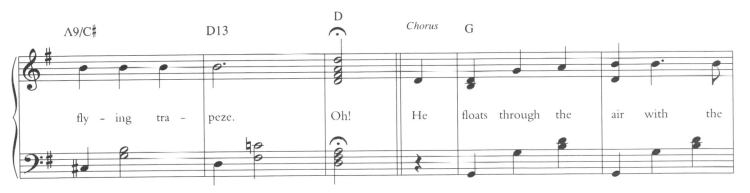

fly - ing tra - peze. Oh! He floats through the air with the

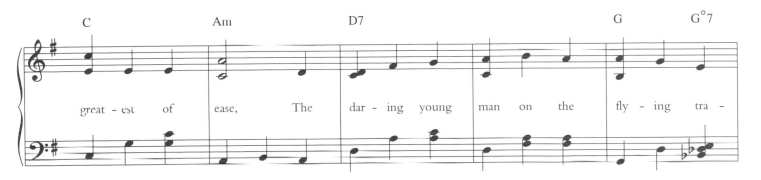

great - est of ease, The dar - ing young man on the fly - ing tra -

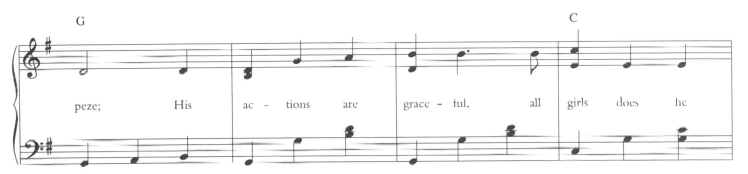

peze; His ac - tions are grace - ful, all girls does he

please, And my love he has sto - len a - way. _____

2. Now the young man by name was Señor Boni Slang,
   Tall, big, and handsome, as well-made as Chang.
   Where'er he appeared, how the hall loudly rang,
   With ovations from all people there.
   He'd smile from the bar on the people below,
   And one night he smiled on my love;
   She winked back at him, and she shouted "Bravo!"
   As he hung by his nose from above.
   Chorus

3. Her father and mother were both on my side,
   And tried very hard to make her my bride;
   Her father, he sighed, and her mother, she cried,
   To see her throw herself away.
   'Twas all no avail, she went there ev'ry night,
   And threw her bouquets on the stage,
   Which caused him to meet her--how he ran me down,
   To tell it would take a whole page.
   Chorus

4. One night I, as usual, went to her dear home,
   And found there her mother and father alone;
   I asked for my love, and soon 'twas made known,
   To my horror, that she'd run away.
   She packed up her boxes and eloped in the night,
   With him with the greatest of ease;
   From two stories high he had lowered her down,
   To the ground on his flying trapeze.
   Chorus

5. Some months after that, I went into a hall;
   To my surprise I found there on the wall,
   A bill in red letters which did my heart gall,
   That she was appearing with him.
   He'd taught her gymnastics, and dressed her in tights,
   To help him live at ease;
   He'd made her assume a masculine name,
   And now she goes on the trapeze.

Final Chorus

She floats through the air with the greatest of ease,
You'd think her a man on the flying trapeze,
She does all the work while he takes his ease,
And that's what's become of my love.

Sippin' Cider Through a Straw

Traditional

Moderately

The pret -ti -est girl _____ I ev - er saw _____

___ Was sip-pin' ci - der through a straw. _____

Chorus

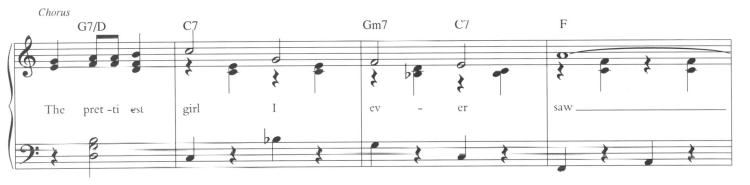

The pret -ti est girl I ev - er saw _____

___ Was sip-pin' ci - der through a straw _____

2. Twas lucky for me,
The straw did slip,
I sipped the cider from her lip.
Chorus

3. She told me that I
Was not her kind,
Then right away she changed her mind.
Chorus

4. Her cheek against mine,
And jaw to jaw,
We both sipped cider through a straw.
Chorus

5. And that's how I got
A mother-in-law,
From sippin' cider through a straw.
Chorus

Under the Bamboo Tree

Words and music by Bob Cole

A - wait -ing there his love to see _____ And then to her he'd sing; _____
You'll hear some Zu - lu ev - 'ry day _____ Gush out this soft re - frain; _____

Chorus

If you lak - a - me, lak I lak - a - you, And we lak - a both the same,

I lak - a say, this ver - y day, I lak - a change your name; ___ 'Cause

I love - a - you, and love-a - you true, And if you - a - love - a - me,

One live as two, two live as one, Un- der the bam - boo tree. _____

Take Me Out to the Ball Game

Words by Jack Norworth
Music by Albert Von Tilzer

Rhythmic waltz

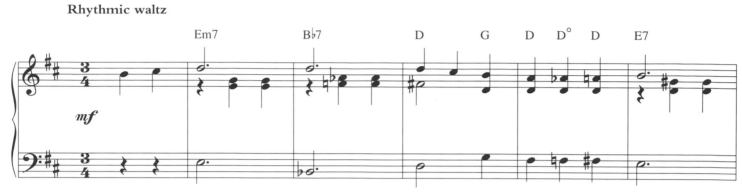

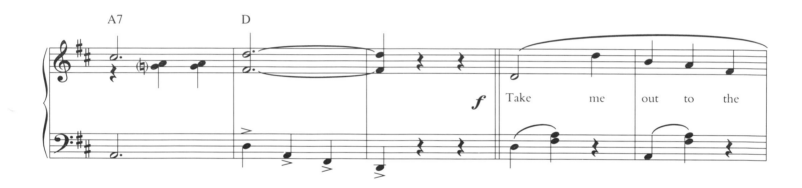

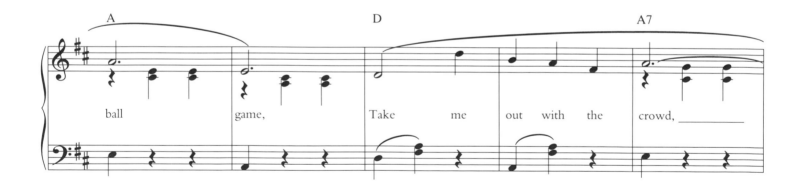

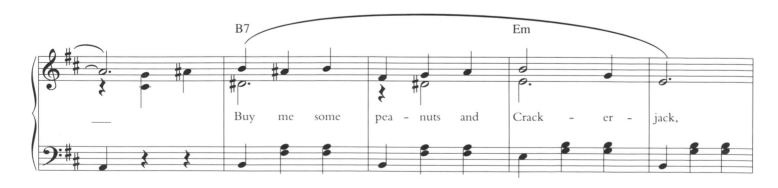

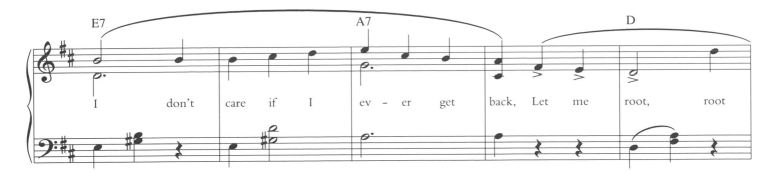

I don't care if I ev – er get back, Let me root, root

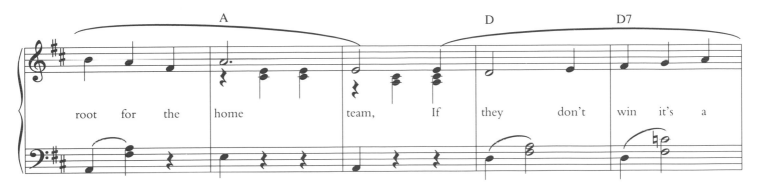

root for the home team, If they don't win it's a

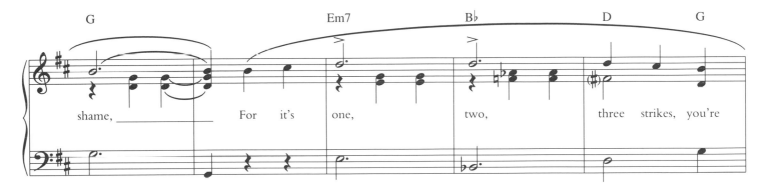

shame, _____ For it's one, two, three strikes, you're

out, At the old ball game. _____

The Band Played On

Words by John F. Palmer
Music by John F. Palmer and Charles B. Ward

Lively waltz tempo

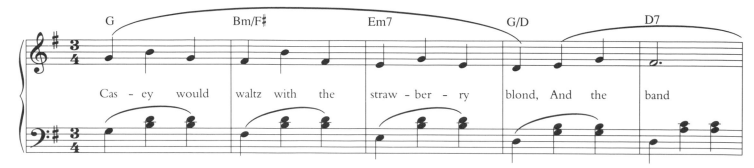

Cas - ey would waltz with the straw - ber - ry blond, And the band

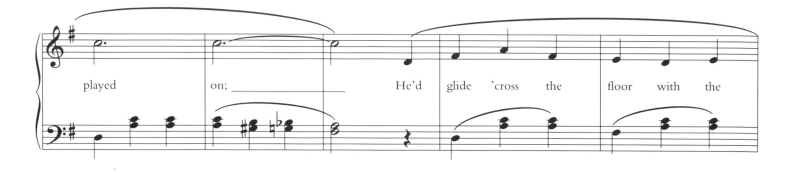

played on; _____ He'd glide 'cross the floor with the

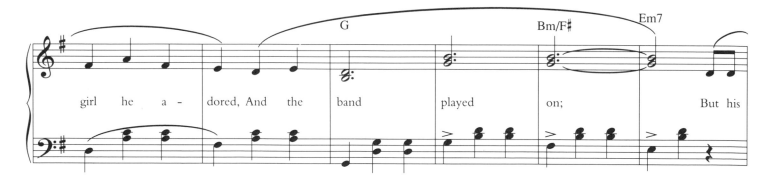

girl he a - dored, And the band played on; But his

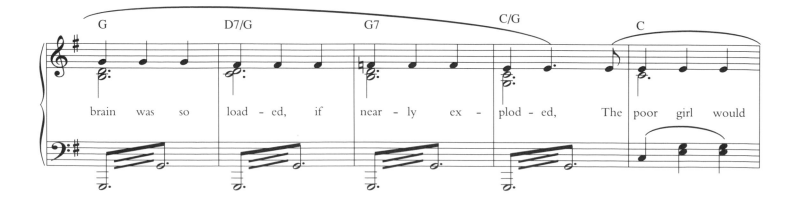

brain was so load - ed, if near - ly ex - plod - ed, The poor girl would

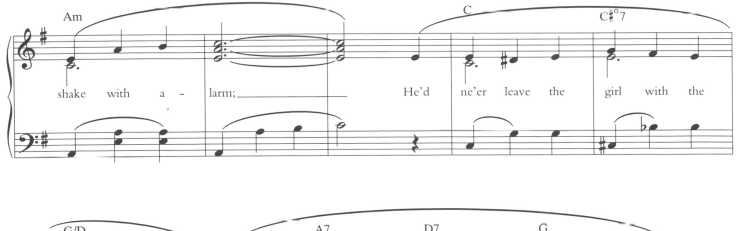

Am .... C ...... C#°7

shake with a - larm;_____ He'd ne'er leave the girl with the

G/D ...... A7 ...... D7 ...... G

straw - ber - ry curl, And the band played on._____

Grandfather's Clock

Words and Music by Henry C. Work

My grand-fa-ther's clock was too large for the shelf, So it stood nine-ty years on the floor; It was tall-er by far than the old man himself, Though it weighed not a pen-ny-weight more. It was bought on the more of the day that he was born, And was al-ways his treas-ure and pride; But it stopped short, nev-er to go a-gain, When the

old man died. Nine - ty years with - out slum - ber - ing,

tick, tock, tick, tock, His life sec - onds num - ber - ing,

tick, tock, tick, tock; It stopped short

nev - er to go a - gain, When the old man died.

2. In watching its pendulum swing to and fro,
   Many hours had he spent while a boy;
   And in childhood and manhood, the clock seemed to know,
   And to share both his grief and his joy;
   For it struck twenty-four when he entered at the door,
   With a blooming and beautiful bride;
   But it stopped short, never to go again,
   When the old man died.
   Chorus

3. My grandfather said that of those he could hire,
   Not a servant so faithful he found;
   For it wasted no time, and had but one desire,
   At the close of each week, to be wound;
   And it kept in its place, not a frown upon its face,
   And its hands never hung by its side,
   But it stopped short, never to go again,
   When the old man died.
   Chorus

4. It rang an alarm in the dead of the night,
   An alarm that, for years, had been dumb;
   And we knew that his spirit was pluming its flight,
   That his hour of departure had come.
   Still the clock kept the time, with a soft and muffled chime,
   As we silently stood by his side;
   But it stopped short, never to go again,
   When the old man died.
   Chorus

Hello! Ma Baby

Words and Music by Ida Emerson and Joseph E. Howard

Lively

Hel - lo! ma ba - by, hel - lo! ma hon - ey, Hel - lo! ma rag - time

gal, Send me a kiss by wire, Ba - by, my heart's on

fire. If you re - fuse me, hon - ey, you'll lose me,

Then you'll be left a - lone; Oh, ba - by, tel - e - phone and

tell me you're my own.

The Teddy Bears' Picnic

Words and Music by John W. Bratton and James B. Kennedy

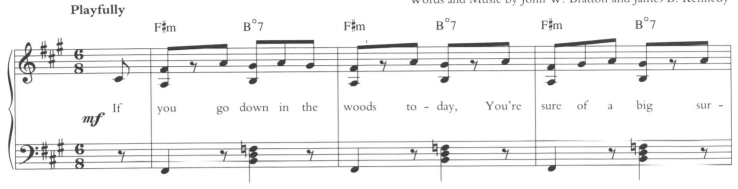

If you go down in the woods to - day, You're sure of a big sur -

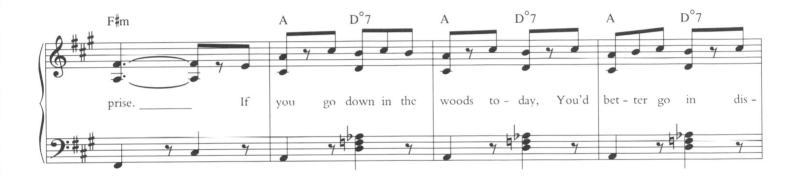

prise. _____ If you go down in the woods to - day, You'd bet - ter go in dis -

guise; _____ For ev - 'ry bear that ev - er there was Will gath - er there for

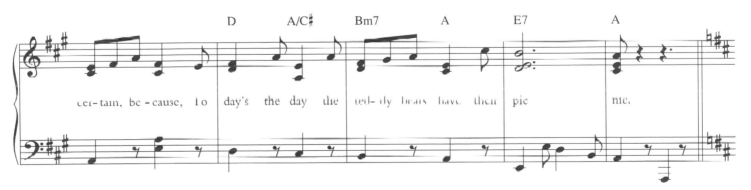

cer - tain, be - cause, To - day's the day the ted - dy bears have their pic - nic.

225

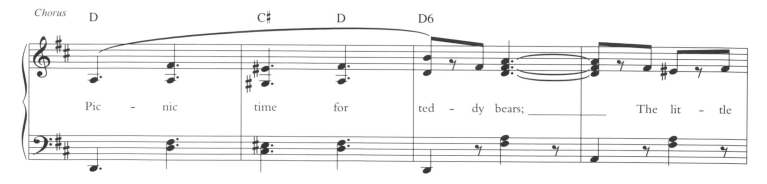

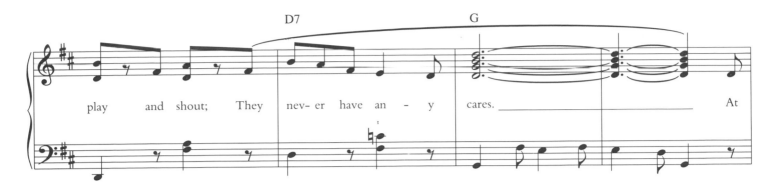

play   and   shout;   They   nev-er   have   an — y   cares._____   At

six   o'-clock their   mum — mies and dad – dies will   take   them home   to   bed,   Be – cause they're

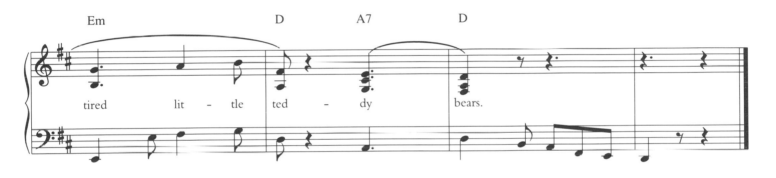

tired   lit – tle   ted – dy   bears.

2. Ev'ry teddy bear who's been good
   Is sure of a treat today.
   There's lots of marvelous things to eat,
   And wonderful games to play.
   Beneath the trees where nobody sees,
   They'll hide and seek as long as they please,
   'Cause that's the way the teddy bears have their picnic.
   Chorus

3. If you go down in the woods today,
   You'd better not go alone.
   It's lovely down in the woods today,
   But safer to stay at home.
   For ev'ry bear that ever there was
   Will gather there for certain, because
   Today's the day the teddy bears have their picnic.
   Chorus

There'll Be a Hot Time in the Old Town Tonight

Words by Joe Hayden
Music by Theodore A. Metz

Vigorously

Come a - long, get you read - y, wear your bran' bran' new gown, For there's

gon - na be a meet - ing in that good, good old town, Where you

know most ev - 'ry - body and they all sure know you, And you've

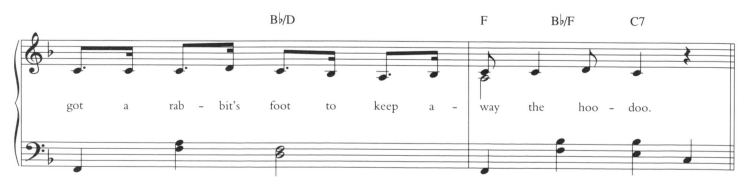

got a rab - bit's foot to keep a - way the hoo - doo.

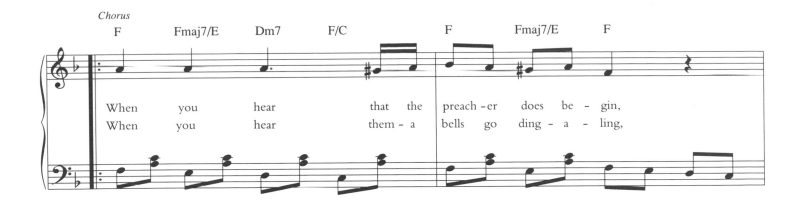

Chorus

When you hear that the preach-er does be-gin,
When you hear them-a bells go ding-a-ling,

Bend down low for to drive a-way your sin, And when you
All join 'round and _____ sweet-y you must sing, And when the

get re - li - gion, you _____ want to dance and sing; There'll be a
verse is all through, In the chor-us, all join in; There'll be a

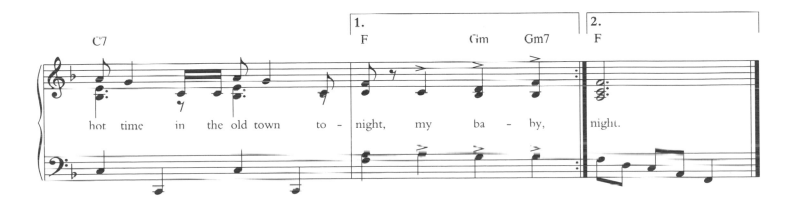

hot time in the old town to - night, my ba - by, night.

TIN PAN ALLEY:
THE POP SONG
COMES OF AGE

(On) Moonlight Bay

Words by Edward Madden
Music by Percy Wenrich

Moderately

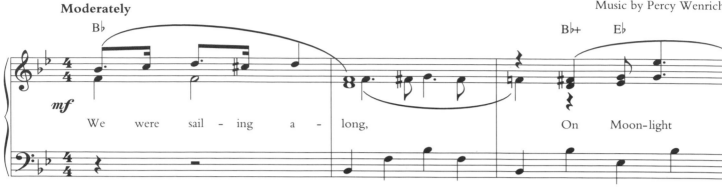

We were sail-ing a-long, On Moon-light

Bay, We could hear the voic-es ring-ing,

___ They seemed to say, "You have sto-len my

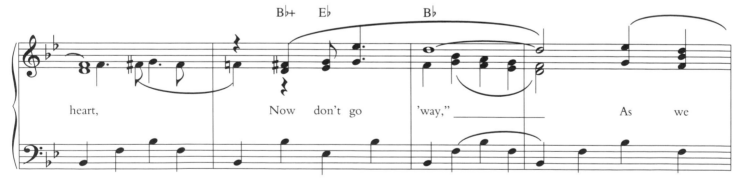

heart, Now don't go 'way," As we

sang "Love's Old Sweet Song" on Moon-light Bay.

Sweet Adeline

Words by Richard H. Gerard
Music by Henry W. Armstrong

Moderately

mp Sweet A - del - ine, _____ My A - del ine,

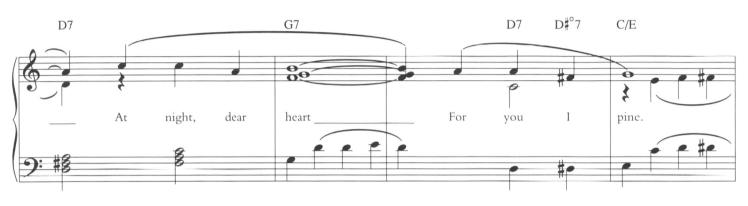

_____ At night, dear heart _____ For you I pine.

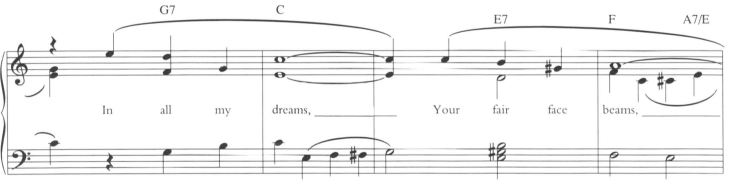

In all my dreams, _____ Your fair face beams,

_____ You're the flow - er of my heart, Sweet A - del - ine. _____

Let Me Call You Sweetheart

Words and Music by Beth Slater Whitson and Leo Friedman

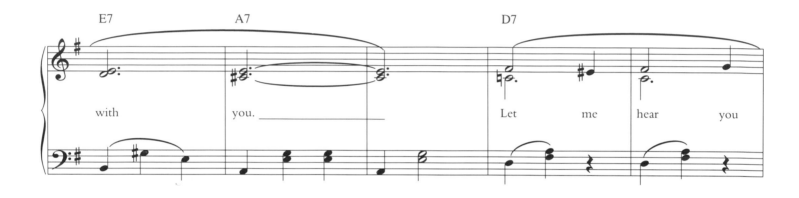

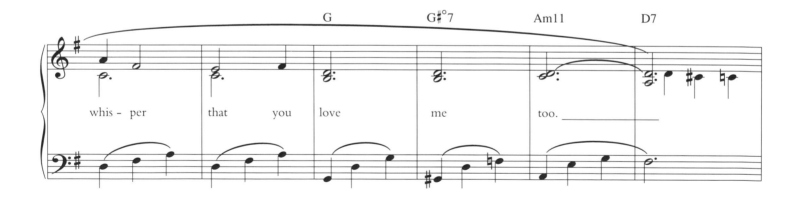

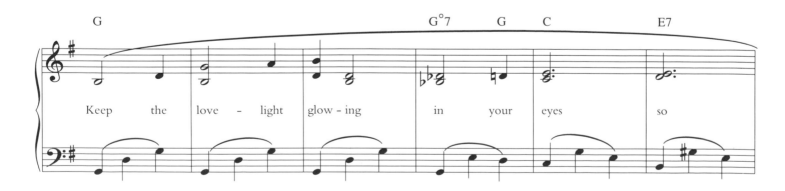

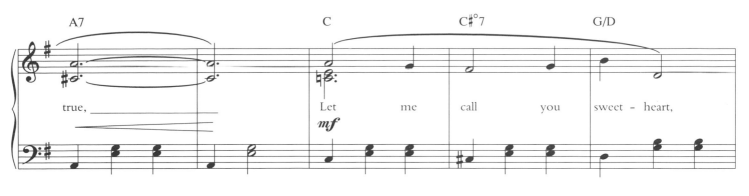

true, _____ Let me call you sweet - heart,

mf

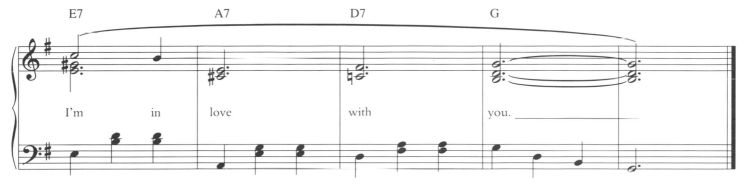

I'm   in   love   with   you. _____

When Irish Eyes Are Smiling

Words by Chauncey Olcott and George Graff, Jr.
Music by Ernest R. Ball

With movement

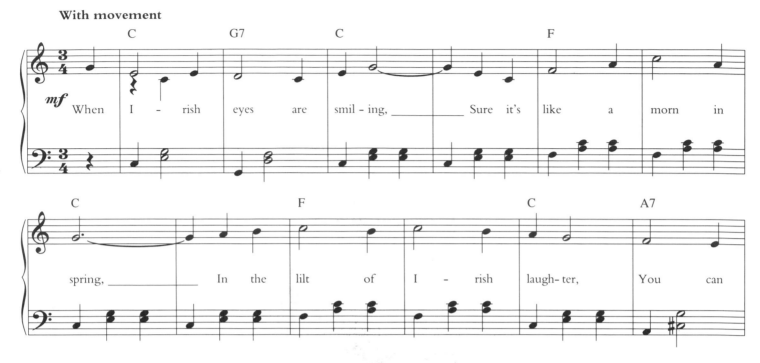

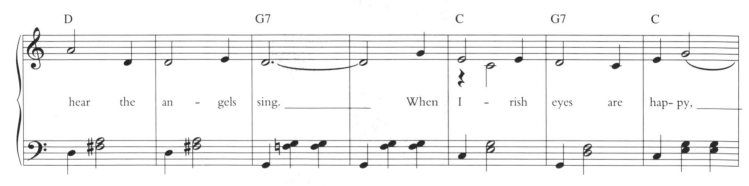

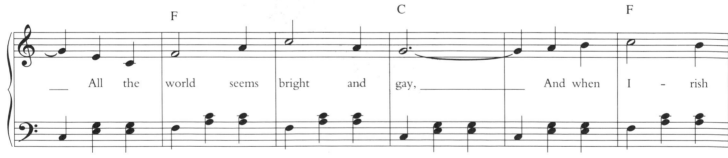

When I - rish eyes are smil - ing, _____ Sure it's like a morn in spring, _____ In the lilt of I - rish laugh-ter, You can hear the an - gels sing. _____ When I - rish eyes are hap-py, _____ All the world seems bright and gay, _____ And when I - rish eyes are smil - ing, Sure they steal ___ your heart a - way. _____

By the Light of the Silvery Moon

Words by Edward Madden
Music by Gus Edwards

With a steady beat

237

In the Shade of the Old Apple Tree

Words by Harry H. Williams
Music by Egbert Van Alstyne

With a lilt

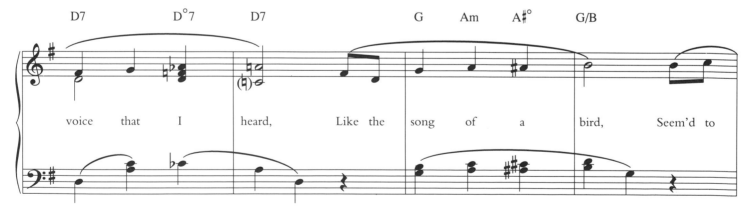

In the shade of the old ap-ple tree, Where the

love in your eyes I could see, When the

voice that I heard, Like the song of a bird, Seem'd to

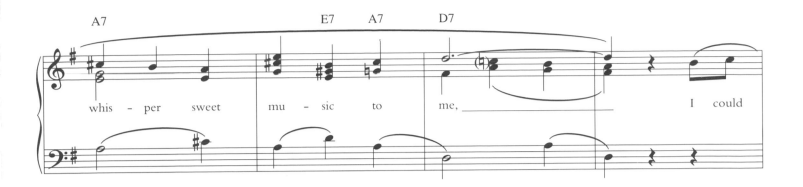

whis – per sweet mu – sic to me, _____ I could

hear the dull buzz of the bee, _____ In the

blos – soms as you said to me, _____ With a

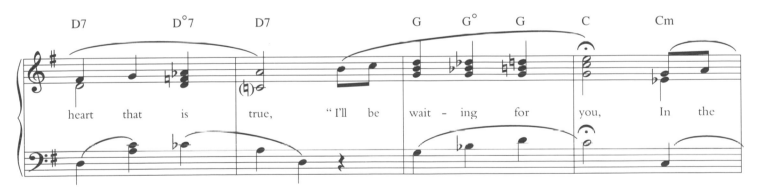

heart that is true, "I'll be wait – ing for you, In the

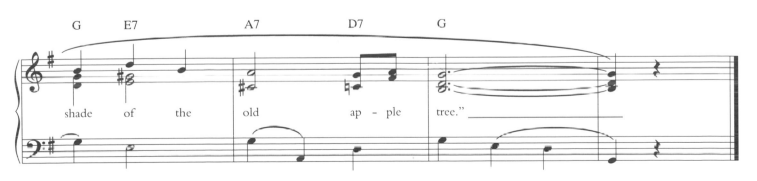

shade of the old ap – ple tree." _____

Goodbye, My Lady Love

Words and Music by Joe E. Howard

Brightly

Good-bye, my la-dy love, Fare-well, my tur-tle dove,

You are the i-dol and dar-ling of my heart, But some day

you will come back to me, And love me ten-der-ly, So

good-bye, my la-dy love, good-bye. _____

Peg o' My Heart

Words by Alfred Bryan
Music by Fred Fisher

Flowingly

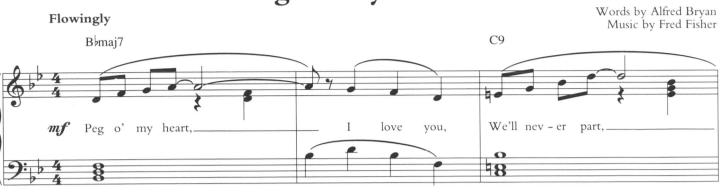

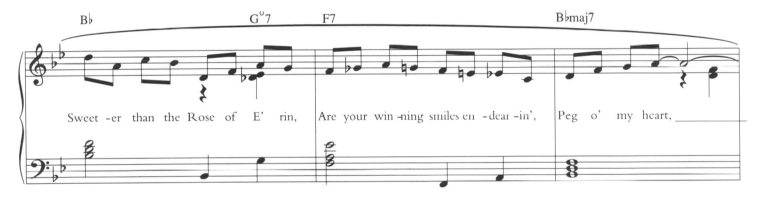

Dark Eyes

Traditional

With passion

Eyes of ec - sta - sy, _____ Al - ways haunt - ing me, _____

_____ Al - ways haunt - ing me _____ With your mys - ter - y;

_____ Tell me ten - der - ly, _____ You be - long to me _____

_____ For e - ter - ni - ty, _____ Dark eyes, talk to me. _____

242

Shine On Harvest Moon

Words by Jack Norworth
Music by Nora Bayes and Jack Norworth

Moderately

mp Oh, shine on, shine on har-vest moon up in the

sky. I ain't had no lov-in' since Jan-u-ar-y, Feb-ru-ar-y,

June, or Ju-ly, Snow time ain't no time to sit out-side and

spoon, So, shine on, shine on har-vest moon for me and my gal.

I Want a Girl—Just Like the Girl
That Married Dear Old Dad

Words by William Dillon
Music by Harry Von Tilzer

With feeling

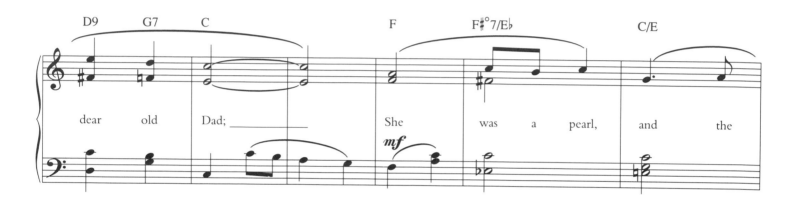

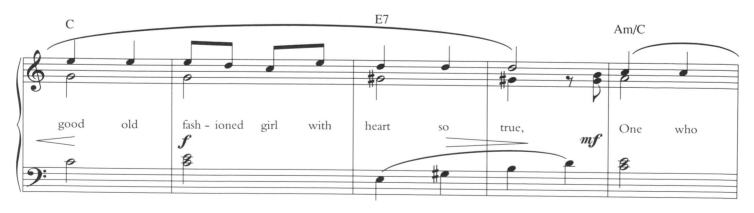

loves no-bod-y else but you; I want a girl, just

like the girl that mar-ried dear old Dad. _____

In the Good Old Summertime

Words by Ren Shields
Music by George Evans

Waltz tempo

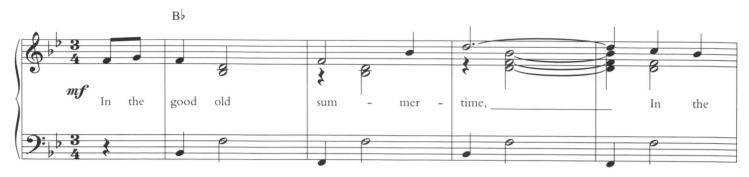

In the good old sum-mer-time, _____ In the

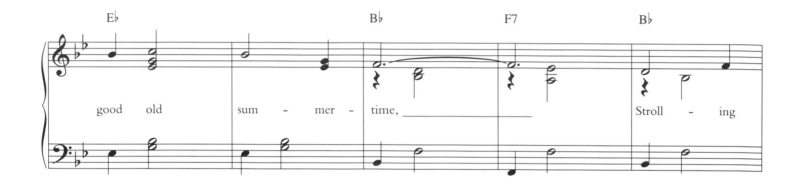

good old sum-mer-time, _____ Stroll - ing

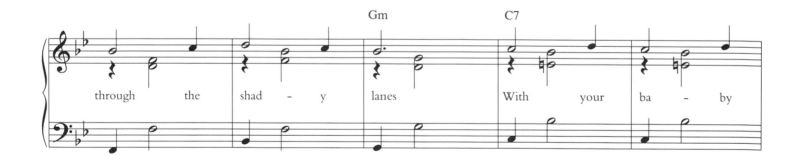

through the shad - y lanes With your ba - by

mine. _____ You hold her hand and she holds

B♭7/F   **E♭**   **B♭**

yours,   And   that's   a   ver - y   good   sign _____

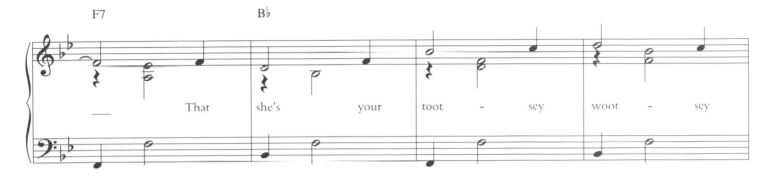

F7   **B♭**

___   That   she's   your   toot - sey   woot - sey

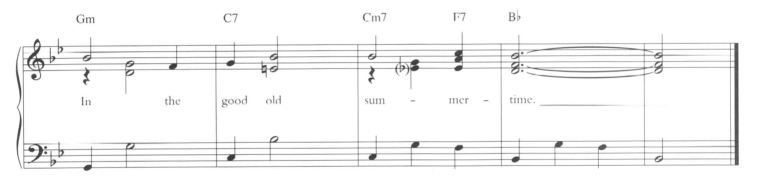

Gm   **C7**   **Cm7**   **F7**   **B♭**

In   the   good   old   sum - mer - time. _____

RAGTIME & THE BIRTH OF THE BLUES

Good Morning Blues

Traditional

2. I got up this morning, blues walkin' 'round my bed.
   I got up this morning, blues walkin' 'round my bed.
   Went to eat my breakfast, blues was in my bread.

3. I sent for you yesterday, here you come today.
   I sent for you yesterday, here you come today.
   You got your mouth wide open, you don't know what to say.

The Maple Leaf Rag

Scott Joplin

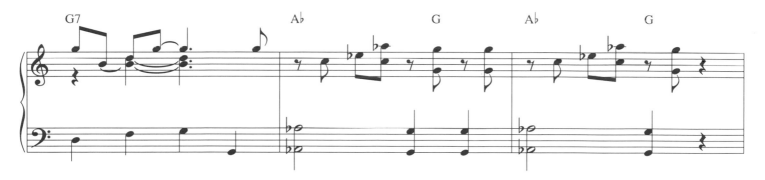

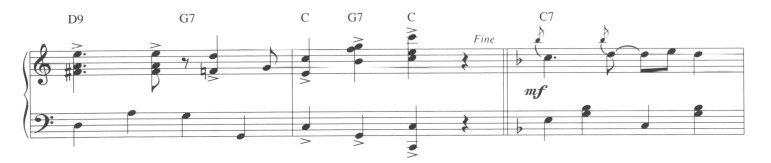

Frankie and Johnny

Traditional

With feeling

Frank - ie and John - ny were

lov- ers, _____ Oh, Lord - y, how they could love. They

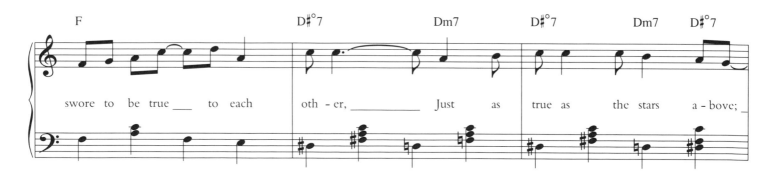

swore to be true ___ to each oth - er, _____ Just as true as the stars a - bove;

___ He was her man, _____ but he done her

wrong.

wrong.

2. Frankie and Johnny went walking,
   Johnny in his brand new suit.
   Oh, "Good Lord," says Frankie,
   "Don't my Johnny look cute."
   He was her man, but he done her wrong.

3. Frankie wnt down to the corner,
   Stopped in to buy her some beer
   Says to the big bartender,
   "Has my Johnny man been here?"
   He was her man, but he done her wrong.

4. "Well I ain't going to tell you no story,
   Ain't going to tell you no lie:
   Johnny went by 'bout an hour ago,
   With a girl named Nellie Bligh.
   He was your man, but he's doin' you wrong."

5. Frankie went home to the hotel.
   She didn't go there for fun.
   Underneath her kimono
   She carried a forty-five gun.
   He was her man, but he's doin' her wrong.

6. Frankie looked over the transom
   To see what she could spy,
   There sat Johnny on the sofa
   Just loving up Nellie Bligh.
   He was her man, but he was doin' her wrong.

7. Frankie got down from the high stool
   She didn't want to see no more;
   Rooty-toot-toot, three times she shot
   Right through that hardwood door.
   He was her man, but he was doin' her wrong.

8. "Oh roll me over so easy,
   Roll me over so slow,
   Roll me over easy boys.
   Why did she shoot so low?
   I was her man, but I done her wrong."

9. Drive out your rubber-tired carriage,
   Drive out your rubber-tired hack.
   There's twelve men going to the graveyard
   And eleven coming back.
   He was her man, but he done her wrong.

10. The sheriff arrested poor Frankie,
    Took her to jail that same day.
    He locked her up in a dungeon cell,
    And threw the key away.
    She shot her man, 'cause he was doin' her wrong.

11. This story has no moral,
    This story has no end.
    This story only goes to show
    That there ain't no good in men.
    He was her man, but he done her wrong.

A Man Without a Woman

Moderato

Traditional

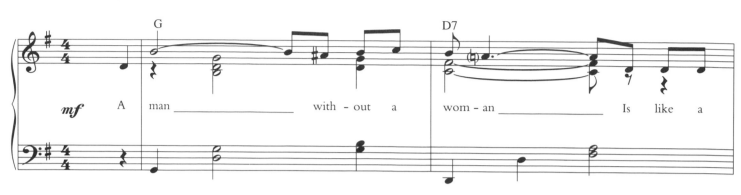

A man _____ with-out a wom-an _____ Is like a

ship _____ with-out a sail, _____ Is like a boat with-out a

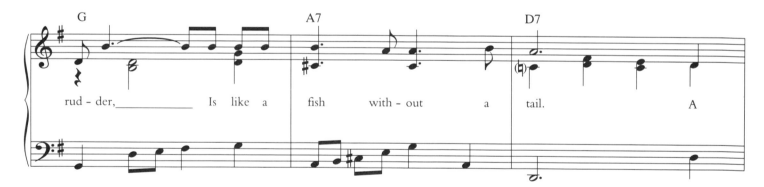

rud-der, _____ Is like a fish with-out a tail. A

man _____ with-out a wom-an _____ Is like a wreck up-on the

sand,_____ But if there's one thing worse in the u - ni - verse, It's a

wom - an,_____ I said a wom - an, It's a wom- an with - out a man._____

The Memphis Blues

Words by George A. Norton
Music by W.C. Handy

You want to be my man, ___ you got to give me for-ty dol-lars

down. You want to be my man, ___ you'll give me

for-ty dol-lars down. If you don't

be my man, ___ your ba-by's gon-na shake this town.

You want to　Mis - ter　Crump don't 'low ___ no

eas - y rid - ers　here.

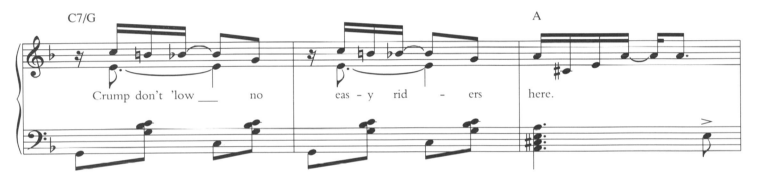

Crump don't 'low ___ no　eas - y rid - ers　here.

We don't care　what Mis - ter　Crump don't 'low ___

We gon - na bar'l - house　an - y - how.　Mis - ter　Crump don't 'low ___ no

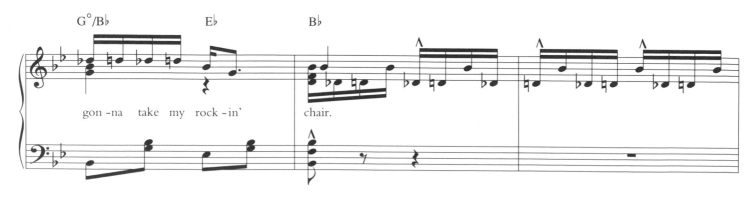

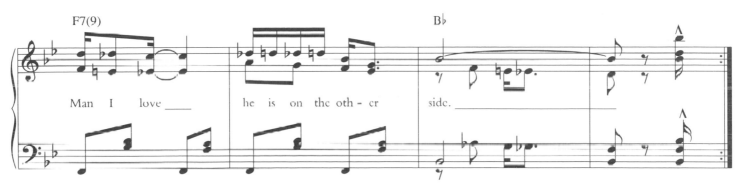

St. James Infirmary

Moderate blues

Traditional

I went down to the St. James In-firm-'ry; _____ I _____

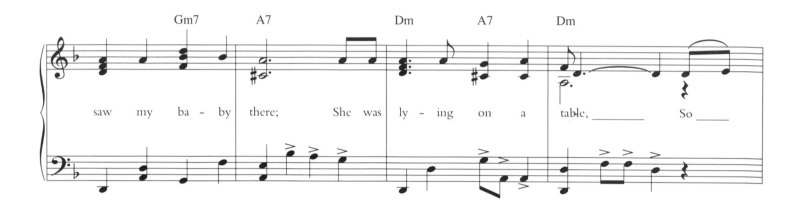

saw my ba-by there; She was ly-ing on a table, _____ So _____

cold, so white, ___ so fair. I went up to see the

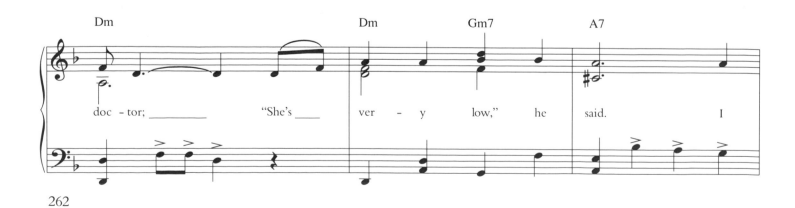

doc-tor; _____ "She's ___ ver-y low," he said. I

went back to see my ba-by, _____ And, good God, she was ly-ing there dead.

2. I went down to old Joe's barroom,
   On the corner by the square;
   The drinks were served as usual
   And the usual crowd was there.
   On my left stood Joe MacKennedy;
   His eyes were bloodshot red;
   He turned to the crowd around him,
   And these are the words he said.

3. Let her go, let her go, God bless her,
   Wherever she may be;
   She may search this wide world over,
   But never find another man like me.
   Now when I die, please bury me
   In a hightop Stetson hat;
   Put a gold piece on my watch chain,
   So the gang will know I'm standing pat.

4. Get six gamblers to carry my coffin,
   Six chorus girls to sing my song;
   Put a jazz band on my tail gate
   To raise hell as we roll along.
   And now that you've heard my story,
   I'll take another shot of booze;
   If anyone should happen to ask you,
   I've got the St. James Infirmary blues.

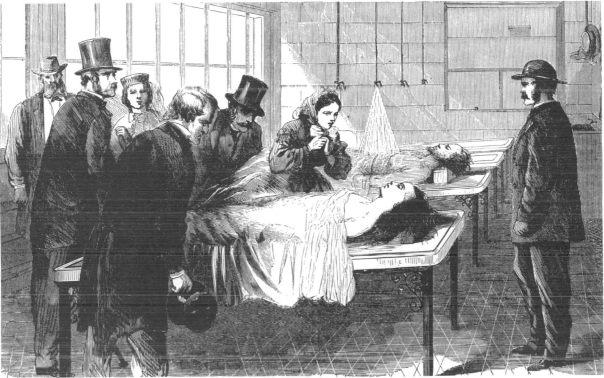

Ragtime Cowboy Joe

Words and music by Lewis F. Muir,
Grant Clarke, and Maurice Abrahams

Moderately fast

Out in Ar-i-zo-na where the bad men are, And the on-ly friend to guide you is an
Dressed up ev-'ry Sun-day in his Sun-day clothes, He ___ beats it to the vil-lage where he

eve-ning star; ___ The rough-est, tough-est man by far ___ Is
al-ways goes; ___ And ev-'ry girl in town is Joe's ___ 'Cause

Rag-time Cow-boy Joe. Got his name from sing-ing to the cows and sheep, ___
he's a rag-time bear. When he starts a-mov-ing on the dance hall floor, ___

Ev-'ry night they say he sings the herd to sleep, In a bas-so
No-one but a lun-a-tic would start a war. Wise men know ___ his

264

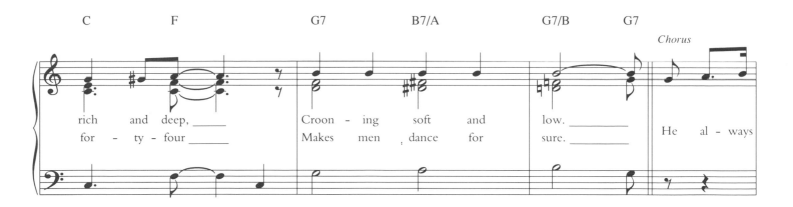

rich and deep, _____ Croon - ing soft and low. _____ He al - ways

for - ty - four _____ Makes men dance for sure. _____

sings rag - gy mu - sic to the cat - tle, As he swings back and

for - ward in the sad - dle, On a horse that is syn - co - pat - ed gait - ed; And there's

such a fun - ny me - ter, To the roar of his re - peat - er. How they run when they

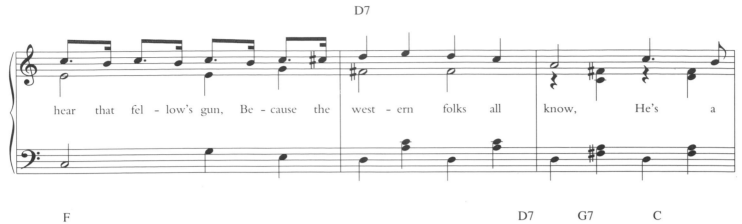

hear that fel - low's gun, Be - cause the west - ern folks all know, He's a

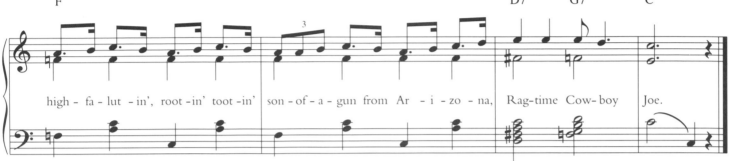

high - fa - lut -in', root -in' toot -in' son -of - a -gun from Ar - i - zo - na, Rag -time Cow -boy Joe.

Careless Love

Smoothly

Traditional

Love, oh love, oh care-less love,

Love, oh love, oh care-less love, Love, oh love, oh

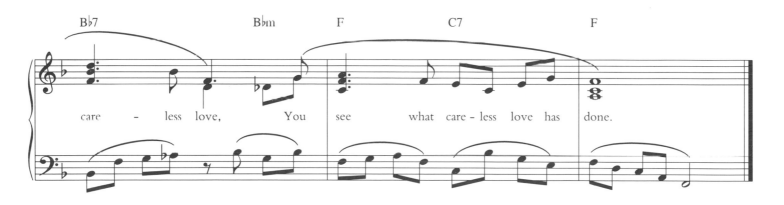

care - less love, You see what care-less love has done.

2. I was happy as can be,
   My days were sunny, bright, and free.
   You came along to do me wrong,
   And you brought your careless love to me.

4. Once I wore my apron low,
   Once I wore my apron low,
   Once I wore my apron low,
   I scarce could keep you from my door.

3. I love my mama and papa too,
   Love my mama and papa too,
   Love my mama and papa too,
   I'd leave them both and go with you.

5. I cried last night and the night before,
   Cried last night and the night before,
   Cried last night and the night before,
   Gonna cry tonight, and cry no more.

Corinna, Corinna

With a steady beat

Traditional

mf

Cor - in - na, Cor - in - na, ___ where you been so long? ___

___ Cor - in - na, Cor - in - na, ___ where you been so long? ___

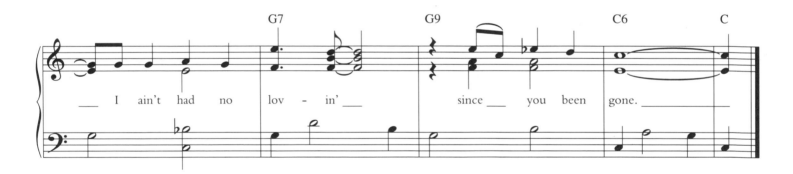

___ I ain't had no lov - in' ___ since ___ you been gone. ___

2. Corinna, Corinna, where'd you stay last night?
Corinna, Corinna, where'd you stay last night?
Your shoes ain't buttoned, girl; don't fit you right.

3. Corinna, Corinna, love you, 'deed I do.
Corinna, Corinna, good Lord knows I do.
But, baby, what's the use? You can't be true.

The Entertainer

Scott Joplin

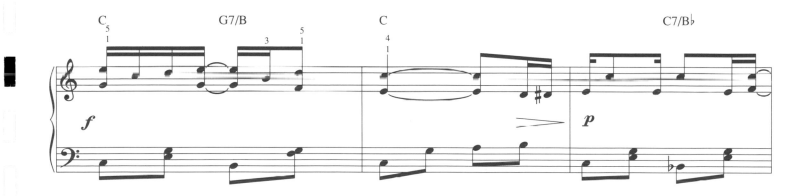

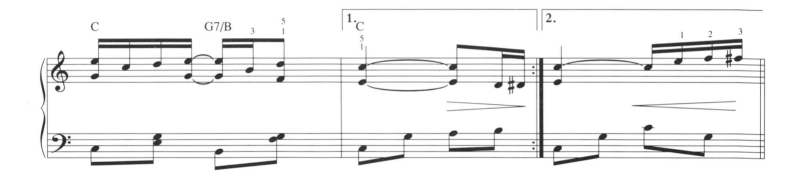

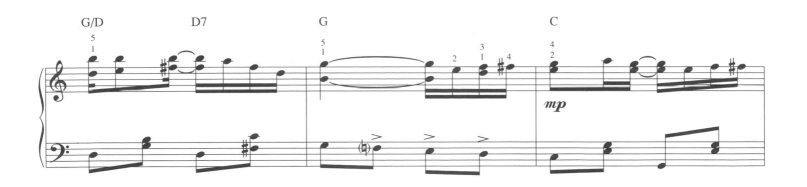

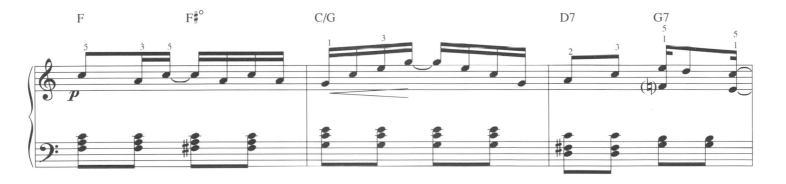

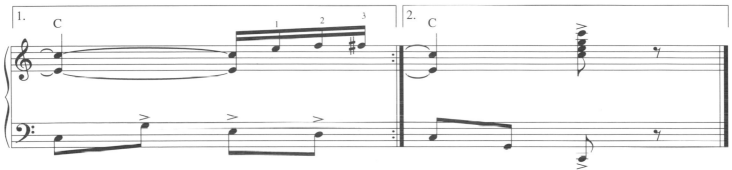

St. Louis Blues

Words and Music by W. C. Handy

Medium blues tempo

I hate to see ___ the eve-nin' sun go down, ___

Hate to see ___ the eve-nin' sun go down, ___

'Cause my ba-by, ___ he done left this town.

Feel-in' to-mor-row like ___ I feel to-day, ___

Feel to-mor-row like ___ I feel to-day,

I'll pack my trunk, ___ make my get - a - way. _____ St. Lou-is

wo - man, _____ with her dia - mond rings, _____ Pulls that

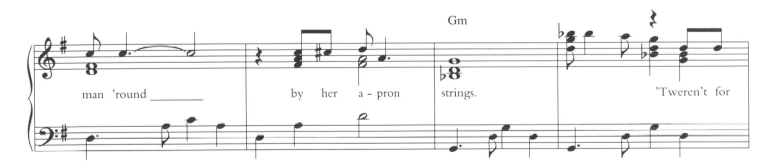

man 'round _____ by her a - pron strings. 'Tweren't for

pow - der _____ and for store - bought hair, _____ The

man I love ___ would not go no - where, no - where. _____

Chorus

Got the St. Lou - is blues, just as blue as ___ I ___ can be,
I ____ love that ___ man like a school - boy ___ loves ___ his pie,

That ___ man got a heart like a rock cast ___ in ___ the sea, ___
Like a Ken - tuck - y Col - 'nel ____ loves his _____ mint ___ and rye, ___

Or _____ else he _____ would - n't have gone ___
I'll _____ love my _____ ba - by _____ till

___ so _____ far ___ from _____ me. ____
___ the ___ day ___ I ____ die. ____

JAZZ & SWING
STANDARDS

You Made Me Love You

Words by Joe McCarthy
Music by James V. Monaco

With a steady beat

Ballin' the Jack

Words by James Henry Burris
Music by Chris Smith

Rhythmically

First you put your two knees close up tight, ____ Then you sway 'em to the left, then you

sway 'em to the right, Step a-round the floor kind of nice and light, ___ Then you

twist a-round and twist a-round with all of your might. ____ Stretch your lov -in' arms straight

out in space, ____ Then you do the Ea - gle Rock with ___ style and grace, ___ Swing your

foot way 'round, then bring it back, __ Now that's what I call Bal - lin' the Jack. ___

A-Tisket A-Tasket

Traditional

Moderately fast

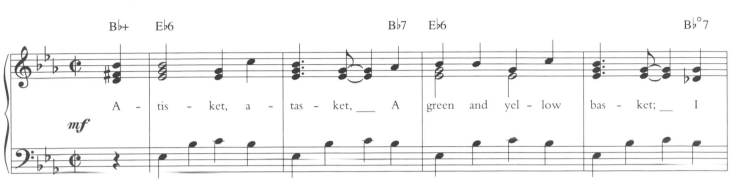

A - tis - ket, a - tas - ket, ___ A green and yel - low bas - ket; ___ I

bought a bas - ket for my love, And on the way I dropped ___ it. ___ I

dropped it, I dropped it, ___ Yes, on the way I dropped it; ___ A

lit - tle girl - ie picked it up, And took it to her love.

Bill Bailey, Won't You Please Come Home?

Words and music by Hughie Cannon

With energy

"Won't you come home, Bill Bai - ley, won't you come

home?" She cried the whole night long.

"I'll do the dish - es hon - ey, I'll pay the

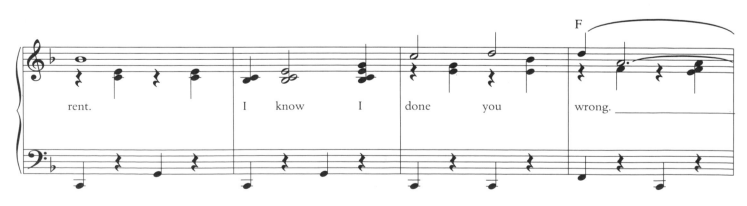

rent. I know I done you wrong.

'Mem – ber that rain – y eve – ning I drove you out

With noth – ing but a fine – tooth

comb? _____ I know I'm to blame; Well

ain't that a shame? Bill Bai – ley, won't you

please come home?" _____

Some of These Days

Words and Music by Sheldon Brooks

Moderately

Some of these days _____ you'll miss _____ me hon - ey, _____

___ Some of these days _____ you'll feel ___ so lone - ly, _____

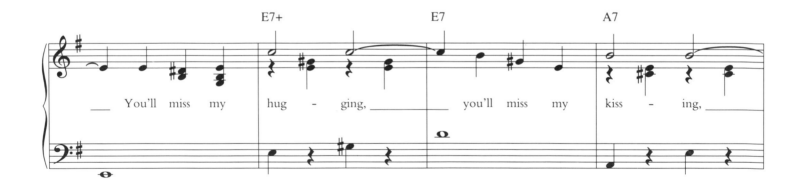

___ You'll miss my hug - ging, _____ you'll miss my kiss - ing, _____

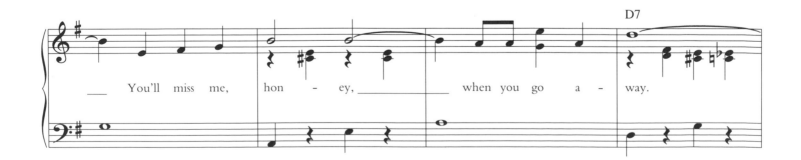

___ You'll miss me, hon - ey, _____ when you go a - way.

I feel so lone – ly _____ just for you on – ly, _____

_____ For you know, hon – ey, _____ you've had your

way; _____ And when you leave me, _____ I know 'twill

grieve me, _____ You'll miss _____ your lit – tle ba – by, _____

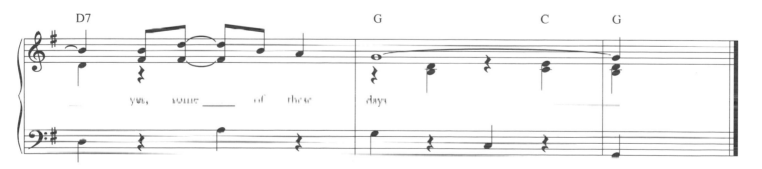

yes, some _____ of these days

Ciribiribin

Words by Rudolf Thaler
Music by Alberto Pestalozza

With movement

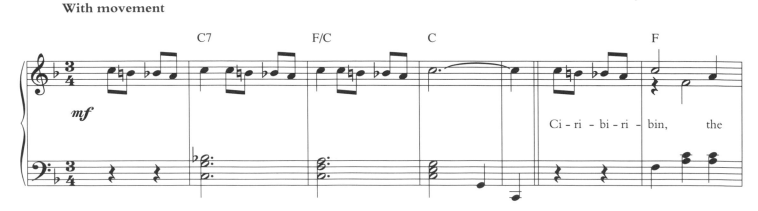

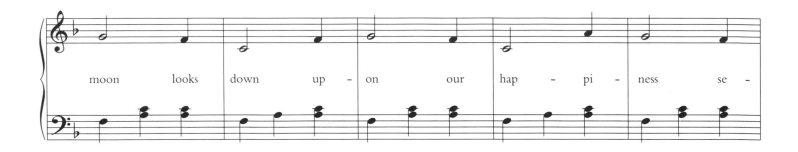

bin,   more   love   than   mine   for   thee   the   world   has

nev – er   seen. _____   Ci – ri – bi – ri – bin, _____   Ci – ri – bi – ri –

bin, _____   Ci – ri – bi – ri – bin,   my   ra – diant   queen. _____

Melancholy Baby

Words by George A. Norton
Music by Ernie Burnett

Play a Simple Melody

Words and music by Irving Berlin

Moderately

Won't you play a sim - ple mel - o - dy,

Like my moth -er sang to me;

One with good old fash - ioned har - mo - ny.

Play a sim - ple mel - o - dy.

Mu -si - cal de - mon, set your hon - ey a - dream - in'; Won't you play me some rag?__

Just change that clas - si - cal nag __ To some sweet beau - ti - ful drag. __

If you will play from a cop - y of a tune that is chop - py. You'll get

all my ap - plause; __ And that is simp - ly be - cause __ I want to lis- ten to

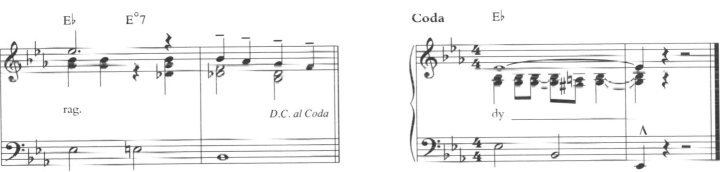

rag.   *D.C. al Coda*

Coda

dy _____

Glow Worm

Music by Paul Lincke
Words by Lila Cayley Robinson

Lightly

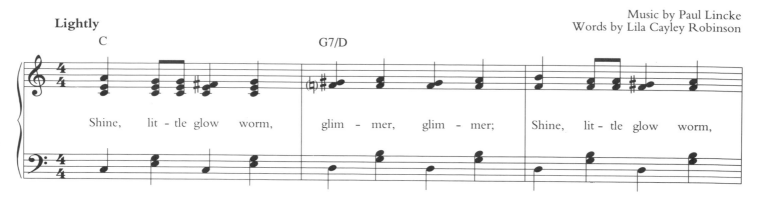

Shine, lit - tle glow worm, glim - mer, glim - mer; Shine, lit - tle glow worm,

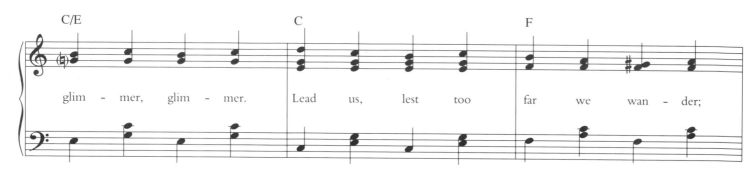

glim - mer, glim - mer. Lead us, lest too far we wan - der;

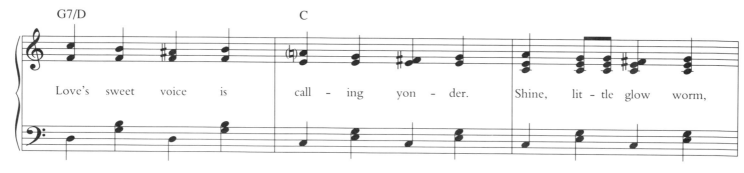

Love's sweet voice is call - ing yon - der. Shine, lit - tle glow worm,

glim - mer, glim - mer; Shine lit - tle glow worm, glim - mer. glim - mer.

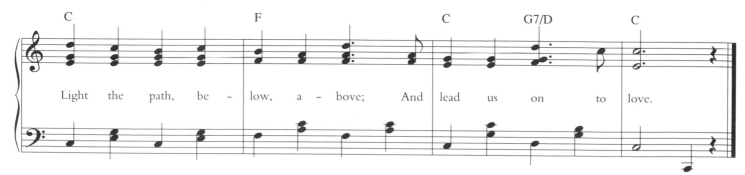

Light the path, be - low, a - bove; And lead us on to love.

Every Little Movement
(Has a Meaning All Its Own)

Words by Otto Harbach
Music by Karl Hoschna

With movement

mf Ev – 'ry lit – tle move – ment has a mean – ing all its own,

Ev – 'ry thought and feel – ing by some pos – ture can be

shown, _____ And ev – 'ry love thought _____ that comes a – steal – ing o'er your

be – ing _____ must be re – veal – ing All its sweet ness _____ in some ap –

peal – ing lit – tle ges – ture, _____ All, all its own.

291

When the Saints Go Marching In

Words by Katharine E. Purvis
Music by James M. Black

With spirit
Introduction

I am just a

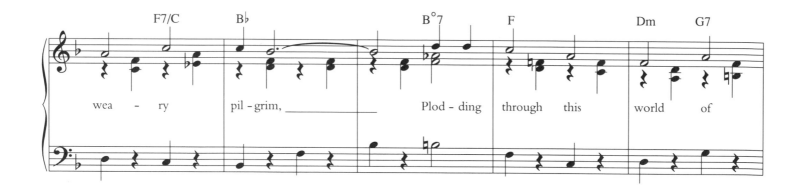

wea — ry pil - grim, _____ Plod - ding through this world of

sin, _____ Get - ting read - y for that day, _____

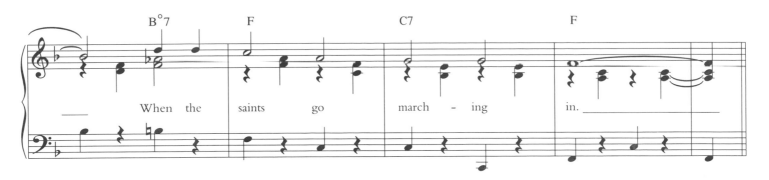

When the saints go march - ing in. ____

Chorus

Oh, when the saints go march - ing in, Oh, when the saints go

march - ing in, Lord, I want to be in that

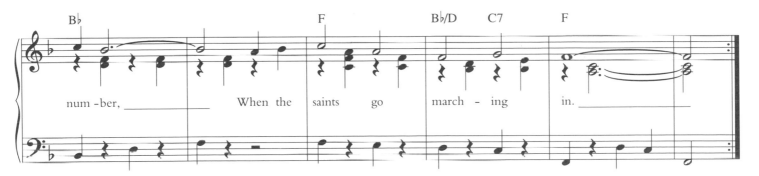

num - ber, ____ When the saints go march - ing in. ____

2. So I pray each day to heaven,
   For the strength to help me win;
   Want to be in that procession,
   When the saints go marching in.
   Chorus

3. Come and join me in my journey,
   'Cause it's time that we begin;
   And we'll be there for that judgment,
   When the saints go marching in.
   Chorus

Additional Choruses

I want to join the heav'nly band,
I want to join the heav'nly band,
Want to hear the trumpets a-blowing,
When the saints go marching in.

I want to wear a happy smile,
I want to wear a happy smile,
Want to sing and shout "Hallelujah,"
When the saints go marching in.

I want to see those pearly gates,
I want to see those pearly gates,
Want to see those gates standing open,
When the saints go marching in

Little Brown Jug

Lively

Words and Music by Joseph E. Winner

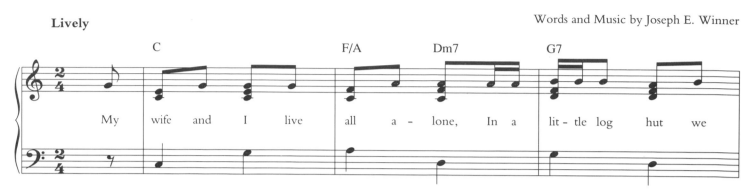

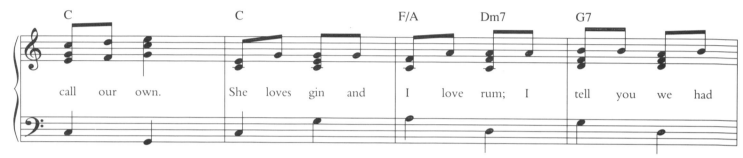

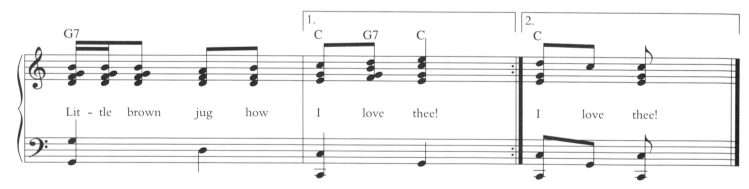

2. 'Tis you who makes my friends and foes,
   'Tis you who makes me wear old clothes.
   Here you are so near my nose,
   So tip her up and down she goes.
   Chorus

3. When I go toiling on my farm,
   Little brown jug under my arm,
   Place him under a shady tree,
   Little brown jug, don't I love thee?
   Chorus

4. Crossed the creek on a hollow log,
   Me and the wife and the little brown dog.
   The wife and the dog fell in, kerplunk,
   But I held on to the little brown jug.
   Chorus

5. One day when I went out to my barn,
   Little brown jug under my arm.
   Tripped me toe and down I fell,
   Broke that little jug all to hell.
   Chorus

THE BROADWAY STAGE
& THE SILVER SCREEN

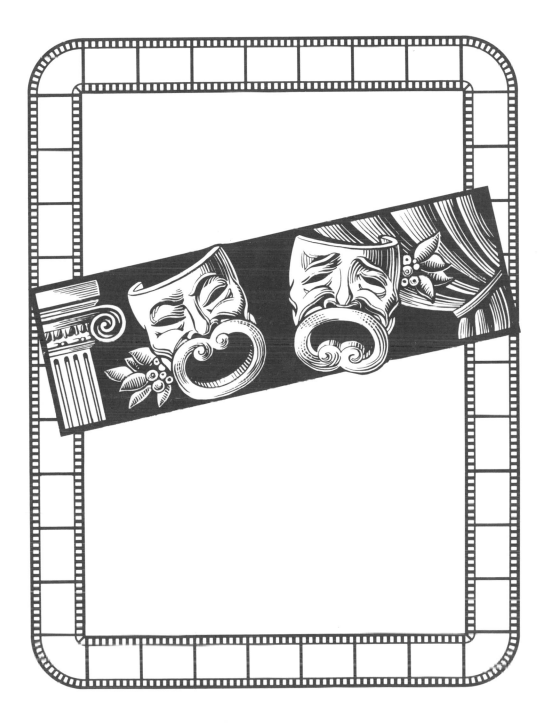

Give My Regards to Broadway

Words and Music by George M. Cohan

Spirited

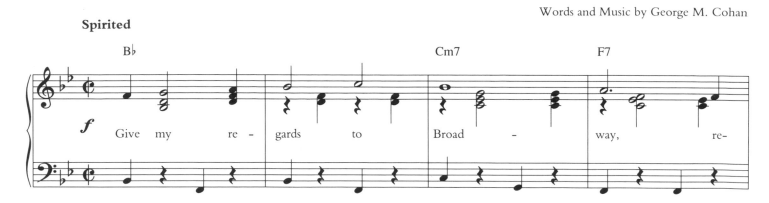

Give my re- gards to Broad - way, re-

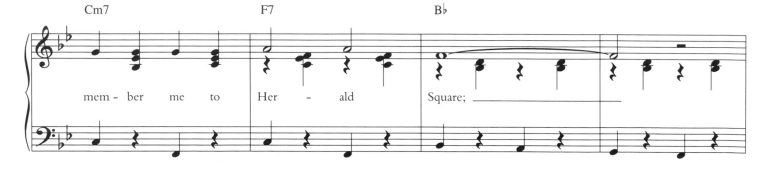

mem- ber me to Her - ald Square;

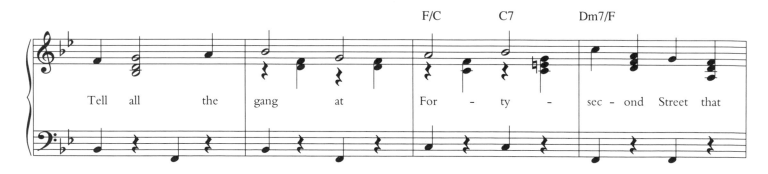

Tell all the gang at For - ty - sec - ond Street that

I will soon be there.

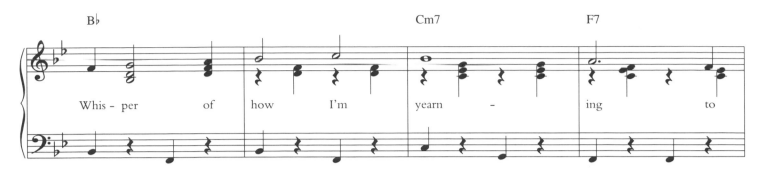

Whis - per of how I'm yearn - ing to

min - gle with the old time throng;

Give my re - gards to old Broad - way and say that

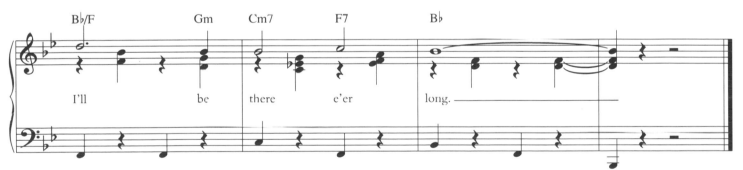

I'll be there e'er long.

Meet Me in St. Louis, Louis

Words by Andrew B. Sterling
Music by Kerry Mills

Brightly

Meet me in in St. Lou - is, Lou - is, Meet me

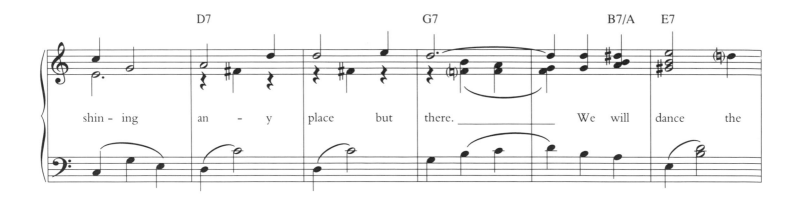

at the fair, _____ Don't tell me the lights are

shin - ing an - y place but there. _____ We will dance the

Hoo - chee Koo - chee, _____ I will be your toot - sie

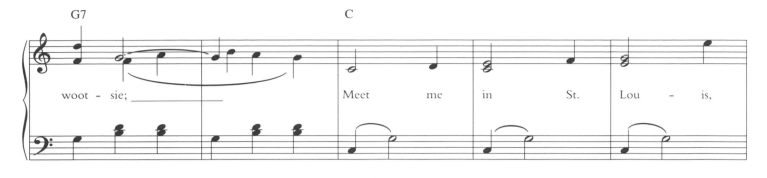

woot - sie; _____ Meet me in St. Lou - is,

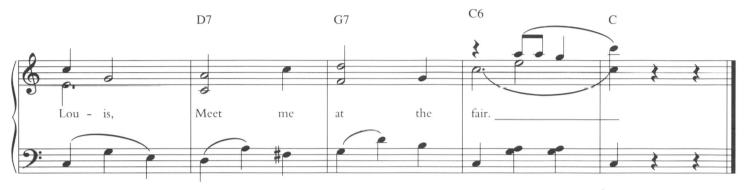

Lou - is, Meet me at the fair. _____

The Bowery

Words by Charles H. Hoyt
Music by Percy Gaunt

With movement

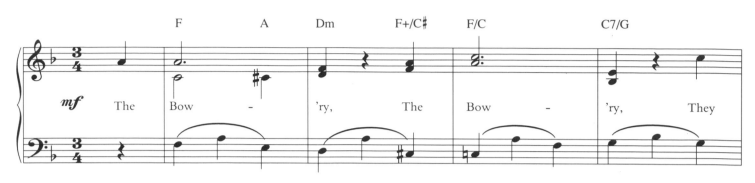

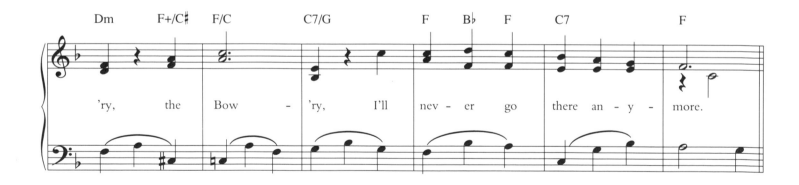

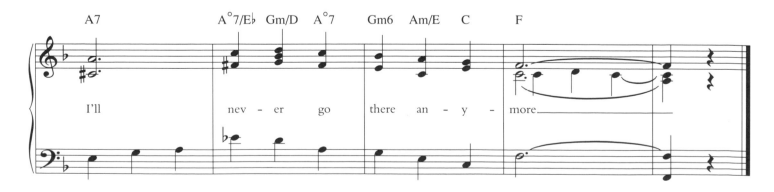

The Man That Broke the Bank at Monte Carlo

Words and music by Fred Gilbert

Alexander's Ragtime Band

Words and music by Irving Berlin

Rhythmically

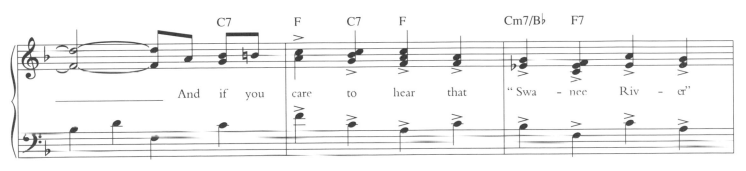

I Wonder Who's Kissing Her Now

Words by Mill M. Hough and Frank R. Adams
Music by Joseph E. Howard and Harold Orlob

Easy waltz tempo

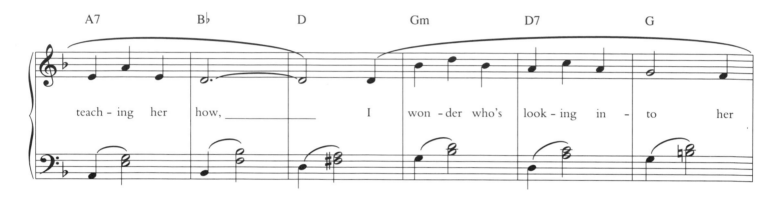

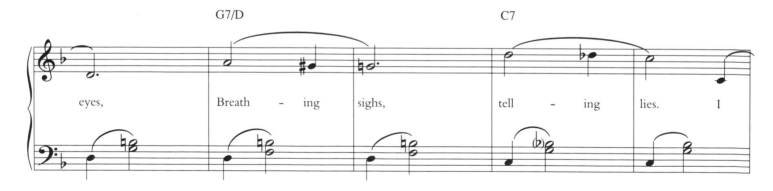

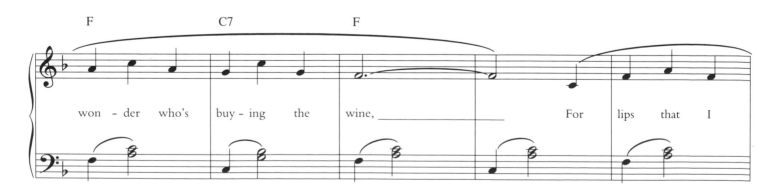

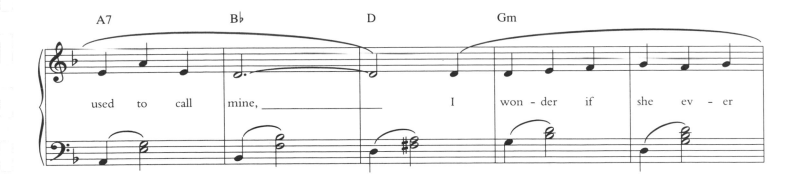

used to call mine, _____ I won - der if she ev - er

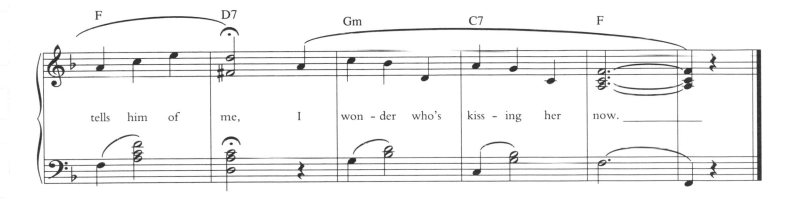

tells him of me, I won - der who's kiss - ing her now. _____

The Yankee Doodle Boy

With energy

Words and Music by George M. Cohan

ly. _____ I've got a Yan - kee Doo - dle sweet -

heart, She's my Yan - kee Doo - dle joy. _____

Yan - kee Doo - dle came to Lon - don just to ride a po - ny;

I am that Yan - kee Doo - dle boy.

The Sidewalks of New York

Moderate Waltz

Words and music by Charles B. Lawlor
and James W. Blake

Down in front of Ca - sey's _____ Old brown

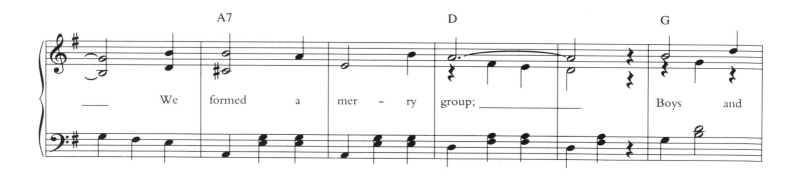

wood - en stoop, _____ On a sum - mer's eve - ning, _____

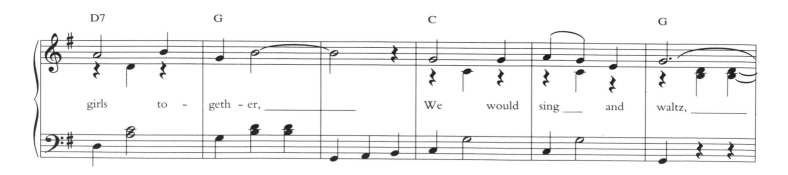

_____ We formed a mer - ry group; _____ Boys and

girls to - geth - er, _____ We would sing ___ and waltz, _____

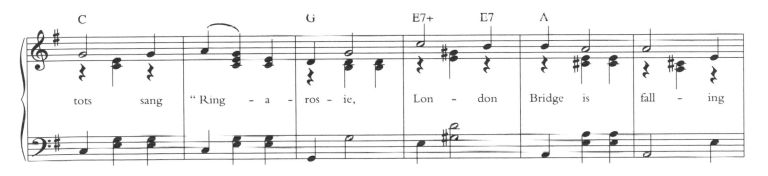

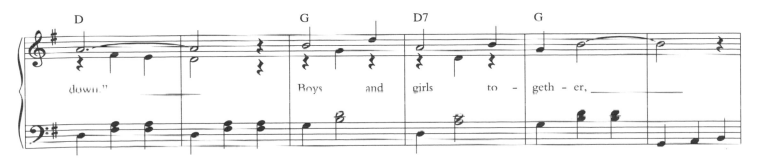

Me and Ma - mie O' - Rourke, _____ Tripped the light ___ fan -

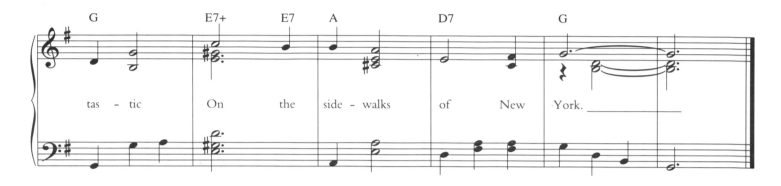

tas — tic   On   the   side - walks   of   New   York. _____

Oh! You Beautiful Doll

Words by A. Seymour Brown
Music by Nat D. Ayer

Moderately

Oh! you beau-ti-ful doll, __ You great big, beau-ti-ful doll, __

Let __ me put my arms a - round you, I __ could nev-er live with - out you,

Oh! you beau-ti-ful doll, __ You great big, beau-ti-ful doll, __ If you

ev-er leave __ me, how my heart will ache, __ I want to hug __ you, but I

fear you'd break. __ Oh! Oh! Oh! Oh! Oh! you beau-ti-ful doll

I Don't Care

Words by Jean Lenox
Music by Harry O. Sutton

Brightly

1. I don't care, ___ I don't care, ___ What peo - ple
2. I don't care, ___ I don't care, ___ If peo - ple

think of me. ___ I'm hap - py go luck - y, Men
don't like me. ___ I'll try to out - live it, I

say I am pluck - y, So jol - ly and care -
know I'll for - give it, And live con - tent - ed -

free. I don't care, ___ I don't care, ___
ly. I don't care, ___ I don't care, ___

If I   do   get that mean and ston - y stare;
If peo - ple   do not try to treat me fair;

Slower

If I'm   nev - er   suc - cess - ful,   It won't be dis -
There is   naught can   a - maze me,   Dis - like can - not

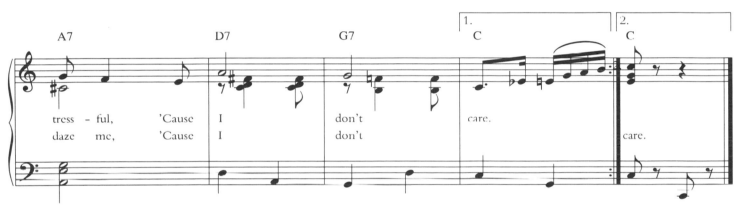

tress - ful,   'Cause   I   don't   care.
daze   me,   'Cause   I   don't   care.

Forty-five Minutes From Broadway

With a lilt

Words and music by George M. Cohan

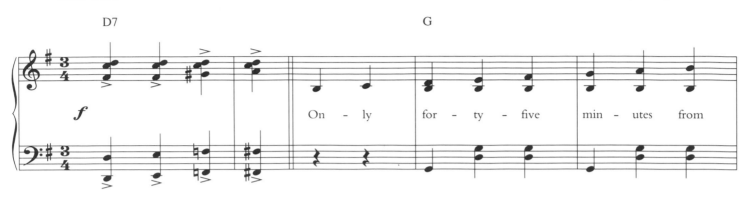

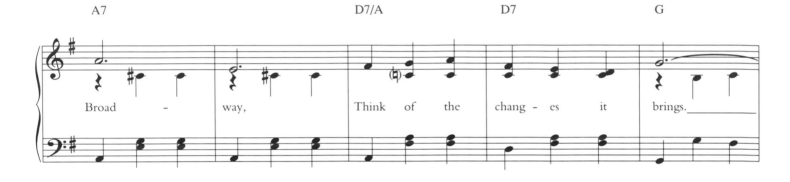

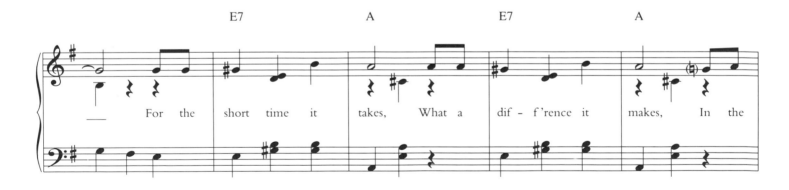

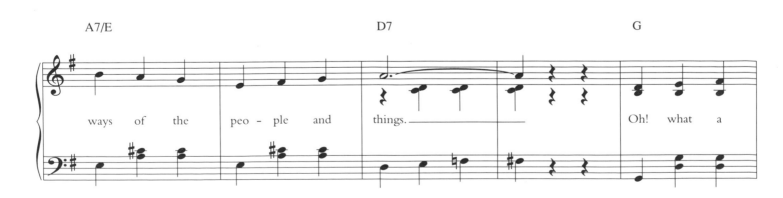

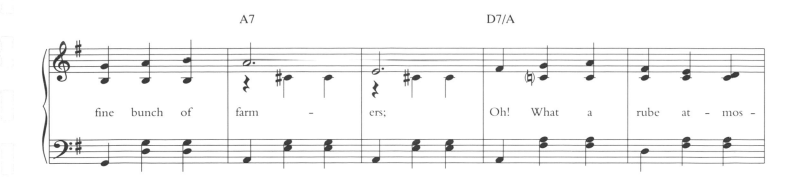

fine bunch of farm - ers; Oh! What a rube at - mos -

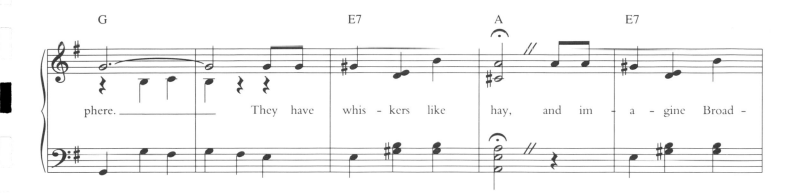

phere. _____ They have whis - kers like hay, and im - a - gine Broad -

way On - ly for - ty - five min - utes from here. _____

CLASSIC FAVORITES

Bridal Chorus
(from Lohengrin*)*

Richard Wagner

Moderately slow

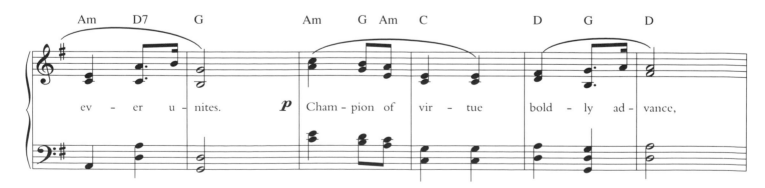

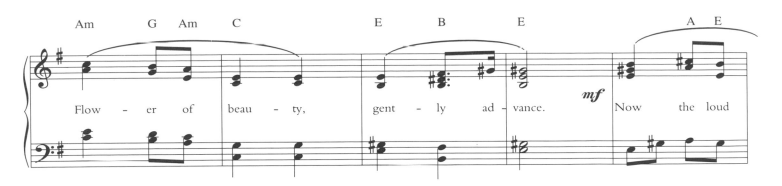

Flow — er of beau — ty, gent — ly ad — vance. Now the loud

mirth of rev — 'ling is end — ed, Night bring-ing peace and

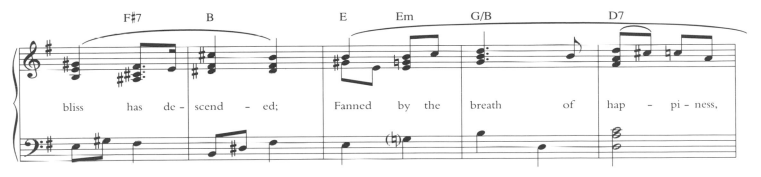

bliss has de — scend — ed; Fanned by the breath of hap — pi — ness,

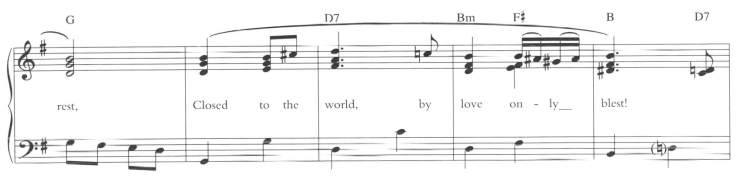

rest, Closed to the world, by love on — ly__ blest!

Guid — ed by us, thrice hap — py pair, En — ter the door — way, 'tis
Home joys di — vine, home joys so pure, Love ev — er faith — ful and

love that in - vites; }   love ev - er sure; }   All that is brave,   All that is fair,

Love now tri - um - phant for - ev - - - er u - nites. **ff**

Toyland

Words by Glen MacDonough
Music by Victor Herbert

Toy – land! toy – land! Lit – tle girl and boy – land;

While you dwell with – in it, _____ You are ev – er hap – py then.

Child – hood's joy – land, Mys – tic, mer – ry toy – land;

Once you pass its bor – ders, You can nev – er re – turn a – gain.

Cradle Song
(Brahms Lullaby)

Words by Karl Simrock
Translation by Arthur Westbrook
Music by Johannes Brahms

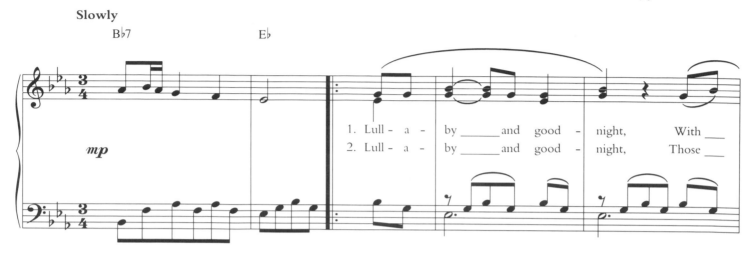

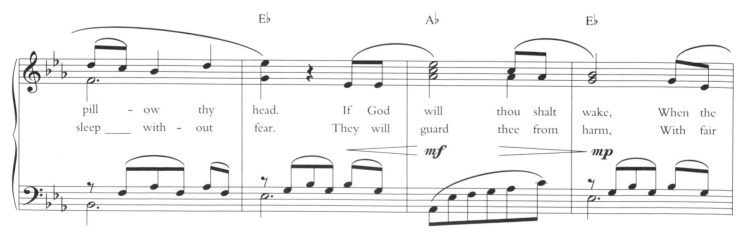

1. Lull - a - by _____ and good - night, With ___ ros - es _____ de - light. _____ Creep ___ in - to thy ____ bed, There ___ pill - ow thy head. If God will thou shalt wake, When the

2. Lull - a - by _____ and good - night, Those ___ blue eyes _____ close tight. _____ Bright ___ an - gels are ____ near, So ___ sleep ____ with - out fear. They will guard thee from harm, With fair

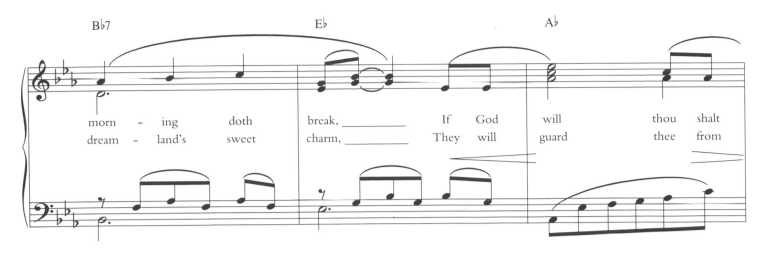

morn - ing doth break, _____ If God will thou shalt
dream - land's sweet charm, _____ They will guard thee from

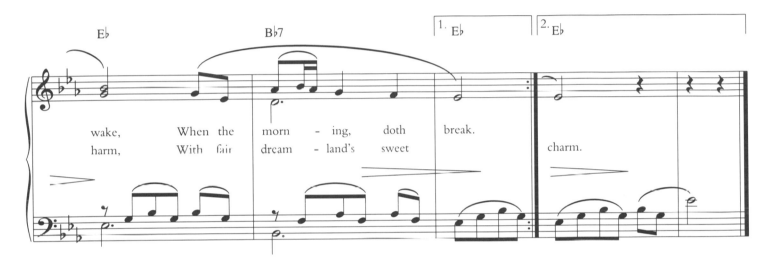

wake, When the morn - ing, doth break.
harm, With fair dream - land's sweet charm.

La Donna È Mobile

Words by Francèsco Maria Piave
Music by Guiseppi Verdi

Allegretto
Introduction

La don - na è mo-bi - le qual piuma al ven - to, mu - ta d'ac -

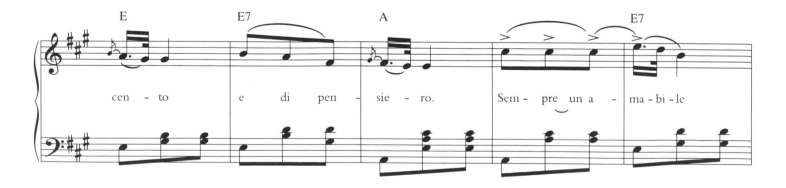

cen - to e di pen - sie - ro. Sem - pre un a - ma - bi - le

leg - gia - dro vi - so, in pian - to in ri - so, è men - zo -

gne - ro. La don - ne è mo - bil qual piu - ma al ven - to,

mu - ta d'ac - cen - to e di pen - sier,

e di pen - sier, e,

è di pen - sier.

I Am the Monarch of the Sea

Words by W.S. Gilbert
Music by Sir Arthur Sullivan

aunts, _____ And we are his sis- ters and his cous- ins and his aunts, His

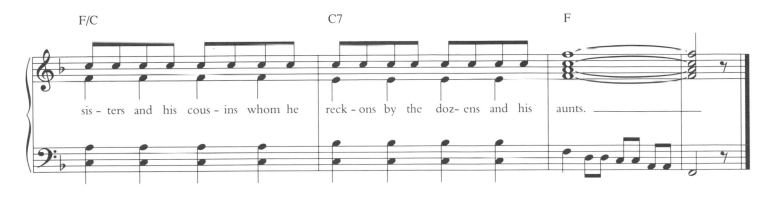

sis- ters and his cous- ins whom he reck- ons by the doz- ens and his aunts. _____

Funeral March of a Marionette

Charles Gounod

Mysteriously

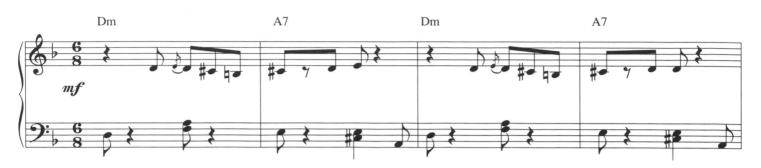

A Wand'ring Minstrel

Words by W.S. Gilbert
Music by Sir Arthur Sullivan

Allegretto con grazia

A wan - d'ring min - strel I, a thing of shreds _____ and patch - es, Of bal - lads, songs, and snatch - es, And dream - y lul - la - by. _____ My cat - a - logue is long, Thro' ev - 'ry pas - sion rang - ing, And to your hu - mors chang- ing, I tune ____ my sup - ple song! _____ I tune ___ my sup - ple song! _____

Ave Maria

Franz Schubert

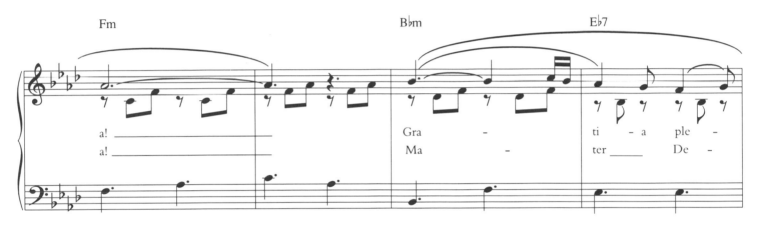

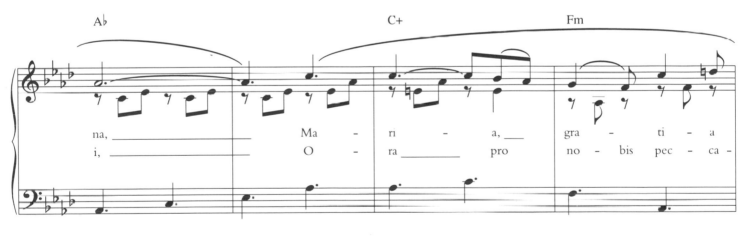

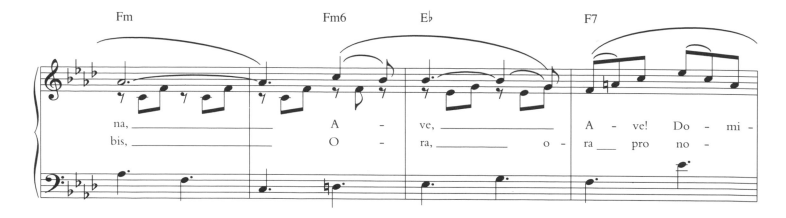

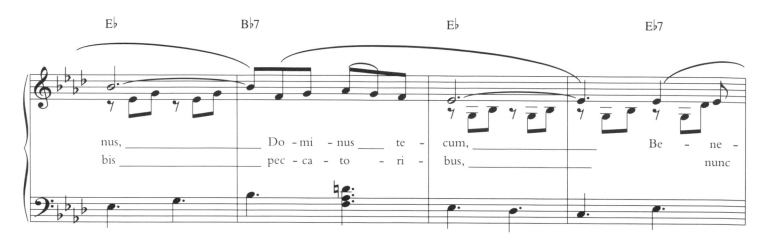

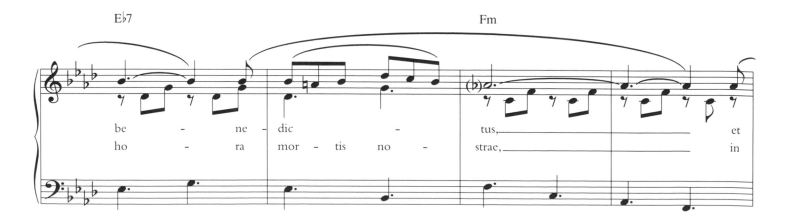

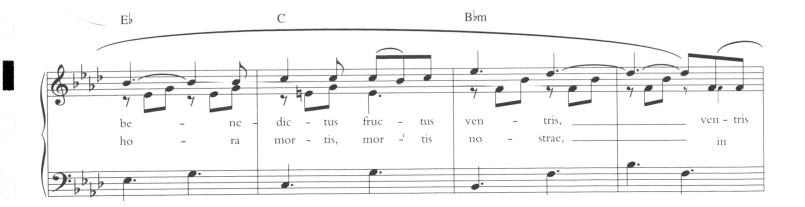

be — ne — dic — tus fruc — tus ven — tris, _____ ven — tris
ho — ra mor — tis, mor — tis no — strae, _____ in

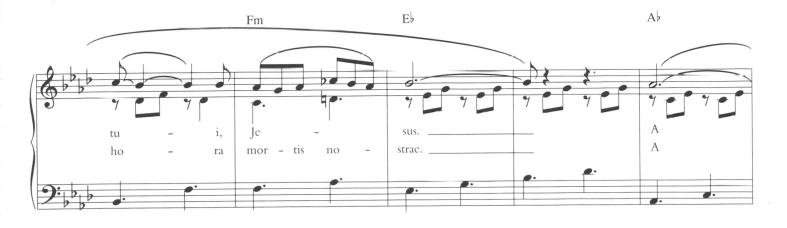

tu — i, Je — sus. _____ A
ho — ra mor — tis no — strae. _____ A

— ve Ma — ri — a! _____
— ve Ma — ri — a! _____

I'm Falling in Love With Someone

Words by Rita Johnson Young
Music by Victor Herbert

Slow waltz tempo

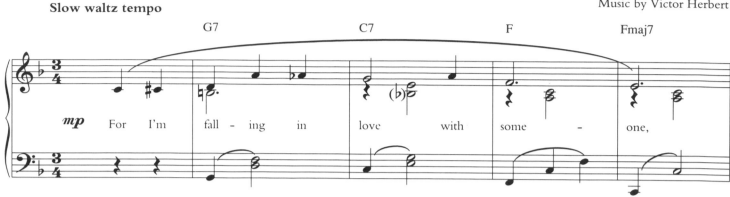

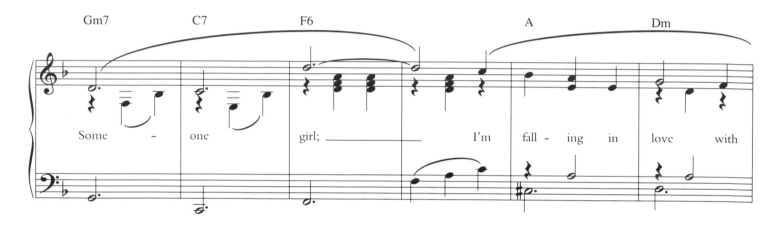

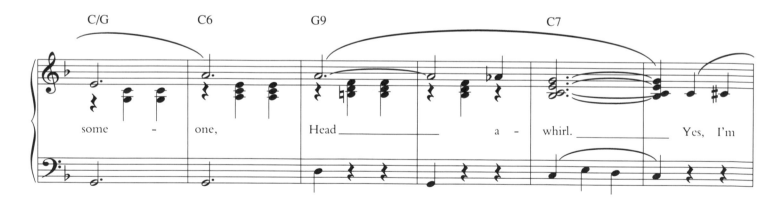

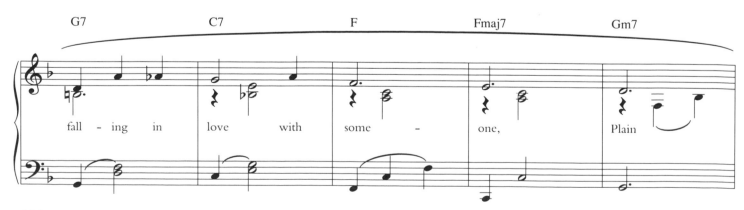

to see;   I'm sure I could love some - one

rall.

mad - ly, If some - one would on - ly love me.

Pomp and Circumstance

Slow march

Edward Elgar

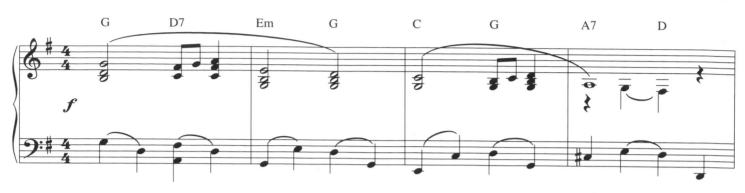

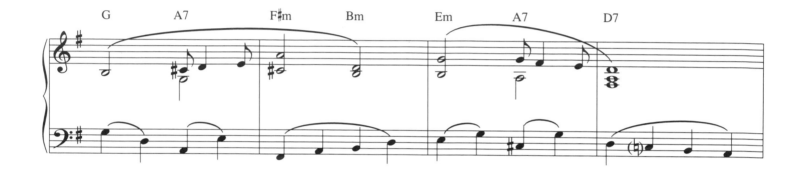

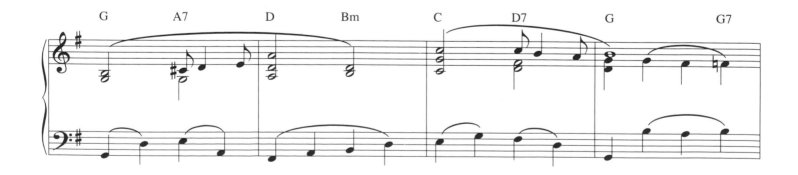

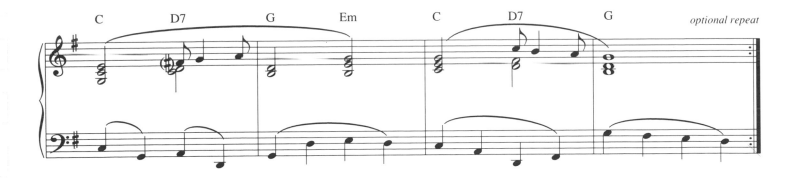

optional repeat

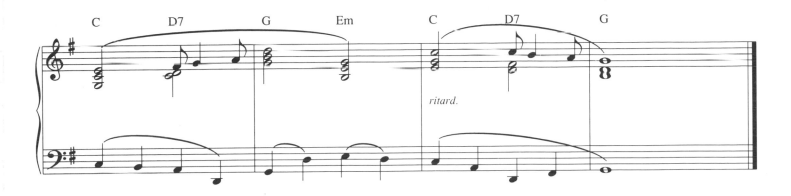

ritard.

The Freedom Movement

Oh Freedom

With feeling

Traditional

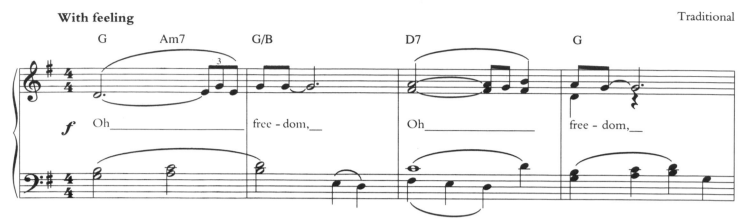

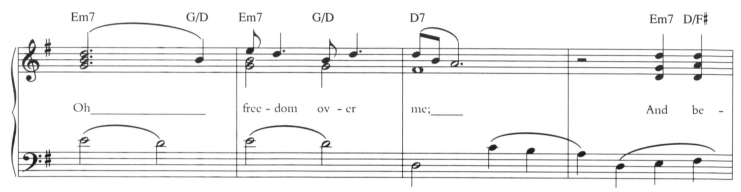

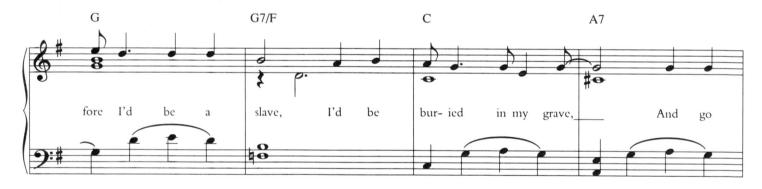

2. No more mourning, no more mourning,
   Nomore mourning over me;
   And before I'd be a slave,
   I'd be buried in my brave,
   And go home to my Lord and be free.

3. No more weeping, no more weeping,
   No more weeping over me; *etc.*
   Chorus

4. No more fighting, no more fighting,
   No more fighting over me;

5. There'll be singing, there'll be singing,
   There'll be singing over me;

Keep Your Eyes on the Prize

Traditional

2. Paul and Silas began to shout,
   Jail door opened and they walked out,
   Keep your eyes on the prize,
   Hold on, hold on.
   Chorus

3. Freedom's name is mighty sweet,
   Soon one day we're gonna meet, *etc.*
   Chorus

4. Got my hand on the gospel plow,
   Wouldn't take nothing for my journey now,
   Chorus

5. The only chain that a man can stand,
   Is that chain of hand in hand,
   Chorus

6. The only thing that we did wrong,
   Stayed in the wilderness a day too long,
   Chorus

7. But the one thing that we did right,
   Was the day we started to fight,
   Chorus

8. We're gonna board that big Greyhound,
   Carryin' love from town to town,
   Chorus

9. We're gonna ride for civil rights,
   We're gonna ride for both black and white,
   Chorus

10. We've met jail and violence too,
    But God's love has seen us through,
    Chorus

11. Haven't been to heaven, but I've been told,
    Streets up there are paved with gold,
    Chorus

341

Down by the Riverside

Traditional

Chorus

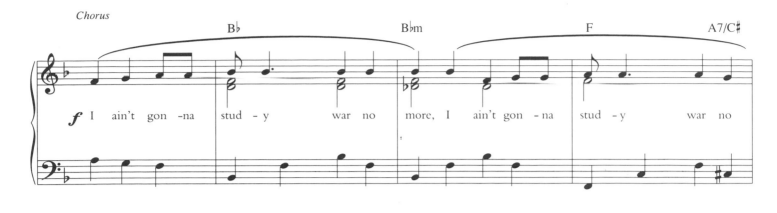

I ain't gon-na stud-y war no more, I ain't gon-na stud-y war no

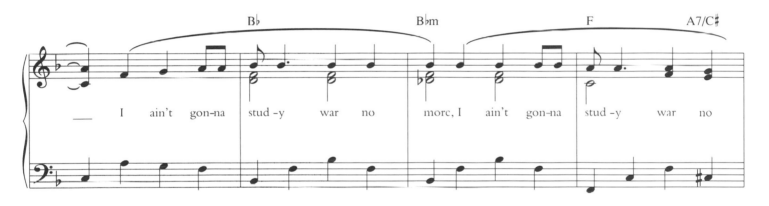

more, I ain't gon-na stud-y war no more.

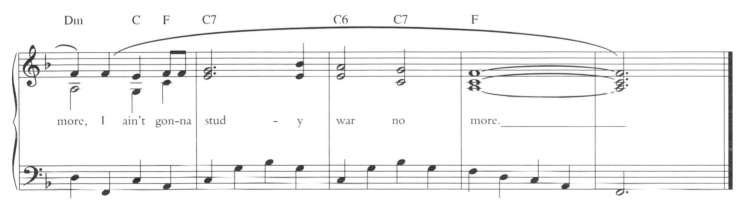

I ain't gon-na stud-y war no more, I ain't gon-na stud-y war no

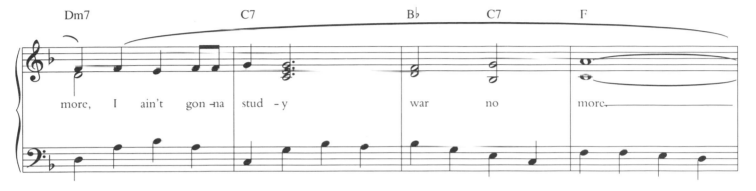

more, I ain't gon-na stud-y war no more.

2. Gonna walk with the Prince of Peace,
Down by the riverside,
Down by the riverside,
Down by the riverside.
Gonna walk with the Prince of Peace,
Down by the riverside,
I'll study war no more.
Chorus

3. Gonna shake hands around the world,
Down by the riverside,
Down by the riverside,
Down by the riverside.
Gonna shake hands around the world,
Down by the riverside,
I'll study war no more.
Chorus

343

We Shall Overcome

Traditional

With conviction

We shall o - ver - come, _____ We shall o - ver - come, _____

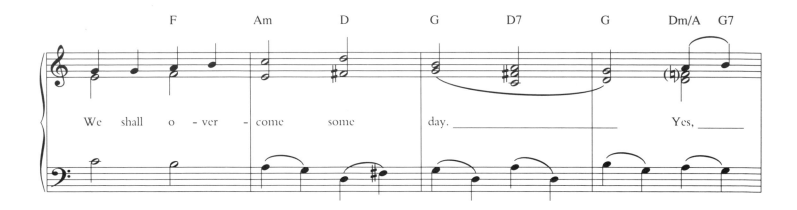

We shall o - ver - come some day. _____ Yes, _____

deep in my heart I do be - lieve

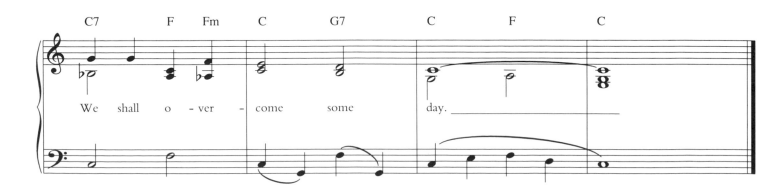

We shall o - ver - come some day. _____

Go Down, Moses

Traditional

2. The Lord told Moses what to do,
   Let my people go!
   To lead the Hebrew children through,
   Let my people go!
   Chorus

3. As Israel stood by the waterside,
   At God's command it did divide,
   Chorus

4. And when they reached the other shore,
   They sang a song of triumph o'er.
   Chorus

5. Then Pharaoh said he'd go across,
   But Pharaoh and his host were lost.
   Chorus

6. Your foes shall not before you stand,
   And you'll possess fair Canaan's Land
   Chorus

7. We need not always weep and mourn,
   And wear these slavery chains forlorn.
   Chorus

345

The Cruel War

Traditional

Sadly

Introduction

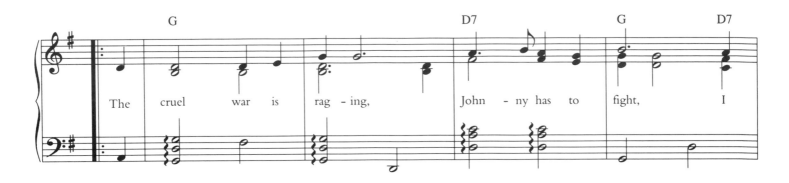

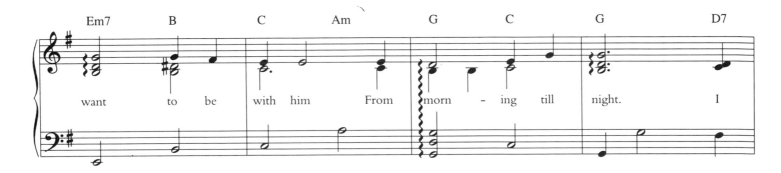

let me go with you? No, my love, no.

2. I'd go to your captain, get down on my knees,
   And ten thousand gold guineas I'd give for your release.
   Ten thousand gold guineas, it grieves my heart so.
   Won't you let me go with you? No, my love, no.

3. Tomorrow is Sunday, Monday is the day,
   That your captain will call you, and you must obey.
   Your captain will call you, it grieves my heart so.
   Won't you let me go with you? No, my love, no.

4. I'll tie back my hair, men's clothing I'll put on,
   And I'll pass as your comrade as we march along.
   I'll pass as your comrade, no one will ever know.
   Won't you let me go with you? No, my love, no.

5. Oh, Johnny, oh, Johnny, I fear you are unkind,
   For I love you far better than all of mankind.
   I love you far better than words can e'er express.
   Won't you let me go with you? Yes, my love, yes.

I'm on My Way to Freedom Land

Traditional

2. I asked my brother to come with me,
   I asked my brother to come with me,
   I asked my brother to come with me.
   I'm on my way, great God, I'm on my way.

3. I asked my sister to come with me,

4. I asked my boss to let me go,

5. If he says no, I'll go anyhow,

6. If you won't go, let your children go,

7. If you won't go, let your mother go,

8. I'm on my way, and I won't turn back,

Woke Up This Morning
(With My Mind on Freedom)

Moderately

Traditional

I woke up this morn - ing with my mind, _____ it was stayed on free - dom, ___ I woke up this morn - ing with my mind, _____ it was stayed on free - dom, ___ I woke up this morn - ing with my mind, _____ it was stayed on free - dom, ___ Hal - le - lu, ___ hal - le - lu, hal - le - lu - jah!

Kumbaya

Traditional

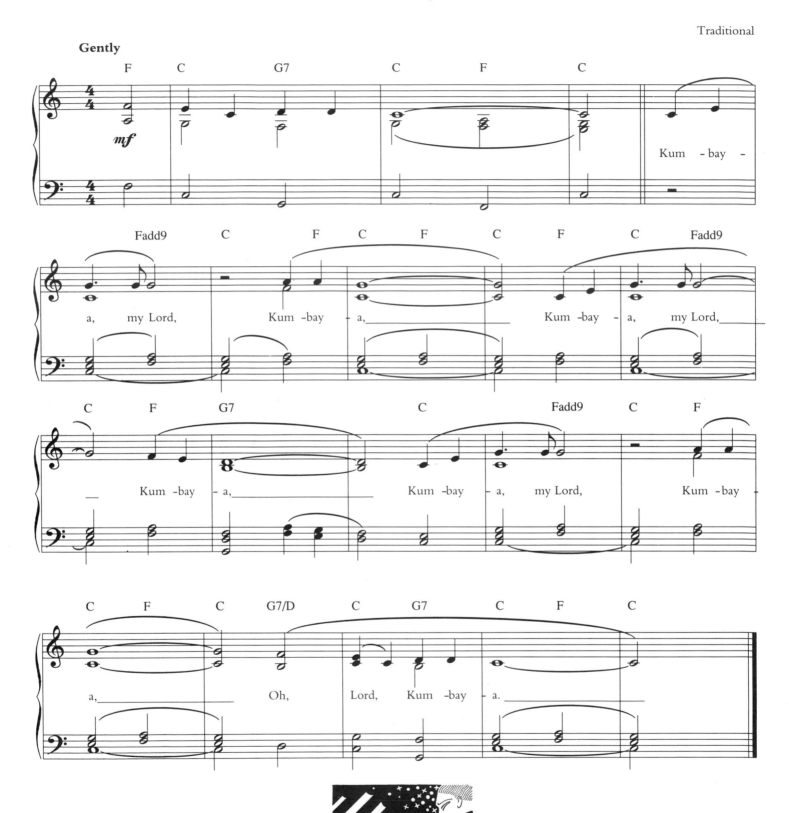

2. Someone's crying, Lord, kumbaya, *etc.*

3. Someone's singing, Lord, kumbaya,

4. Someone's praying, Lord, kumbaya,

5. Someone's sleeping, Lord, kumbaya,

ROCK & POP REVIVAL

Scarborough Fair

Traditional

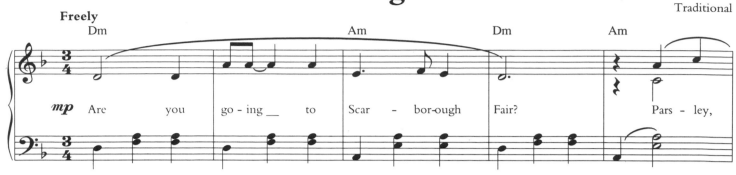

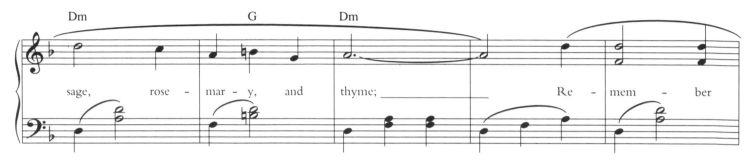

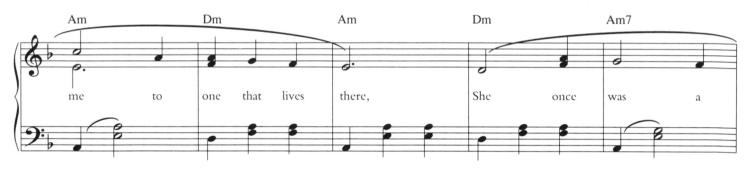

2. Tell her to make me a cambric shirt,
   Parsley, sage, rosemary, and thyme;
   Without a seam or fine needlework,
   And then she'll be true love of mine.

3. Tell her to wash it in yonder dry well,
   Parsley, sage, rosemary, and thyme;
   Where water ne'er sprung, nor drop of rain fell,
   And then she'll be a true love of mine.

4. Tell her to dry it on yonder thorn,
   Parsley, sage, rosemary, and thyme;
   Which never bore blossom since Adam was born,
   And then she'll be a true love of mine.

5. Oh, will you find me an acre of land,
   Parsley, sage, rosemary, and thyme;
   Between the sea foam and the sea sand,
   Or never be a true love of mine?

6. Oh, will you plough it with a lamb's horn,
   Parsley, sage, rosemary, and thyme;
   And sow it all with one peppercorn,
   Or never be a true love of mine?

7. Oh, will you reap it with a sickle of leather,
   Parsley, sage, rosemary, and thyme;
   And tie it up with a peacock's feather,
   Or never be a true love of mine?

8. And when you've done and finished your work,
   Parsley, sage, rosemary, and thyme;
   Then come to me for your cambric shirt,
   And you shall be a true love of mine.

House of the Rising Sun

Traditional

Moderately

mp There is a ___ house in New Or-

leans, They call the Ris - ing ___ Sun; ___

___ It's been the ru - in of man-y a poor

boy, And God, I know I'm ___ one. ___

2. My mother was a tailor,
   She sewed my new blue jeans.
   My father was a gambling man,
   Way down in New Orleans.

3. The only thing a gambler needs,
   Is a suitcase and a trunk;
   And the only time he's satisfied,
   Is when he's on a drunk.

4. Oh, mothers, tell your children,
   Not to do what I have done,
   To live in sin and misery,
   In the House of the Rising Sun.

5. One foot on the platform,
   The other's on the train;
   I'm going down to New Orleans,
   To wear that ball and chain.

6. Going back to New Orleans,
   My race is almost run;
   I'm going to spend the rest of my life,
   Beneath that Rising Sun.

Morning Has Broken

With movement

Introduction

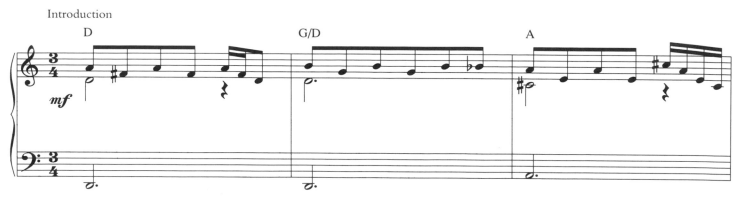

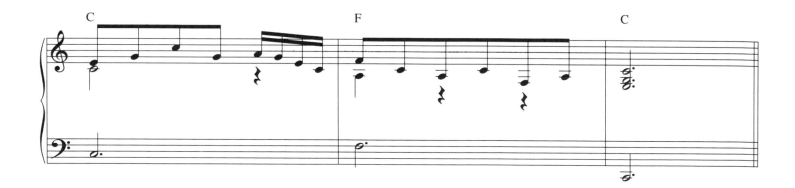

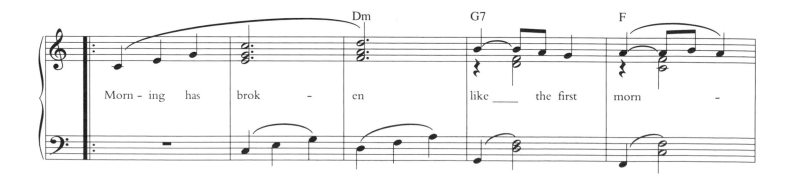

Morn - ing has brok - en   like ____ the first   morn -

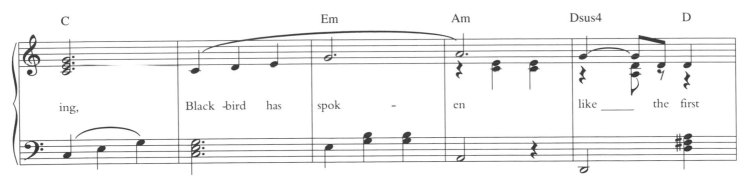

ing, Black -bird has spok - en like _____ the first

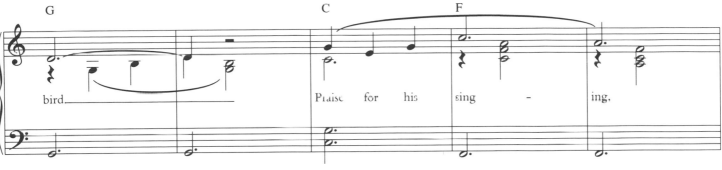

bird_____ Praise for his sing - ing,

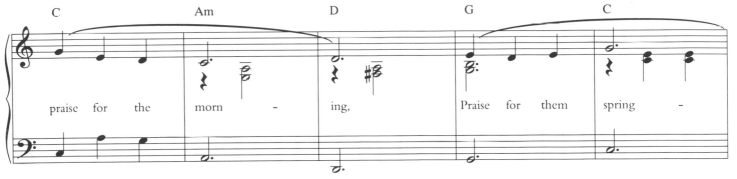

praise for the morn - ing, Praise for them spring -

ing fresh from ___ the Word.

2. Sweet the rain's new fall, sunlit from heaven,
   Like the first dewfall on the first grass.
   Praise for the sweetness of the wet garden,
   Sprung in completeness where His feet pass.

3. Mine is the sunlight, mine is the morning,
   Born of the one light Eden saw play.
   Praise with elation, praise ev'ry morning,
   God's re-creation of the new day.

Sloop John B.

Moderately

Traditional

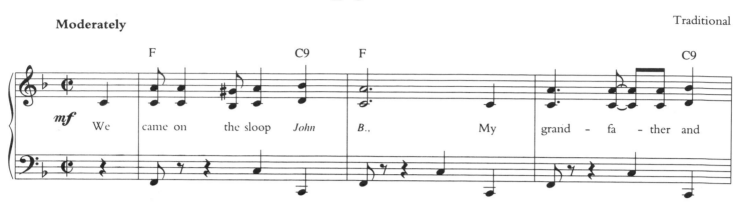

We came on the sloop *John B.,* My grand – fa – ther and

me, A – round Nas – sau town we ____ did

roam; ____ Drink –ing all night,

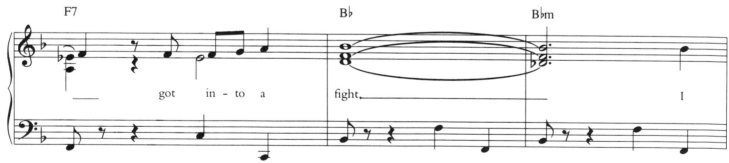

____ got in – to a fight, ____ I

feel so break up, I want to go home. ____

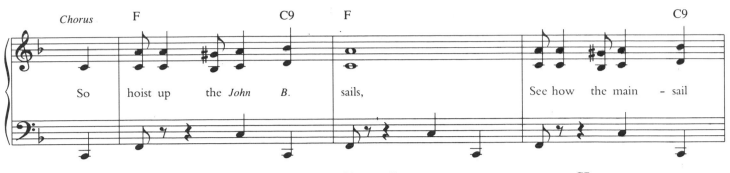

Chorus

So hoist up the *John B.* sails, See how the main - sail

sets, Call for the cap -tain a -shore, let me go home._____

Let me go home,_____ I want to go home,_____ I

feel so break up, I want to go home._____

2. The first mate, he got drunk,
   Broke in the captain's trunk,
   Constable had to come and take him away.
   Sheriff John Stone, please let me alone,
   I feel so break up, I want to go home.

3. The poor cook, he took fits,
   Threw away all the grits,
   Then he took and ate up all of the corn.
   Let me alone, I want to go home,
   This is the worst trip I've ever been on.

Tom Dooley

Moderately

Traditional

2. You dug her grave four feet long,
   You dug it three feet deep,
   You rolled the cold clay over her,
   And tromped it with your feet.
   Chorus

3. 'Round this time tomorrow,
   Wonder where I'll be?
   Down in some lonesome valley,
   Hangin' from a white oak tree.
   Chorus

4. Take my fiddle off the wall,
   Play it all you please,
   For at this time tomorrow,
   It'll be no use to me.
   Chorus

Wabash Cannonball

Traditional

Moderately

mf From the great At - lan - tic O - cean To the wide Pa - ci - fic's

shore, From the ones we leave be - hind us To the ones we see once

more. She's might - y tall and hand- some, And quite well known by

all, She's a mod ern com - bin - a - tion Called the Wa - bash Can - non ball.

2. Hear the bell and whistle calling,
   Hear the wheels that go "clack clack,"
   Hear the roaring of the engine,
   As she rolls along the track.
   The magic of the railroad
   Wins hearts of one and all,
   As we reach our destination
   On the Wabash Cannonball.

3. Listen to the jingle,
   The rumble and the roar,
   Riding through the woodlands,
   To the hill and by the shore.
   Hear the mighty rush of engines,
   Hear the lonesome hobo squall;
   Riding through the jungles
   On the Wabash Cannonball.

4. Now the eastern states are dandies,
   So the western people say
   From New York to St. Louis
   And Chicago by the way,
   Through the hills of Minnesota
   Where the rippling waters fall
   No chances can be taken
   On the Wabash Cannonball.

I'm Henery the Eighth, I Am

Words and music by
R.P. Weston and Fred Murray

With gusto

I'm Hen -er -y the Eighth, I am!

Hen -er -y the Eighth, I am, I am!

I got mar -ried to the wid -ow next door, She's been

mar -ried sev -en times be -fore; And ev -'ry

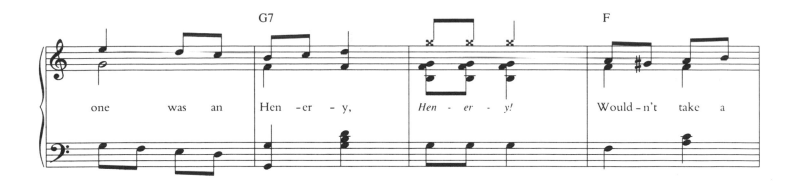

one was an Hen -er -y, *Hen - er - y!* Would –n't take a

Wil -lie or a Sam, *No Sam!* I'm her eighth old man named

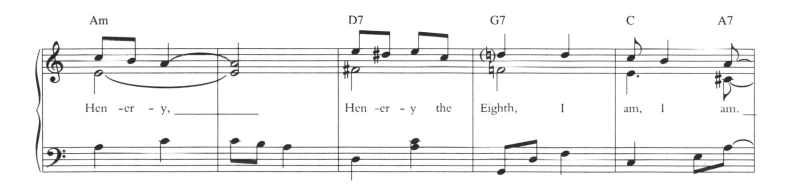

Hen -er -y, _____ Hen -er -y the Eighth, I am, I am.

_____ Hen -er -y the Eighth, I am! _____

Midnight Special

Traditional

Moderate rock tempo

You get up in the morn - in.' You hear the ding - dong

ring. Now you look ___ up - on the ta - ble,

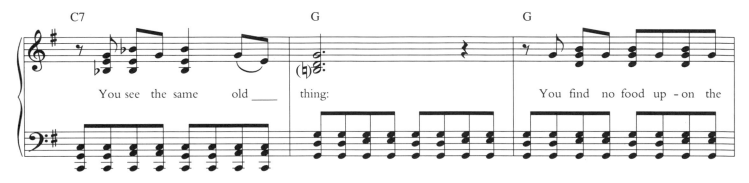

You see the same old ___ thing: You find no food up - on the

ta - ble, ___ Noth - ing ___ up in the pan, ___

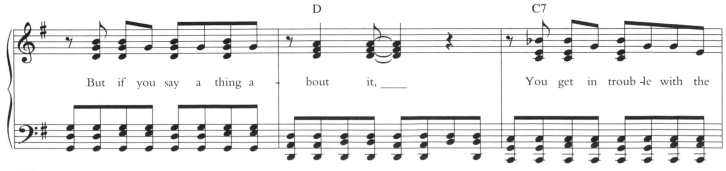

But if you say a thing a - bout it, ___ You get in troub - le with the

man. So, let the Mid - night ___ Spe - cial ___

shine a light on me, ___ Oh, let the Mid - night ___

Spe - cial ___ shine its ev - er -lov -in' light on me. ___

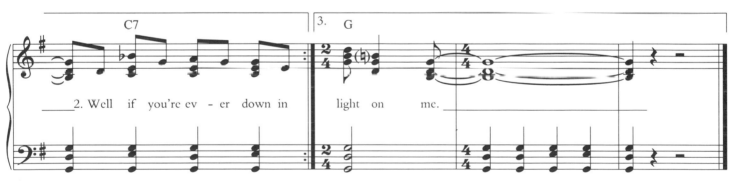

___ 2. Well if you're ev - er down in light on me. ___

2. Well, if you're ever down in Houston
    You'd better walk on by;
    Oh, you'd better not gamble,
    And, you'd better not fight;
    Because the sheriff will arrest you,
    His boys will pull you down,
    And then, before you know it,
    You're penitentiary bound.
    Chorus

3. Yonder comes Miss Lucy.
    How in the world do you know?
    I can tell her by her apron,
    And the dress she wore.
    Umbrella on her shoulder,
    Piece of paper in her hand;
    She's gonna see the sheriff,
    To try and free her man.
    Chorus

La Bamba

Traditional

Latin beat

Pa - ra bai - lar la bam-

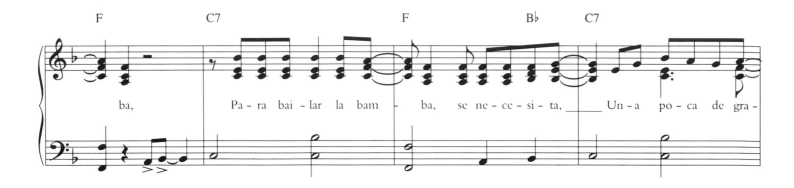

ba, Pa - ra bai - lar la bam - ba, se ne - ce - si - ta, Un - a po - ca de gra-

cia, Un - a po - ca de gra - cia, par' - mi par' - tia. Ay ar - ri - ba, yar - ri-

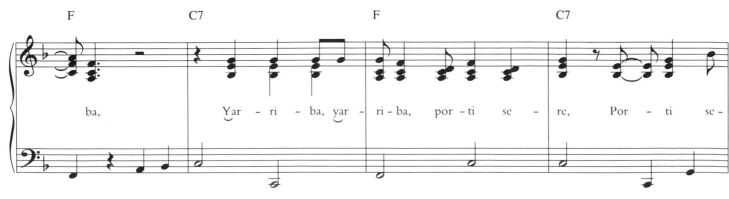

ba, Yar - ri - ba, yar - ri - ba, por - ti se - re, Por - ti se-

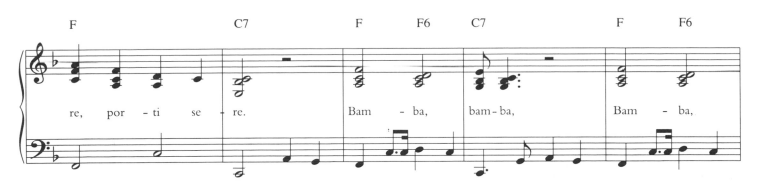

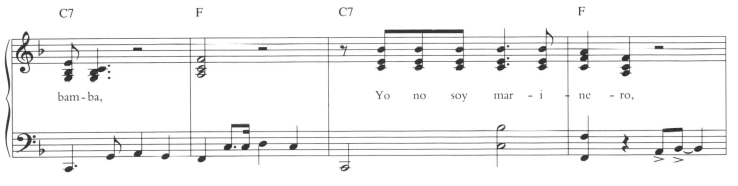

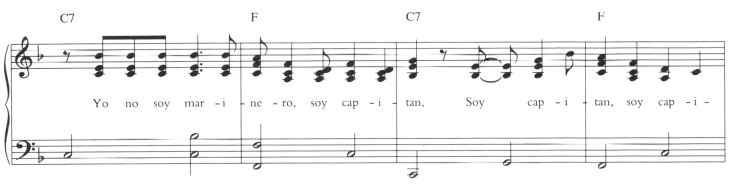

365

Wimoweh

Traditional

Bouncy

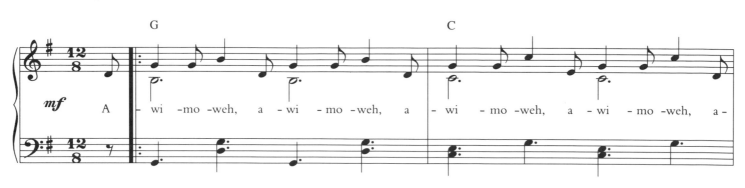

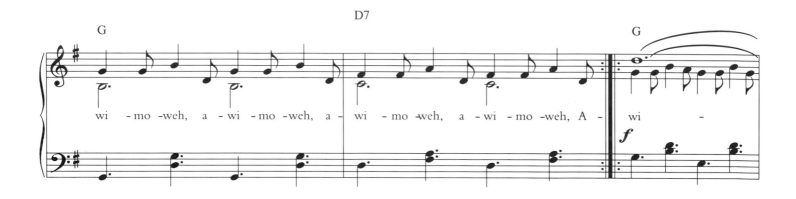

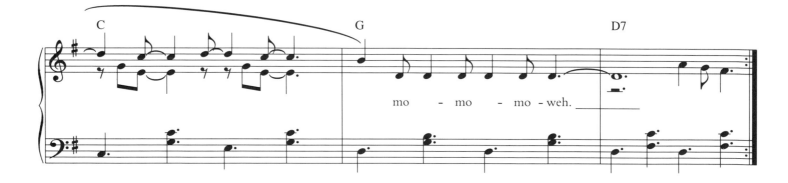

Wi -mo -weh, a -wi -mo -weh, a - wi -mo -weh, a -wi -mo -weh, a-

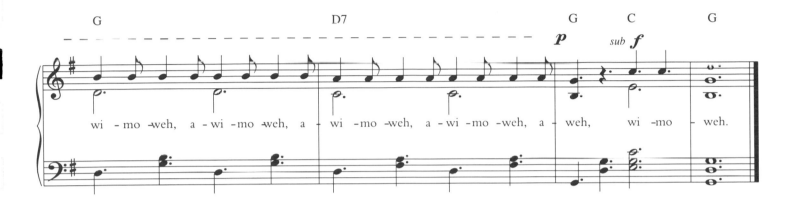

wi -mo -weh, a -wi -mo -weh, a - wi -mo -weh, a -wi -mo -weh, a - weh, wi -mo - weh.

C. C. Rider

Rhythmically

Traditional

C. C. Rid - er, see what you have done,

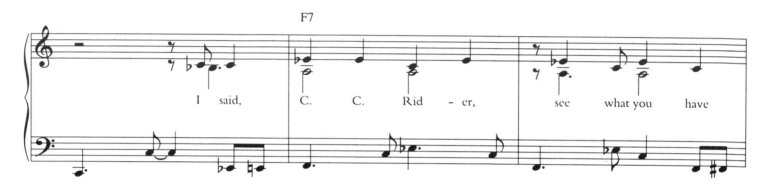

I said, C. C. Rid - er, see what you have

done, Well, you made me love you,

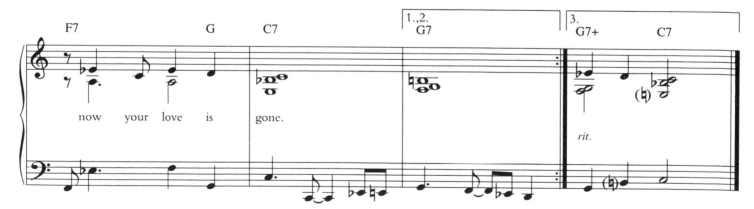

now your love is gone.

2. C.C. Rider, love you, 'deed I do,
   C.C. Rider, love you, 'deed I do,
   There isn't one thing, darlin', I wouldn't do for you.

3. C.C. Rider, I need you by my side,
   C.C. Rider, I need you by my side,
   You're the only one who keeps me satisfied.

Michael, Row the Boat Ashore

Traditional

2. Jordan's river is chilly and cold, hallelujah,
Kills the body, but not the soul, hallelujah,
Jordan's river is deep and wide, hallelujah,
Meet my mother on the other side, hallelujah.

3. Michael's boat is a music boat, hallelujah,
Michael's boat is a music boat, hallelujah,
Michael, row the boat ashore, hallelujah,
Michael, row the boat ashore, hallelujah.

NOTES ON THE SONGS

After the Ball. A little-known songwriter named Charles K. Harris was commissioned to write this song in 1892 for an extravagant Milwaukee minstrel show entitled *A Trip to Chinatown*. America soon fell in love with this deeply sentimental waltz—and sales of the sheet music broke all existing records. "After the Ball" became the first million-seller in the history of American popular music—and, over the years, created over five million dollars in sales. Charles K. Harris went on to create several other popular sentimental hits—but none is as well remembered today as "After the Ball."

Alexander's Ragtime Band. Irving Berlin wrote this song in 1911 while working as a singing waiter in New York City. Its overwhelming success launched the twenty-three-year-old Berlin on what has been called the most successful songwriting career in American history. In 1938, "Alexander's Ragtime Band" was featured in a musical film of the same title, starring Alice Faye, Jack Haley, and Don Ameche. In 1954, it was heard again in *There's No Business Like Show Business,* with Ethel Merman, Marilyn Monroe, and Donald O'Connor. Today, the song is still counted among Berlin's most successful works—and is widely performed as a jazz standard.

Amazing Grace. This inspiring American hymn first became popular in the early 1800s. The melody is traditional, but may be traced to several Scottish airs of the eighteenth century. The moving words were penned by Reverend John Newton—a slave-ship captain who underwent a spiritual awakening and began a new life in the ministry. This song is performed in many languages throughout the world. It is a particular favorite of the bagpipe corps of America's police and firefighters. As a tribute to the lasting popularity of this song, Judy Collins made it a top-40 hit in 1971. The following year, the Royal Scots Dragoon Guards of Scotland's armored regiment recorded a bagpipe band version of this tune that put it back on the pop charts.

America, the Beautiful. American poetess Katharine Lee Bates wrote the words to this beloved anthem in 1893, after an inspiring visit to the summit of Pike's Peak. Her poem was first published in 1895, and soon after, the melody was adapted from "Materna" by Samuel Augustus Ward.

America *(My Country 'Tis of Thee).* In 1832, the Reverend Samuel F. Smith wrote new words to the British national anthem, "God Save the King," and produced this popular patriotic anthem. "America" was first performed at a children's Fourth of July celebration in Boston. It did not achieve nationwide fame until the Civil War. Today, it is the most well known and frequently performed patriotic song in the nation.

Anchors Aweigh. Written by Charles A. Zimmerman, this march was originally entitled "Sail Navy Down the Field"—and served as a fight song for the United States Naval Academy at Annapolis (class of 1907). Captain Alfred Hart Miles and R. Lovell wrote the lyrics to "Anchors Aweigh"—which became a favorite anthem of the United States Navy.

Annie Laurie. William Douglas wrote the words to this beautiful ballad in 1688 while fighting in Flanders. It is said that he died on the battlefield murmuring the name of his beloved Annie Laurie, daughter of Sir Robert Laurie. Annie married another years after her lover William was slain. Her memory lives on in this beautiful ballad, which was set to music by Lady John Scott (also known as Alicia Ann Spottiswoode). "Annie Laurie" was popular in America in the mid-nineteenth century— and remains a favorite sentimental ballad today.

A-Tisket A-Tasket. After winning the Harlem Amateur Hour in 1934, Ella Fitzgerald created a popular sensation with her jazzy rendition of "A-Tisket, A-Tasket." This traditional nursery rhyme first appeared in the 1870s—and has enjoyed over a century of American popular attention—particularly during the swing era. In 1944, it was featured in the musical film *Two Girls and a Sailor,* starring June Allyson, Van Johnson, and Lena Horne.

Auld Lang Syne. Robert Burns adapted this traditional Scottish air in 1711—and added the classic final stanzas. It became popular in America, beginning in the late 1700s. The melody has inspired many other songs (including Princeton's school song, "Old Nassau")—even Beethoven wrote variations on this theme. "Auld Lang Syne" was also Guy Lombardo's signature tune—and is sung the world over to ring in the New Year.

Aura Lee. This all-time favorite sentimental ballad was written in 1861 by W.W. Fosdick and George R. Poulton. "Aura Lee" not only became a barbershop classic, it also inspired two later song successes— "Army Blue," the United States Military Academy theme song, and "Love Me Tender," Elvis Presley's smash hit of 1956.

Ave Maria. Franz Schubert's "Ave Maria" (Opus 52, No. 6) is among the world's favorite inspirational pieces. The original words were taken from Sir Walter Scott's *Lady of the Lake*. The Latin version is derived from Luke 1:28. "Ave Maria" is performed at church and at home to celebrate many spiritual occasions—and it is a particular favorite at traditional Christian weddings.

Ballin' the Jack. This novel dance number was published in 1913 with music by Chris Smith and words by James Henry Burris. In 1915, it was featured in the stage musical *The Passing Show of 1915*— and has since enjoyed numerous popular jazz recordings and a notable Hollywood career. In 1942, "Ballin' the Jack" was featured in the musical film *For Me and My Gal*. It was also heard in the musical films *On the Riviera, Jazz Dance,* and *That's My Boy*.

The Band Played On. A young actor named John F. Palmer wrote this song in 1895. Palmer sold the song for a flat fee to an older performer and songwriter, Charles B. Ward—who made some alterations and published it as his own. Ward promoted the song on the vaudeville circuit and made it a popular success. Casey and his bewildered dance partner are still well remembered today in this energetic waltz song.

The Banks of the Ohio. This traditional ballad originated in the Ohio region. Through the years, its grim tale of love and murder has inspired many popular mystery tales—and several related folk ballads.

Barb'ra Allen. Samuel Pepys mentions this "little Scotch song" in his diary as early as 1666. It became an early American favorite when it was brought to the colonies by the first settlers—and its popularity lives on in numerous versions throughout America and Europe.

The Battle Hymn of the Republic. It is said that Julia Ward Howe was inspired to write these famous lyrics in a dream—and completed the verses just a few hours after waking. The rousing tune is borrowed from another popular Civil War song "John Brown's Body" (formerly "Glory Hallelujah"), which is sometimes attributed to melodist William Steffe. Howe's lyrics first appeared anonymously in the *Atlantic Monthly* in 1862. She received five dollars for her masterful poem, which soon became a favorite war song of the period—and an all-time American national treasure.

Beautiful Dreamer. Stephen Foster wrote this ethereal love song from his bed at the poverty ward of Bellevue Hospital in New York City—just a few days before his death on January 13, 1864. "Beautiful Dreamer" has enjoyed well over a century of world popularity—and was featured in the musical film *Swanee River,* starring Al Jolson and Don Ameche.

The Big Rock Candy Mountain. This traditional American folk song was known to many travelling musicians and hobos of the late 1800s. It was featured in the 1949 film *Nighttime in Nevada,* starring Roy Rogers and Andy Devine. "The Big Rock Candy Mountain" was also repopularized through the memorable recordings and performances of the Weavers and Burl Ives.

Bill Bailey, Won't You Please Come Home? Hughie Cannon wrote this swingy song in 1902. It was so successful that it inspired reply songs, including "Since Bill Bailey Came Home" and "I Wonder Why Bill Bailey Don't Come Home." The song was popular throughout the swing era—and enjoyed many notable jazz recordings. In 1959, "Bill Bailey, Won't You Please Come Home" was featured in the musical film *Five Pennies,* with Louis Armstrong.

Black Is the Color of My True Love's Hair. This Southern Appalachian ballad may be traced to several British sources. The lyrics are based on a ballad entitled "Dark Is the Color of My True Love's Eyes." The tune is a rich variant of another eighteenth century English ballad.

Blow the Man Down. This traditional sailor's work song is probably of English origin. When it was first published in 1880, it was already the favorite shanty of American seamen. This simple call-and-answer song has inspired hundreds of different verses over the years. Like other shanties, the pulsing and regular beat of "Blow the Man Down" helped the crew to maintain a concerted team effort while hoisting the sails, weighing the anchor, or performing other group tasks on shipboard.

The Blue Tail Fly. Also known as "Jimmy Crack Corn," this was a popular minstrel song of the 1840s. At one time, the authorship of "The Blue Tail Fly" was attributed to Dan Decatur Emmett (writer of "Dixie"), but it is more likely of purely traditional origin. The song has abolitionist undertones—and was popular in the North before the Civil War. "Blue Tail Fly" was a favorite of President Lincoln's—and he requested that it be played at the ceremony of his Gettysburg Address.

The Bowery. Percy Gaunt borrowed this popular melody from the traditional Italian song, "La Spagnola." Charles H. Hoyt wrote the lyrics. "The Bowery" debuted in the minstrel show "A Trip to Chinatown" in 1892 (as did the very successful "After the Ball"). The great popularity of this song made property values drop in the Bowery area—and caused public outcry among local property owners and storekeepers.

A Boy's Best Friend Is His Mother. This beloved chestnut was written in 1884 by Joseph P. Skelly (a plumber by profession), who created hundreds of songs as a sideline. Sentimental songs about "Mother" were very popular during this period—and were published in great numbers well into the teens and twenties. This one (and the famous "M-O-T-H-E-R" of 1915) made a lasting impression on the American public—and are still well known today.

Bridal Chorus (from Lohengrin). This stately chorus was written by Richard Wagner for his opera *Lohengrin,* which was composed between 1846 and 1848. It is often performed in the same wedding ceremony as Felix Mendelssohn's "Wedding March" from the opera *A Midsummer Night's Dream* (1844). Wagner's march is best known to some as "Here Comes the Bride"—but is most often performed as an organ instrumental during that important trip down the aisle.

Bright College Years. As the official song of Yale College, "Bright College Years" has enjoyed countless performances on and off campus. The tune was written by Carl Wilhelm—and the words by H.S. Durand (Class of 1881). Although Yale's name is featured prominently in the final phrase of each verse, this beautiful song is sure to move anyone who fondly remembers "the happy, golden, bygone days" of college. During the last line of each verse, it is traditional to wave your handkerchief rhythmically from side to side (beginning from left to right) with each new syllable of the lyric.

Bury Me Not on the Lone Prairie. Sometimes called "The Dying Cowboy," this traditional American cowboy song was adapted from a sailor's ballad, "Oh, Bury Me Not in the Deep, Deep Sea." This sad song of the sea was based on the poem, "The Ocean Burial," written in 1839 by E.H. Chapin—and set to music ten years later by George N. Allen. "Bury Me Not on the Lone Prairie" was popularly revived in 1932.

By the Light of the Silvery Moon. Melodist Gus Edwards (who also wrote the tune to "School Days") teamed with lyricist Edward Madden to write this popular hit in 1909. That year, it was featured in the prestigious *Ziegfeld Follies*—and became an instant smash. This sentimental song is a barbershop favorite—and enjoyed a long Hollywood career in such films as *Birth of the Blues, The Jolson Story, Always Leave Them Laughing,* and *Two Weeks With Love.* It even inspired a motion picture of the same name in 1953, starring Doris Day and Gordon MacRae.

The Caissons Go Rolling Along. Also known as "The U.S. Field Artillery March," this exuberant service song was long attributed to John Philip Sousa—whose stirring band arrangement made it famous in 1918. The march was actually written in 1908 by Brigadier Edmund L. Gruber (while stationed in the Philippines). New lyrics were added by Harold Arberg in 1956—and it became the official song of the United States Army as "The Army Goes Marching Along."

The Camptown Races. Sometimes entitled "Gwine to Run All Night," this song was written by Stephen Foster in 1850 and popularized by the Christy Minstrels. The tune was later adapted for the shanty "Sacramento." "The Camptown Races" was featured in several musical films, including *Swanee River, I Dream of Jeanie,* and *Colorado.*

Careless Love. Music historians consider this lovely Appalachian tune to be the first traditional blues song. The title "Careless Love" is thought to be simply a mispronunciation of an earlier nineteenth century ballad entitled "Kelly's Love." Many blues lyrics focus on lost love, desertion, and broken families—but none as eloquently as "Careless Love"—the oldest American blues.

Carry Me Back to Old Virginny. This song was written in 1878 by James A. Bland, the first successful Black-American songwriter. Besides composing close to seven hundred songs, Bland was an internationally famous music hall performer—as well as the first Black examiner in the United States Patent Office. This popular song was featured in the film *Hullabaloo,* starring Frank Morgan and Billie Burke. It became the official state song of Virginia in 1940.

Casey Jones. On April 29, 1900, a heroic train engineer named John Luther "Casey" Jones realized that his Cannon Ball Express was on a collision course with another train. Casey ordered everyone to jump off, except himself, and died at the throttle. The words to "Casey Jones" are sometimes attributed to Wallace Saunders, the engineer's Black engine-wiper, who adapted the tune from the popular ballad "Jimmie Jones." When "Casey Jones" was popularized in 1909, the lyrics were credited to T. Lawrence Seibert—and the music to Eddie Newton. This song exists in many versions and is generally considered to be a product of our rich folk heritage.

C.C. Rider. This traditional folk song became an all-time favorite blues and rock hit for a wide range of recording artists. Ma Rainey brought this tune to position fourteen on the charts in 1925. In 1957, rhythm and blues singer Chuck Willis had a career-making hit with this song—and inspired the dance craze called "The Stroll." In 1963, rhythm and blues singer Lavern Baker recorded her hit version of this tune (entitled "See See Rider"). The magic had still not worn off this powerful rhythm number—for Eric Burdon & the Animals made "See See Rider" a hit once again for seven weeks in 1966.

Chester. Written in 1778 by William Billings, "Chester" was the first original popular song written by an American-born composer. This rousing, patriotic anthem served as a marching song for Colonial troops throughout New England—and was heard at many important battle sites during the Revolutionary War.

Cindy. This spirited folk song originated in the Southern Appalachian region in colonial times—and was a popular singalong and square dance tune in the mid-nineteenth century.

Ciribiribin. This popular big band number was actually written in 1898 by Alberto Pestalozza. The lilting, romantic melody received many notable arrangements during the swing era—and served as theme song for Harry James. In 1934, "Ciribiribin" was featured in the musical film *One Night of Love*. In 1955, it was heard in another musical film, *Hit the Deck*—and featured again in the 1978 film *Heaven Can Wait*.

Clementine. The words and music to this song are often attributed to Percy Montrose—but many authorities feel it is a product of the folk process. "Clementine" first appeared forty years after the California Gold Rush. This comic view of one pioneer girl's terrible fate provides a cynical comment on forty-niners—who seemed willing to sacrifice anything for the promise of gold.

Colorado Trail. This lonesome love song originated in the Rocky Mountain region—and was well known among wranglers and rodeo men at the beginning of this century. The melody is of Irish origin, but the lyrics are as American as a ten-gallon hat.

Columbia, the Gem of the Ocean. This inspiring anthem was published in 1843 as "Columbia the Land of the Brave" with words and music credited to Thomas A. Becket and David T. Shaw. The song was conceived by Shaw, who asked Becket to help him write it for a benefit performance at the Chestnut Theatre. This rousing national treasure is also known as "The Red, White, and Blue" and "The Army and Navy Song." It has been suggested that this melody may be traced to England—but the earliest published record of the English version ("Britannia, the Pride of the Ocean") occurs in 1852.

Comin' Thro' the Rye. Robert Burns wrote this poem in 1796—probably with the traditional Scottish tune in mind. The song was popularly performed at the Royal Circus in its day and has remained an American favorite since colonial times.

Corinna, Corinna. This traditional Black-American blues song has been recorded by many blues artists over the decades. Its hard-driving rhythm and earthy lyric made it a natural choice for several prominent rhythm and blues band as well—and it was also recorded by country and western artists and swing bands. In 1961, "Corinna, Corinna" became a hit on the pop charts for Ray Peterson.

Cradle Song *(Brahms Lullaby)*. This beautiful work by Johannes Brahms is surely the world's most famous lullaby. It was published in 1868 in a collection of five songs for voice and piano (Opus 49). The German words are often attributed to Karl Simrock. Arthur Westbrook translated the lyric into English (and another English version is credited to Mrs. Natalia MacFarren). The English title "Cradle Song" is a translation of the German title "Wiegenlied"—still, this gentle waltz is known to many simply as "Brahms Lullaby."

Cripple Creek. This energetic fiddle tune is traditionally performed at country hoedowns and singalongs in the American South and West. With its relentless dance rhythm and fun-loving lyrics, "Cripple Creek" is famous for its ability to fire up the crowd—and set feet aflying.

The Cruel War. The Civil War fostered many songs and poems that expressed antiwar sentiments. In "The Cruel War," a young girl conspires to disguise herself as a soldier so that she may accompany her beloved into battle. This ageless theme occurs in several earlier British ballads—but "The Cruel War" remains the most powerful and best-known of these laments.

Cumberland Gap. This spirited dance tune celebrates the gateway of the Cumberland Mountains of Kentucky, which was discovered by Thomas Walker in 1750. "Cumberland Gap" was an early Appalachian favorite. Like most mountain tunes, it is traditionally performed as an energetic fiddle tune or sung a capella.

Daisy Bell. Also known as "A Bicycle Built for Two" and "Daisy, Daisy," this quaint waltz was written in 1892 by Harry Dacre. The song was first performed on the London music hall stage—and quickly became a favorite in Europe and America. The tandem bicycle was a common sight during the 1890s—and was especially popular with young couples.

Danny Boy. Frederick Weatherly wrote new words to the traditional Irish song "Londonderry Air" and published "Danny Boy" in 1913. This affecting love song is known throughout the world for its ability to move the heart (especially if the heart is Irish)—and enjoyed thirteen weeks on the pop charts when Conway Twitty recorded it in 1959.

The Daring Young Man (On the Flying Trapeze). This famous comic song was published anonymously in 1868 as "The Flying Trapeze." The tune was written by Alfred Lee—and the words by George Leybourne. Through the years, this whimsical song has enjoyed a prominent place in the circus and vaudeville repertoires of England and America. It was revived as a popular tune in the 1930s (usually with the shortened title "The Man on the Flying Trapeze").

Dark Eyes. Also known as "Black Eyes," this passionate song is based on a traditional tune of the Russian gypsies entitled "Ochee Chornya" (meaning "dark eyes"). During the 1920s, "Dark Eyes" enjoyed several popular recordings—and it remains today the best-loved gypsy song in America.

Dixie. Composed in 1860 by Black-American minstrel/songwriter Daniel Decatur Emmett, this rousing song was the decided favorite of the Civil War era. Like many other popular Southern songs, "Dixie" was performed in the North with lyrics which favored the Union side. It was first performed as the company finale or "walk-around" in a minstrel show at Bryant's Theatre—and became an instant smash on the minstrel circuit. Emmett died in penury, after being persuaded to sign over the copyright to this popular hit to his publisher for five hundred dollars.

Down by the Riverside. This is among America's oldest antiwar songs—and received wide popular revival as a protest song during the 1960s. As in other American folk songs, here the river symbolizes spiritual awakening—and a renewed commitment to the brotherhood of man.

Down in the Valley. Also known as "Birmingham Jail," this traditional song originated in the Southern Appalachian Mountains in the mid-nineteenth century. It achieved national fame in the early 1900s—and has since become a mainstay of the American folk repertoire.

Drill, Ye Tarriers, Drill. This wry work song originated among Irish railway workers of the late nineteenth century (although it is sometimes attributed to vaudevillian Thomas F. Casey). The word "tarrier" literally means "one who tarries"—and, like any good work song, this one urges the workers to do their level best. Even in the face of dangerous conditions, poor wages, and unfair employers, these men were clearly able to enjoy the irony of their situation in outspoken songs like "Drill, Ye Tarriers, Drill." Such songs paved the way for the prominent labor songs of the later union movements.

Drink to Me Only With Thine Eyes. The words to this beautiful love song are from Ben Jonson's poem "To Celia," published in 1616. The tune first appeared in print in 1780—and is thought to be the work of Colonel R. Mellish.

The Eddystone Light. This merry sea shanty first became popular in the early eighteenth century. Sometimes known as "The Keeper of the Eddystone Light," it is traditionally performed as a jaunty hornpipe.

The Entertainer. Scott Joplin wrote "The Entertainer" in 1902. This classic piano rag (along with his very successful "Maple Leaf Rag" of 1899) are still widely popular today. In 1973, Marvin Hamlisch adapted compositions of Scott Joplin to create the score for the Academy Award-winning film *The Sting.* "The Entertainer" served as the theme song for the movie—and became a gold-record hit for Hamlisch in 1974. The popular movie soundtrack and hit single created a renewed public interest in ragtime music—and made Scott Joplin's name a household word.

The Erie Canal. The Erie Canal was completed in 1825—and served as an important conduit of goods between New York City and the Great Lakes region. The "canawlers" were a rough breed of watermen who invented many folk songs and stories to amuse themselves as they drove their mule-drawn barges on this slow, four-hundred-mile journey. Also known as "Low Bridge, Everybody Down," this traditional American folk song was adapted and published in 1913 by Thomas S. Allen.

Every Little Movement (Has a Meaning All Its Own). Otto Harbach and Karl Hoschna created this lovely ballad for the musical *Madame Sherry,* which opened in America in 1910. "Every Little Movement" remained popular throughout the swing era—and was featured in the 1951 musical film *On Moonlight Bay,* starring Doris Day and Gordon MacRae.

The First Noel. This traditional Christmas carol became popular in the early 1800s. Although the song is probably of English origin, the word *Noël* is French—and was a common expression of glad tidings on Christmas Day. The lyric recounts the biblical story of Christ's birth with timeless simplicity and beauty.

The Foggy, Foggy Dew. This traditional folk song originated in England in the early 1700s. It is thought to have been brought to the American Midwest by English settlers in the early 1800s. The original version of this song is actually quite ribald—but most know it today in this milder setting as a charming tale of lost love.

For He's a Jolly Good Fellow. The melody of this well-known song is centuries old—and may be traced to French folk sources. An early version (entitled "Malbrouk" or "Marlborough," after the Duke of Marlborough) was among Napoleon Bonaparte's favorite military airs. Beethoven featured this popular melody in his "Battle Symphony" of 1813. There are several versions of the lyric, including "We Won't Come Home Until Morning" and "The Bear Went Over the Mountain." The familiar version "For He's a Jolly Good Fellow" has been a part of college life for decades—and is widely performed at celebrations and convivial gatherings of all kinds.

Forty-five Minutes From Broadway. George M. Cohan wrote this comic song in 1905 for a musical of the same name starring Fay Templeton and Victor Moore. Officials of New Rochelle, New York, felt the show contained defamatory statements about their township and formally boycotted *Forty-five Minutes From Broadway* throughout its run. This classic show song remained popular throughout the swing era—and was featured in the 1942 musical film *Yankee Doodle Dandy.* "Forty-five Minutes From Broadway" was revived on Broadway in 1968 in the musical tribute to Cohan's life, *George M!*

Frankie and Johnny. This is easily the most famous blues in musical history. A stark tale of love and murder, "Frankie and Johnny" was recorded by many great blues and popular artists—and was a signature tune for Mae West. As a testament to this song's versatility, rhythm and blues singer Brook Benton put it on the charts for four weeks in 1961; soul singer Sam Cooke put it on the charts for seven weeks in 1963; and Elvis Presley, the king of rock and roll, made it a hit once again for five weeks in 1966.

Froggy Went A-Courtin'. This fanciful song was written in England in the late 1500s. It was entitled "A Most Strange Weddinge of the Froge and the Mouse" when first published in 1611—and became an early favorite in colonial America. Though considered a children's song, "Froggy Went A-Courtin'" has long been enjoyed by adults (and may have originally been a political satire of Queen Elizabeth's suitor, the Duke of Anjou).

Funeral March of a Marionette. This famous instrumental piece was composed by Charles Gounod in 1872. Although it has no lyrics, it certainly qualifies as one of America's well-loved musical compositions. Many know it best as the mysterious theme of the popular television series *Alfred Hitchcock Presents*.

Gaudeamus Igitur. This is perhaps the oldest student song still in popular use. The words may be traced to a thirteenth century Latin manuscript. The tune became popular in the late eighteenth century. "Gaudeamus Igitur" (meaning, "now let us be happy") celebrates the idyllic life of the student. In 1932, Sigmund Romberg featured a classic male-chorus arrangement of this song in his operetta *The Student Prince*.

Give My Regards to Broadway. George M. Cohan wrote this all-time showstopper in 1904 for the Broadway production of *Little Johnny Jones*. The song was revived on Broadway in the 1968 tribute to the composer *George M!*, starring Bernadette Peters and Joel Gray. It has been featured in numerous musical films, including *Yankee Doodle Dandy, Broadway Melody, Jolson Sings Again,* and *With a Song in My Heart*. This classic show tune also inspired a dramatic film of the same name in 1948.

Glow Worm. German composer Paul Lincke wrote the music and German words to this song—and Lila Cayley Robinson wrote the English lyrics. "Glow Worm" was first published in 1902—and became a hit in the musical *The Girl Behind the Counter*. Johnny Mercer added his own lyrics to this tune in the early 1950s—but it is frequently performed as a swing or jazz instrumental piece.

Go Down, Moses. This traditional Black-American spiritual first appeared in the early 1860s. "Go Down, Moses" recounts the deliverance of the Israelites from Egyptian bondage—a natural metaphor for the abolition of slavery in America. A century later, this song served the Civil Rights Movement as a powerful outcry against racial oppression and inequality.

Goodbye, My Lady Love. Joe E. Howard wrote this song in 1904. He based the melody on a contemporary instrumental piece entitled "Down South" (which was composed by W.H. Myddleton). Howard's other enduring hits, "Hello! Ma Baby" (of 1889) and "I Wonder Who's Kissing Her Now" (of 1909), were written with collaborators—but "Goodbye, My Lady Love" was entirely his creation.

Good Morning Blues. This classic twelve-bar blues song has been recorded by many of the great blues masters. Like other traditional Black-American blues, this song uses bluesy harmonies and repetition to create a powerful, lonesome feeling.

Goodnight, Ladies. This popular song was written by E.P. Christy for performance by his troupe, the Christy Minstrels. It appears as early as 1847. In later years, it became a popular college song and a favorite of the barbershop quartet. The first section of the melody of "Goodnight Ladies" is similar to one of "I've Been Working' on the Railroad" (beginning with "Someone's in the kitchen with Dinah . . ."). The second part of "Goodnight Ladies" clearly inspired Sarah Josepha Hale's "Mary Had a Little Lamb" of 1867.

Grandfather's Clock. Abolitionist and inventor Henry Clay Work wrote this song in 1876. It was performed in minstrel shows of the time—and remains a popular sentimental ballad to this day. Many of Work's other songs deal with Abolitionist and Prohibitionist themes. This beautifully crafted song tells the story of one man's mortal bond with his treasured floor clock (which we call a "grandfather's clock" to this day).

Greensleeves. This time-honored English ballad is often attributed to King Henry VIII (an accomplished amateur musician and songwriter). The words were published as early as 1580. A popular Elizabethan dance tune, "Greensleeves" is mentioned twice in Shakespeare's *Merry Wives of Windsor*. The melody was later used for the Christmas carol "What Child Is This?"

Hail! Hail! the Gang's All Here. Theodore Morse based this melody on themes from Gilbert and Sullivan's *Pirates of Penzance* (in which the melody served as an amusing parody of Verdi's "Anvil Chorus"). Morse's wife, Theodora, is credited with coauthorship of the lyrics of "Hail! Hail! the Gang's All Here," which became popular in the late teens. Today, this song is still a natural favorite at community and college celebrations—or, for that matter, at any occasion that inspires friends to unite their voices in song.

Hail to the Chief. Sir Walter Scott's poem "The Lady of the Lake" of 1810 provides the words to this majestic song. The music is often attributed to James Sanderson. "Hail to the Chief" first became popular in 1812—and was performed at the inauguration of President James Polk in 1845. To this day, the march is played to herald the arrival of the President of the United States.

Hanukkah Song. Hanukkah, the Jewish Festival of Lights, commemorates the biblical revolt of the Maccabees. The *menorah* is a ritual candelabra used during the eight-day festival. On each day of Hanukkah, one more candle of the menorah is lit using a special candle called a *shamos*. This beautiful song takes its melody from an old Yiddish folk song—and it is sung every year in midwinter wherever Hanukkah is celebrated.

Havah Nagilah. This traditional Hebrew folk song is a favorite accompaniment for the *hora*—an energetic traditional dance performed at Jewish celebrations and festivals. "Havah Nagilah" is traditionally performed at a spirited dance tempo, and accelerates to breakneck speed during its last sections.

Hello! Ma Baby. The telephone was invented in 1875 by Alexander Graham Bell—and it was still quite a novelty when this song was written in 1889. Of the many songs written about this remarkable invention, this is certainly the most memorable. Joe Howard wrote several other notable hits later in his career, including "Goodbye, My Lady Love" and "I Wonder Who's Kissing Her Now."

He's Got the Whole World in His Hands. This early Black-American spiritual was popularized in the 1920s. Over the years, people of many sects and creeds have found it easy to identify with this simple treatment of God's powerful love for all mankind. "He's Got the Whole World in His Hands" enjoyed several popular recordings in the 1950s—and was a natural choice for peace and civil rights advocates of the 1960s. Few traditional religious songs ever make it to the pop charts—but, this appealing spiritual (as recorded by Laurie London) was a number one hit for four weeks in 1958.

Home on the Range. Originally entitled "My Western Home," this folk song first appeared in the 1870s. It was, for a time, the official state song of Kansas—and was a known favorite of President Franklin D. Roosevelt. Its authorship has been the subject of controversy and litigation over the years—but historians generally agree that it is a product of our rich American folk heritage.

Home, Sweet Home. Actor John Howard Payne wrote the words to this famous song—and the music was adapted by Henry R. Bishop from a piece entitled "Sicilian Air." The song was first introduced in England in Payne's little-known opera of 1823, *Clari, the Maid of Milan*. "Home, Sweet Home" was soon a great success in England and America—but sadly, Payne was cut off from his rightful credit or royalties. Throughout his life, he thought it ironic that his popular song made so many people "boast of the delights of home" when he himself had been orphaned at an early age and "never had a home of his own."

House of the Rising Sun. This gritty folk song depicts the seamy side of life in the New Orleans red light district. In some versions, the House of the Rising Sun is the "ruin of many a poor girl"—while others depict the downfall of a dissolute gambler. This powerful song became a well-known rock ballad when the Animals made their number-one hit recording in 1964. Frijid Pink then put this hard-driving song on the charts again for eleven weeks in 1970.

I Am the Monarch of the Sea. This whimsical song is from Gilbert and Sullivan's comic opera *H.M.S. Pinafore,* which was first performed in 1878. With "I Am the Monarch of the Sea," we are first introduced to the story's farcical patriarch—The Rt. Hon. Sir Joseph Porter K.C.B., First Lord of the Admiralty (and his multitudinous lady relatives). When Queen Victoria heard this strong satire on her Navy, it is reported that she said, "We are not amused." However, many thousands of theatregoers were.

I Don't Care. This delightful novelty song was written in 1905 by Jean Lenox and Harry O. Sutton. It enjoyed a wide popular revival in the 1940s—and was featured in the 1949 musical film *In the Good Old Summertime,* starring Judy Garland, Van Johnson, and Buster Keaton.

I'll Take You Home Again, Kathleen. Thomas P. Westendorf wrote this song in 1876 in the style of a traditional Irish ballad. Immigrants from many nations were instantly touched by thoughts of homeland and family expressed in this deeply sentimental song (particularly, of course, those from Ireland). Westendorf wrote this song for his wife Jennie who was unhappy about their relocation to Kentucky—and yearned for her home in the East.

I Love You Truly. This song was written by Carrie Jacobs-Bond at the turn of the century. In the 1930s it enjoyed a wide popular revival—and has since become a mainstay of wedding and anniversary celebrations worldwide.

I'm Falling in Love With Someone. Victor Herbert and Rita Johnson Young created this lovely ballad for the operetta *Naughty Marietta,* which was first performed in 1910. A film version of the work was made in 1935, starring Nelson Eddy and Jeanette MacDonald. The song was also featured in the 1939 film tribute to Herbert's life and work *The Great Victor Herbert,* starring Mary Martin and Allan Jones.

I'm Henery the Eighth, I Am. This clever novelty song was written in 1910 by R.P. Weston and Fred Murray. "I'm Henery the Eighth, I Am" was popularized on the English music hall stage by an energetic star named Harry Champion. The British rock group Herman's Hermits revived this classic song in 1965—and brought it to the number one position on the pop charts.

I'm on My Way to Freedom Land. Originally entitled "I'm on My Way to Canaan Land," this old spiritual is thought to have had special significance to Underground Railroad organizers and escapees. It was revived during the Freedom Movement—and inherited many new impromptu verses at rallies and demonstrations.

In Good Old Colony Times. This traditional American drinking song originated in 1830—when "Good Old Colony Times" were already a thing of the past. The comic tale of three colonial rogues who meet a grim end "because they could not sing" makes a perfect subject for high-spirited group singing.

In the Good Old Summertime. This memorable song was written in 1902 by Ren Shields and George Evans. The melody was composed by Evans (nicknamed "Honey Boy") who led a famous minstrel troupe. Shields, a vaudeville comedian, wrote the lyrics. Stage songstress Blanche Ring debuted the song that year in a musical entitled *The Defender*. In 1949, "In the Good Old Summertime" served as the title song in a popular musical film starring Judy Garland and Van Johnson.

In the Shade of the Old Apple Tree. This sentimental ballad was published in 1905, with words by Harry H. Williams and music by Egbert Van Alstyne. It soon enjoyed wide popularity—and remains well known to this day. Harold Arlen was even inspired to write a spinoff of this old favorite entitled "In the Shade of the New Apple Tree."

I Ride an Old Paint. This traditional cowboy song originated in the late nineteenth century when cattlemen were already well established in the American West. The beloved pinto pony, "Old Paint," and the bovine "little doggies" appear in several other cowboy songs of the period—most notably, "Goodbye, Old Paint (I'm Leaving Cheyenne)."

I've Been Working on the Railroad. Also known as "The Levee Song" and "Someone's in the Kitchen With Dinah," this traditional American work song originated in the 1880s. In 1903, the melody was published with new lyrics as "The Eyes of Texas (Are Upon You)."

I Want a Girl—Just Like the Girl That Married Dear Old Dad. This charming ballad was first published in 1911, with lyrics by William Dillon and music by Harry Von Tilzer. During the 1940s, this song had a popular revival in such films as *Show Business* and *The Jolson Story*.

I Want to Be in Dixie. Irving Berlin wrote the lyrics to this swingy song in 1912, at the age of twenty-four. Just one year earlier (while working as a singing waiter) he'd had his first big songwriting success with "Alexander's Ragtime Band." Although "I Want to Be in Dixie" never achieved the great popularity of many of Berlin's later songs, it is an early milestone in his great and prolific career—and a delightful tribute to the American South.

I Wonder Who's Kissing Her Now. Melodist Joe Howard (who also wrote "Goodbye, My Lady Love" and "Hello! Ma Baby") teamed with lyricists Will M. Hough and Frank R. Adams to create this popular sentimental ballad in 1909. The melody was originally attributed to Joe Howard only—but after heated litigation, Harold Orlob established himself as a cowriter of the music. "I Wonder Who's Kissing Her Now" was featured in the Broadway musical *The Prince of Tonight* in 1909. It enjoyed a popular revival during the 1940s and was featured in the 1946 musical film *The Time, the Place and the Girl*. In 1947, it served as the title song in a musical film tribute to the life and work of Joe Howard.

Jesse James. The most famous outlaw of the American West is commemorated in this ballad, which originated in the Missouri region. The songwriter, Billy Gashade, is attributed in the final verse. The story is a true one: Jesse James (alias James Howard) was betrayed by one of his own accomplices, Robert Ford, who shot him in order to receive reward money and amnesty from the authorities. Like Robin Hood, Jesse goes down in history as an outlaw hero who had a generous spirit and many true friends.

Jingle Bells. This Christmas song was written in 1857 by J.S. Pierpont. Although the days of sleighing are well behind us, this exhilarating winter ride is affectionately mentioned in many more recent yuletide songs—and the jingling sleigh bells have earned an important place in the Christmas orchestra.

John Henry. The Industrial Revolution brought astounding new inventions to the American frontier—many of which made their way into folk stories and songs of the day. "John Henry" became popular during the 1870s. It tells the story of a mythical railroad worker who refused to be replaced by the steam drill—and dies proving his superiority to the machine. John Henry is the workingman's hero—and his story is equally pertinent today as new technologies and automation are applied to many tasks that were once accomplished by human labor alone.

Johnny Has Gone for a Soldier. Like several other American folk songs, this Revolutionary War ballad is based on the Irish tune, "Shule Aroon." While most of the colonial war songs express patriotic optimism and zeal, this one deals with the sad aspects of war from the point of view of one broken-hearted woman. "Johnny Has Gone for a Soldier" is also commonly known as "Buttermilk Hill." This affecting ballad has remained an American favorite since colonial times. It served as a popular Civil War song—and as a powerful song of protest during the Vietnam War.

Joy to the World. This beloved Christmas carol became popular in the early 1800s. The melody is by Lowell Mason, who was inspired by several themes from Handel's *Messiah*. The words were written by Isaac Watts, as inspired by Psalm 98. This jubilant song has enjoyed millions of performances and recordings over the years—and remains an American holiday favorite to this day.

Just Before the Battle, Mother. George Root wrote this affecting war ballad in 1863. His "Tramp! Tramp! Tramp!" and "Battle Cry of Freedom" were also quite popular—and the latter song is mentioned in the third verse of "Just Before the Battle Mother." Like Walter Kittredge's "Tenting Tonight," this song focuses on the sad aspects of war and the soldier's yearning for home and loved ones.

Keep Your Eyes on the Prize. This memorable freedom song was adapted from the great spiritual, "Mary Had a Golden Chain" (also called "Hold on"). "Keep Your Eyes on the Prize" was an important Freedom Riders' Song for SNCC (the Student Nonviolent Coordinating Committee)—and inspired an award-winning television documentary of the same name about the Civil Rights Movement.

Kentucky Babe. Over the years, a surprising number of songs have been written about life in Kentucky—and this minstrel lullaby is perhaps the most beautiful. "Kentucky Babe" was written in 1896— with words by Richard Buck and music by Adam Geibel.

Kumbaya. This beautiful folk tune is of African origin—and was brought by slaves to America in the early part of the nineteenth century. The word "kumbaya" is thought to be a dialect pronunciation of "come by here." The folk revival and freedom movement of the 1960s brought renewed fame to this lovely song—with popular recordings by the Weavers and other noted folk artists.

La Bamba. This traditional Mexican tune has enjoyed many years of popularity—and several revivals. Rock and roll star Ritchie Valens made a hit with "La Bamba" in 1959—and a movie of the same name based on his life was made in 1987. This film featured a soundtrack by the Latin-American rock quintet Los Lobos. Their version of this terrific Latin tune held the number one position on the charts for three weeks.

La Donna È Mobile. This spirited aria is from Giuseppe Verdi's opera *Rigoletto,* which was first performed in 1851. The opera is based on a melodrama by French writer Victor Hugo entitled *Le Roi s'amuse*. Francesco Maria Piave translated and adapted the play into an effective libretto. The gondoliers of Venice were known for finding out about choice arias—and spoiling their debuts by singing them before the opera opened. As a precaution, Verdi did not show the lead tenor the music for "La donna è mobile" until two days before opening night.

Let Me Call You Sweetheart. This classic love song was published in 1910, with words and music credited to Beth Slater Whitson and Leo Friedman. (Just one year earlier this team had a popular success with "Meet Me Tonight in Dreamland.") Soon after "Let Me Call You Sweetheart" was published, barbershop quartets throughout the country included the song in their repertoire of favorites. This beautifully crafted waltz is still widely known and loved today as a model work of its period.

Little Brown Jug. Attributed to Joseph E. Winner, this fun song first appeared in 1869. The Weatherwax Brothers popularized "Little Brown Jug" in 1911—and Glenn Miller made it world famous in 1939 with his popular swing arrangement.

Listen to the Mockingbird. Philadelphian songwriter and publisher Septimus Winner wrote the words to this great tune after he overheard it performed by its composer, Richard Milburn, a Black guitarist and whistler (and freelance barber). This minstrel ballad was published in 1855—and became a huge success in America and Europe. For years, its authorship was credited to a pseudonym of Winner's—Alice Hawthorne. Winner dedicated the song to bachelor President James Buchanan's niece and First Lady, Harriet Lane. Although this song is most often performed as a sentimental ballad, some of us remember it best as the jaunty theme music of "The Three Stooges."

Long, Long Ago. This sentimental ballad was written in 1833 by Thomas Haynes Bayly. Although "Long, Long Ago" is still well loved today in its original form—it also inspired the melody of the 1942 song hit "Don't Sit Under the Apple Tree (With Anyone Else But Me)."

Love's Old Sweet Song. This classic Victorian ballad was written in 1884 by G. Clifton Bingham and James Lyman Molloy. "Love's Old Sweet Song," has remained an American sentimental favorite for almost a century—and was featured in the 1952 musical film *Wait Till the Sun Shines Nellie*.

The Man That Broke the Bank at Monte Carlo. This charming character song first became popular in the English music hall, as performed by Charles Corborn. Written in 1892 by Fred Gilbert, the song is thought to portray DeCourcey Bower, a famous gambler of the period. The "Bwa Boolong" mentioned in the lyric refers to Paris's famous avenue, the *Bois du Bologne*. "The Man That Broke the Bank at Monte Carlo" was featured in the musical film *In Old Sacramento* of 1946—and is still considered a novelty classic today.

A Man Without a Woman. This traditional song first appeared during the 1890s. Its natural, jaunty rhythm made it a perfect subject for later ragtime and jazz arrangements. While other songs of the 1890s may now seem dated and quaint, "A Man Without a Woman" seems as fresh and natural today as it did a century ago.

The Maple Leaf Rag. Black-American composer Scott Joplin was a pianist at the Maple Leaf Club in Sedalia, Missouri, when he wrote this rag. It is easily the most popular and famous of all of his works—and indeed, the most successful ragtime composition in musical history. Sidney Brown added lyrics to the piece in 1903—but it is the instrumental version that remains well-known today. In 1974, Marvin Hamlisch featured "The Maple Leaf Rag" in the soundtrack of *The Sting*.

The Marines' Hymn. The melody of this stirring service song is based on the "Gendarme Duet" from Jacques Offenbach's opera *Geneviéve de Brabant* of 1867. The author of the lyrics is not known. "The Marines' Hymn" was published in 1918—and became a favorite of servicemen during World War II.

Meet Me in St. Louis, Louis. Lyricist Andrew B. Sterling and melodist Kerry Mills wrote this song to commemorate the St. Louis Exposition of 1904. This brilliant song has had a long popular career—and has been singled out time after time as a model work of its period. In 1944, it was made the title song in the classic musical film starring Judy Garland and Mary Astor. "Meet Me in St. Louis" enjoyed another revival in 1989 in the Broadway musical of the same name.

Melancholy Baby. Ernie Burnett composed the tune to this all-time favorite song and George A. Norton wrote the words. "Melancholy Baby" was first published in 1912 as "Melancholy"—and has since enjoyed countless popular recordings and performances. It was featured in the musical film *Birth of* *the Blues,* starring Bing Crosby and Mary Martin—and was also performed in the musical film *Both Ends of the Candle.*

The Memphis Blues. Copyrighted in 1910, this historic piece was W.C. Handy's first published blues. Lyrics by George A. Norton were added in 1912, when it became the campaign song of Memphis politician Edward Crump. "The Memphis Blues" enjoyed great popularity throughout the jazz era. In 1941, it was featured in the musical film *Birth of the Blues,* starring Bing Crosby and Mary Martin. This historic blues was also heard in the 1958 musical film tribute to W.C. Handy's life and work, *St. Louis Blues* (starring Nat "King" Cole and Eartha Kitt).

Michael, Row the Boat Ashore. This lilting Black-American sea shanty comes from the Georgia Sea Islands. First published in 1867, "Michael, Row the Boat Ashore" was rediscovered in the 1950s—and was subsequently recorded by several folk artists. One recording by the Highwaymen became a number one hit on the pop charts in 1961.

Midnight Special. This bluesy folk song is thought to memorialize the midnight run of the Golden Gate Limited, whose shining headlight could be seen by inmates of the Texas State Prison. "Midnight Special" was revived by Paul Evans, who brought it to position sixteen on the pop charts in 1960. Singer/songwriter Johnny Rivers also had a pop hit with this enduring song in 1965.

A Mighty Fortress Is Our God. This famous chorale was written in 1527 by Martin Luther, who based the lyric on Psalm 46. It became a popular battle song among Protestant soldiers of the time (who knew it as "Ein' Feste Burg Ist Unser Gott"). E.H. Hedge translated the song in 1853 and produced the familiar English version, "A Mighty Fortress Is Our God." Today, this classic hymn is performed in scores of languages throughout the world.

(On) Moonlight Bay. Lyricist Edward Madden (who wrote the words to "By the Light of the Silvery Moon") teamed with melodist Percy Wenrich to create this wonderful song in 1912. It has enjoyed many decades of popularity, including a Hollywood career. In 1940, "(On) Moonlight Bay" was featured in the musical film *Tin Pan Alley,* starring Betty Grable and Alice Faye. In 1951, it was featured as the title song in a musical film starring Doris Day and Gordon MacRae.

Morning Has Broken. This beautiful folk hymn, with a lyric by Eleanor Farjeon, became a favorite of singer/songwriter Cat Stevens—whose hit recording of the song stayed on the pop charts for eleven weeks in 1971.

My Old Kentucky Home. It's thought that this song was inspired by Harriet Beecher Stowe's popular novel, *Uncle Tom's Cabin,* which opens with this line: "Oh, goodnight, goodnight poor Uncle Tom, grieve not for your old Kentucky home." This great minstrel tune by Stephen Foster was published in 1853—and popularized by the Christy Minstrels. "My Old Kentucky Home" became the official state song of Kentucky in 1928—and is played each year before the running of the Kentucky Derby. It was also featured in the musical films *Swanee River* and *I Dream of Jeanie.*

Nobody Knows the Trouble I've Seen. This Black-American spiritual originated in Civil War times—and was popularized after the turn of the century. It's easy to see how early blues songs emerged from this type of mournful, down-to-the-ground spiritual.

Oh Freedom. This classic spiritual was used as a marching song by Black regiments of the Civil War. "Oh Freedom" was revived as a song of protest during the Freedom Movement, which inspired many new pertinent verses like "No more violence" and "Free to be honest."

Oh, Susanna. Written in 1848 by Stephen Foster, this minstrel song was immensely popular in its day—a particular favorite of the Gold Rush forty-niners as they travelled West in search of a claim. The widespread success of this song established Foster as a leading American songwriter. "Oh, Susanna" was featured in several films, including *Swanee River,* with Al Jolson and Don Ameche. The song enjoyed new popularity during the 1970s with pop singer James Taylor's classic recording.

Oh! You Beautiful Doll. This energetic novelty song was written in 1911 by A. Seymour Brown and Nat D. Ayer. It has since been featured in numerous musical films including *Wharf Angel, The Story of Vernon and Irene Castle,* and *For Me and My Gal.* This ever-popular standard inspired a musical film of the same name in 1949.

Old Folks at Home. Stephen Foster sold this song for fifteen dollars to E.P. Christy of the Christy Minstrels in 1851. The overwhelming success of this classic minstrel song put Florida's little Swanee River on the map, and established Foster as America's most important songwriter. "Old Folks at Home" is Florida's state song—and was featured in the musical film *I Dream of Jeanie,* starring Ray Middleton and Bill Shirley.

Old Hundredth *(The Doxology).* This beautiful song has been a mainstay of the Protestant hymnal for over four hundred years—and is considered the oldest English song still in popular use. The tune was composed for Psalm 134 of the *Genevan Psalter* of 1551 by Louis Bourgeois. Ten years later, William Kethe's metrical version of Psalm 100 provided the lyrics (thus the name, "Old Hundredth"). A century later, another version (sometimes known as "Praise God From Whom All Blessings Flow") featured the words from the last verse of Bishop Thomas Ken's *Morning and Evening Hymns.* Shakespeare mentions this popular hymn in *Merry Wives of Windsor.*

On Top of Old Smoky. This folk song comes from the Smoky Mountain region—so named for the mists which rise from the hills and hover in the valleys. It is based on an earlier folk song, "My Little Mohee," which may be traced to British sources. "On Top of Old Smoky" was repopularized in the 1950s with recordings by Burl Ives and the Weavers. Gene Autry also sang this song in the 1951 film *Valley of Fire.*

Over the River and Through the Wood. This song originally featured only the first and third stanzas—and was not associated with a particular holiday. When the second stanza was added some sixty years ago, "Over the River and Through the Wood" became a favorite Thanksgiving song.

Peg o' My Heart. This charming love song was written in 1913 by melodist Fred Fisher and lyricist Alfred Bryan—both accomplished and prolific collaborators. "Peg o' My Heart" was featured in *The Ziegfeld Follies of 1913*—and was an instant success. It enjoyed several popular recordings in the 1940s and was featured in the 1949 musical film *Oh, You Beautiful Doll.*

Play a Simple Melody. Irving Berlin wrote this memorable song early in his prolific songwriting career. It was published in 1914—and debuted that year in the stage musical *Watch Your Step.* "Play a Simple Melody" enjoyed wide popular revival in the 1950s—and was featured in the 1954 musical film *There's No Business Like Show Business.*

Pomp and Circumstance. Edward Elgar composed this stately march (Opus 39, No. 1) for the coronation of King Edward VII in 1901. The title is taken from Shakespeare's *Othello.* The original words (written by Arthur Benson) have long been forgotten—but Elgar's grand theme is used today as processional music at graduation ceremonies throughout the world. Few classical pieces ever make it to the pop charts—but this one did in 1961 with Adrian Kimberly's recording (retitled "The Graduation Song").

Poor Wayfaring Stranger. This traditional American ballad appears in "shape-note" hymnbooks of the early 1800s. Later versions of the song display the earthy, mournful character of other so-called "white spirituals." This song was repopularized during the folk revival of the 1950s.

Prayer of Thanksgiving. This hymn is based on a Dutch hymn melody which may be traced to the beginning of the seventeenth century. The English version, translated by Dr. Theodore Baker in 1894, is also known as "We Gather Together (To Ask the Lord's Blessing)"—and remains among the popular Thanksgiving songs in the Protestant hymnal.

Ragtime Cowboy Joe. This novel ragtime song was published in 1912. It was featured in the 1943 musical film *Hello, Frisco, Hello,* starring Alice Faye and John Payne—and again, in 1945 in *Incendiary Blonde,* starring Betty Hutton.

Rally Round the Flag. This Union battle song (published as "The Battle Cry of Freedom") was written in 1863 by George Frederick Root. At this point in the war, the Union Army was tired and depleted. The song was an instant success in the ranks—and did much to boost spirits in Union camps throughout the remainder of the war. Today, this historic song is a cherished reminder of the many brave Americans that fought and died for human freedom.

Red River Valley. This traditional cowboy song is based on a popular song of the 1890s, entitled "In the Bright Mohawk Valley," which may be traced to Canadian folk sources. The musical film *King of the Cowboys,* with Roy Rogers and Smiley Burnette, pays tribute to this favorite American ballad.

The Riddle Song. Also known a "I Gave My Love a Cherry," this traditional folk song emerged in the mid-1800s—and may be traced to various Elizabethan folk sources. This version of the song comes from the Kentucky mountain region—and enjoyed a popular revival during the folk movement of the 1950s.

Rock-a My Soul. This traditional Black-American spiritual originated in the early 1800s. Like other uptempo spirituals, "Rock-a My Soul" extols the redemptive power of prayer with contagious joy and excitement. Its powerful beat and syncopated melody make it a gospel choir favorite.

Sailing, Sailing. This sea shanty was written in 1880 by Godfrey Marks (also known as James Frederick Swift). Sometimes entitled "Sailing" or "Sailing, Sailing Over the Bounding Main," it remains today the best-known song of the sea in American history.

St. James Infirmary. This traditional blues first appeared in the 1890s as "Gambler's Blues." It enjoyed a popular revival in the 1930s—and was featured in the Broadway musical, *Blackbirds of 1934.* In 1941, "St. James Infirmary" was featured in the musical film classic *The Birth of the Blues,* starring Bing Crosby and Mary Martin. Over the years, prominent musicians have performed and recorded this terrific song in a variety of musical settings—including jazz, swing, blues—and even rock-blues.

St. Louis Blues. Alec Wilder, the songwriter and eminent popular song historian, once said, "I don't believe any American song is better known or has had more performances than 'St. Louis Blues.'" Indeed, this song is a classic entry in the annals of popular music. W.C. Handy (sometimes called "the father of the blues") wrote the music and lyrics in 1914. "St. Louis Blues" has since enjoyed worldwide popularity—as well as a distinguished Hollywood career. The song inspired the musical film of the same name in 1928, featuring Bessie Smith. It was the title song of another musical film in 1958, with Nat King Cole. In 1929, "St. Louis Blues" was featured in the musical film *Is Everybody Happy,* starring Ted Lewis—who appeared in another version of this film in 1943. In 1941, "St. Louis Blues" was featured in *The Birth of the Blues,* starring Bing Crosby and Mary Martin. Louis Armstrong and Ann Miller appeared in the 1944 musical film *Jam Session,* which also featured this enduring and popular blues.

Scarborough Fair. Also known as "Parsley, Sage, Rosemary, and Thyme," this folk song was brought to America by its earliest British colonists. "Scarborough Fair" enjoyed wide popular revival in 1966 with a recording by Paul Simon and Art Garfunkel. The following year, their version of "Scarborough Fair" was featured in the award-winning film *The Graduate,* with Anne Bancroft and Dustin Hoffman.

School Days. Will D. Cobb and Gus Edwards wrote "School Days" in 1907 after several other successful collaborations (including "Sunbonnet Sue," which was published the previous year). "School Days" is the world's most famous song about life at school—and is affectionately quoted in many songs, musicals, and films. In 1945, this sentimental favorite was featured in the musical film *Sunbonnet Sue,* with Gale Storm and Phil Regan.

She'll Be Comin' Round the Mountain. The Black-American spiritual "When the Chariot Comes" inspired this popular folk song at the turn of the century. It was a well-known dance and singalong song—and a favorite with railroad workers, who added several alternate verses.

Shenandoah. Like the Shenandoah River, this lovely shanty takes its name from a prominent American Indian chief. It recounts the tale of a fur trader who falls in love with the daughter of Shenandoah. Although the Shenandoah River courses mainly through Virginia, it is likely that this folk song originated among the traders travelling the Missouri River during the early 1800s.

(Around Her Neck) She Wore a Yellow Ribbon. Also known as "Around My Hat," this traditional song originated in the mid-nineteenth century. In its day, it was performed as a slow and sad ballad—but it enjoyed a wide popular revival during the 1950s as an energetic pop chorus number.

Shine On Harvest Moon. This beautiful barbershop favorite was written in 1908 by Jack Norworth and songstress Nora Bayes. "Shine On Harvest Moon" debuted in the *Ziegfeld Follies (1908)*. It was revived for the *Ziegfeld Follies (1931)* and enjoyed many popular recordings during the 1930s. It has been featured in several musical films over the years, including *Ever Since Eve, Nancy Goes to Rio,* and *The Eddy Duchin Story*. In 1944, it served as the title song in a musical film tribute to Nora Bayes.

The Sidewalks of New York. This rousing song (sometimes known as "East Side, West Side") has been a favorite theme song of New York City for almost a century. It was written in 1894 by Charles B. Lawlor and James W. Blake—and has since enjoyed countless performances and recordings throughout the world. "The Sidewalks of New York" served as the campaign song for Al Smith's Presidential run in 1928—and was featured in the musical film *Beau James,* starring Bob Hope, in 1957.

Silent Night. On Christmas Eve of 1818, the organ broke down in St. Nicholas Church in the village of Oberdorf, Austria. The curate, Joseph Mohr, quickly penned the words to this classic carol and asked the organist, Franz Gruber, to write the music. "Silent Night" was first heard at midnight mass that night with guitar accompaniment. This lovely carol is enjoyed in many languages throughout the world—and is a particular American favorite.

Silver Threads Among the Gold. The words to this beautiful song were written by Eben E. Rexford—and were published as a poem in a small Wisconsin newspaper. In 1873, melodist Hart P. Danks bought the poem from Rexford for three dollars and set it to music. The resulting sentimental classic remains popular to this day.

Sippin' Cider Through a Straw. This whimsical song was published in 1919 with words and music credited to Mack David and Larry Shay. The song was actually popular during the 1890s—and was inspired by the traditional cowboy song "Drinkin' Whiskey With My Pals." In recent years, "Sippin' Cider Through a Straw" was repopularized by Madison Avenue in a well-known series of beverage commercials.

Sloop John B. Originally a West Indian folk song, the "Sloop John B." captured the attention of the Beach Boys in 1966. Their recording of this classic tune stayed on the pop charts for ten weeks.

Some of These Days. This terrific jazz standard was written in 1910 by Black composer Sheldon Brooks. It was featured in several films, including the Marx Brothers' *Animal Crackers* and *Rose Marie,* starring Jeannette MacDonald and Nelson Eddy. "Some of These Days" became an immense commercial success when Sophie Tucker made it her theme song—but the composer never benefitted, as he had sold the song for a flat fee of thirty dollars at the time of publication.

Sometimes I Feel Like a Motherless Child. First published in 1918 (as adapted and arranged by Henry Thacker Burleigh), this Black-American spiritual is thought to have originated in the late 1890s. The lyric does not feature the typical Christian language and imagery found in other spirituals. Instead, the image of the wandering orphan serves as a powerful metaphor for one who has strayed from the faith.

Sourwood Mountain. This traditional dance tune comes from the Southern Appalachians—and takes its title from a section of the Blue Ridge Mountains of Virginia. No square dance in this area would be complete without a lively fiddle version of this fun song.

Springfield Mountain. Also known as "The Pesky Serpent," this is thought to be America's first homegrown folk song. It commemorates Lieutenant Thomas Myrick of Springfield Mountain, Massachusetts, who died of a rattlesnake bite in 1761 (and whose tombstone still stands today). Although this ballad is an authentic colonial product, it enjoyed a popular revival during the 1800s. In its original version, "Springfield Mountain" is a moralistic elegy about the untimely death of a young colonist. The most popular version is a gentle parody—and includes his hapless wife trying to "sip" the poison from his body with her "two ruby red lips." Some hilarious spoof versions also exist.

The Star-Spangled Banner. The words to our national anthem were written by Francis Scott Key— a witness to the British naval attack on Fort McHenry. After a night of relentless bombardment from enemy ships, the American flag still waved atop the fort at dawn. This experience inspired Key to write the poem "The Star-Spangled Banner" which was soon after set to the familiar English drinking melody, "To Anacreon in Heaven" (credited to John Stafford Smith). "The Star-Spangled Banner" was made the American national anthem in 1931 by an act of Congress.

Stewball. This traditional Irish ballad was first published in 1822 as "Skuball," after a famous horse of the day who won a big race against thoroughbreds without the benefit of a pedigree. The song was soon popular in America—and is traditionally performed as a country waltz with a steady, loping beat. Peter, Paul and Mary brought their charming version of "Stewball" to the pop charts in 1963.

The Streets of Laredo. Also known as "The Cowboy's Lament," this folk song is based on a similar ballad of Irish origin entitled "A Handful of Laurel," about a dying soldier. The sad fate of the young cowboy in "The Streets of Laredo" served as a strong warning to cowboys of the day that intemperance and wild ways could be fatal in the rough society of the American West.

Sweet Adeline. Undoubtedly the most popular barbershop song in history, "Sweet Adeline" was made famous in 1903 by the Quaker City Four—America's best-loved male quartet. Henry Armstrong was only seventeen years old when he wrote this brilliantly simple melody. Richard H. Gerard wrote the words and titled the song after the popular Italian opera star Adelina Patti (inspiring many American parents of the day to give their baby daughters this unusual and lovely name.)

Sweet Betsy From Pike. This traditional song was published anonymously in 1853—although the lyrics are sometimes attributed to John A. Stone. "Sweet Betsy From Pike" commemorates the rugged life of the Western pioneer in this amusing portrait of two hearty forty-niners journeying by wagon train from Pike County, Missouri, to California.

The Sweetheart of Sigma Chi. Byron D. Stokes and F. Dudleigh Vernor (both members of the Alpha Pi fraternity) wrote this melodious college song in 1912 as a tribute to the Sigma Chi sorority at Albion College. The song was repopularized in the late twenties—and may still be heard on college campuses throughout the country.

Sweet Molly Malone. This folk song originated in Ireland in the 1750s—and soon after became an American favorite. Over the years, the musical cries of the mongers of Dublin and London have inspired many songs—but none has captured as many hearts as "Sweet Molly Malone."

Swing Low, Sweet Chariot. A Black-American spiritual originating in the later part of the nineteenth century, this is perhaps the most widely performed song of its kind. In 1976, "Swing Low, Sweet Chariot" was featured in the hit musical *Bubbling Brown Sugar*.

Take Me Out to the Ball Game. Lyricist Jack Norworth and melodist Albert Von Tilzer wrote this song in 1908. The surging national interest in baseball made it an instant success—and today, it is known and loved as the unofficial theme song of this thrilling spectator sport.

The Teddy Bears' Picnic. This whimsical song was written in 1913 by John W. Bratton and James B. Kennedy. It enjoyed several recordings during the forties and fifties by popular vocal groups and solo performers, including Bing Crosby. Today, "The Teddy Bears' Picnic" is still a favorite novelty song—and Madison Avenue has even given it some national airplay.

Tenting Tonight. Walter Kittredge, a Northerner, wrote this famous Civil War song (sometimes titled "Tenting on the Old Camp Ground") in 1864. Unlike most other patriotic songs of the period, this ballad focuses on the futility and sadness of the war as viewed from both sides. There are several first-hand accounts of both Union and Confederate soldiers in different campgrounds uniting their voices over some distance in a rendition of this song. "Tenting Tonight" makes a powerful plea for "the war to cease"—and may be considered the most popular antiwar song in American history.

There Is a Tavern in the Town. Although once credited to William H. Hills, "There Is a Tavern in the Town" was published anonymously in 1883—and may be traced to Cornish folk sources. This lively song recounts the age-old story of love gone astray from a woman's point of view—and has been a favorite on the college campus for decades.

There'll Be a Hot Time in the Old Town Tonight. Also known as "A Hot Time in the Old Town," this song is attributed to two minstrel showmen—singer/dancer Joseph Hayden and bandleader Theodore Metz. The song first appeared in 1896 and soon became a favorite on the minstrel stage. In later years, Theodore Roosevelt's Rough Riders adopted the song as their unofficial anthem—and even sang a chorus of it as they charged San Juan Hill. In 1975, "There'll Be a Hot Time in the Old Town Tonight" was featured in Broadway's musical tribute to Bessie Smith—*Me and Bessie*.

This Train. The locomotives that blazed and thundered through the American South represented hope and freedom to many of its rural inhabitants. For many Black Southerners, the railroad track pointed the way to a better life in the more tolerant atmosphere of the industrial North. The "freedom train" and "glory train" appear in many Southern folk songs, but nowhere more vividly than in "This Train."

Tom Dooley. This traditional American ballad was a number one hit for the Kingston Trio in 1958—and remained on the pop charts for eighteen weeks. It is said that this song was written by Thomas C. Dula just days before he was hung for the murder of Laura Foster in North Carolina in 1868. Tom publicly confessed to the murder from the gallows—and his lover and accomplice, Annie Selton, owned up to the crime many years later upon her deathbed.

Toyland. Victor Herbert and Glen MacDonough created this whimsical song for the very successful musical *Babes in Toyland*—first performed in 1903. Along with "The March of the Toys," this song quickly became popular with the American public (especially among the young and the young at heart). Stan Laurel and Oliver Hardy starred in the 1934 film adaptation of *Babes in Toyland,* which inspired another movie in 1961.

The Trail of the Lonesome Pine. The scenic Blue Ridge Mountains of Virginia are portrayed in this touching love song. The words were written by Ballard MacDonald, and the music by Harry Carroll. "The Trail of the Lonesome Pine" tells the age-old story of separated lovers—and seems as simple and fresh today as it did when it was first heard in 1913.

Turkey in the Straw. This traditional fiddle tune is based on "Old Zip Coon," an early minstrel song which was published anonymously in 1834. The tune is thought to be of Irish origin—and became a mainstay of the American square dance. Over the years, "Turkey in the Straw" has inspired hundreds of different verses and adaptations, among them, "There Was an Old Soldier Who Had a Wooden Leg."

Under the Bamboo Tree. Composed by Black-American songwriter Bob Cole in 1902, this success-ful novelty song made its debut that year in the stage musical *Sally in Our Alley.* The song's lovely, syncopated melody and endearing portrait of Zulu romance captured the attention of the American public. In 1903, "Under the Bamboo Tree" was back on Broadway in *Nancy Brown.* The song enjoyed a popular revival in the 1944 musical film *Meet Me in St. Louis,* starring Judy Garland and Mary Astor. It remains today among the well-loved novelty songs of all time.

Wabash Cannonball. This hard-driving railroad song was the signature tune of Roy Acuff, the king of country music. Acuff starred in the original Grand Ole Opry—and introduced the nation to country music. Although the great train commemorated in the lyrics is long since gone, the song is immortalized in many popular recordings, as well as the 1941 dramatic film "Rolling Home to Texas."

A Wand'ring Minstrel. W.S. Gilbert and Arthur Sullivan wrote this beautiful ballad for their popular operetta *The Mikado.* Set in Imperial Japan, *The Mikado* was first performed in 1885 at the Savoy Theatre in London. "A Wand'ring Minstrel" is the theme song of the story's hero, Nankipoo, a handsome Japanese prince disguised as a poor travelling musician. Like other light operas created by this brilliant team, *The Mikado* was performed throughout the Western Hemisphere (in fact, copyright pirates mounted many unauthorized versions of their operettas, particularly in the United States). Other popu-lar songs from *The Mikado* include "The Flowers That Bloom in the Spring" and "Three Little Maids."

We Shall Overcome. The theme song of the Civil Rights Movement, the traditional "We Shall Overcome" was based on the C.A. Findley hymn "I'll Overcome Some Day" (1901). The music was anonymously adapted from another hymn, "O Sanctissima." In 1946, Black-American tobacco workers seeking better wages first popularized "We Shall Overcome" as a song of protest. During the sixties, this inspiring song was central to many meetings, marches, freedom rides, and sit-ins throughout the United States.

We Wish You a Merry Christmas. This Medieval carol recalls the time when troupes of strolling musicians went "wassailing" from door to door on Christmas Eve seeking coins and holiday fare. "We

Wish You a Merry Christmas" has enjoyed centuries of popularity. It is still performed widely today during the holiday season—and it remains the quintessential door-to-door carolling song.

When Irish Eyes Are Smiling. Many songs have been written about Ireland and Irish-American life—but this sentimental classic is perhaps the most memorable and universally well loved among them. The lyrics were written by Chauncey Olcott and George Graff, Jr.—and the music was composed by Ernest R. Ball. "When Irish Eyes Are Smiling" was first published in 1912—and was featured in the musical *The Isle of Dreams* in 1913.

When Johnny Comes Marching Home. This jubilant march was published in 1863 as "Johnny Fill Up the Bowl." It is attributed to Patrick S. Gilmore, Bandmaster of the Union Army. Gilmore was famous for the spectacular concerts he conducted in Boston—featuring the world's largest orchestra and over ten thousand singers. "When Johnny Comes Marching Home" has inspired countless arrangements and variations—and served as the title song of a musical film starring Allan Jones and Donald O'Connor.

When the Midnight Choo-Choo Leaves for Alabam'. Irving Berlin wrote this terrific song in 1912—just a year after his first big success with "Alexander's Ragtime Band." In 1938, both songs were featured in the musical film *Alexander's Ragtime Band,* starring Alice Faye, Jack Haley, and Don Ameche. In 1954, the songs were featured together again in *There's No Business Like Show Business,* with Ethel Merman, Marilyn Monroe, and Donald O'Connor. "When the Midnight Choo-Choo Leaves for Alabam'" is a high-spirited tribute to the deep South—and a charming portrait of eager lovers reunited at last in their home state.

When the Saints Go Marching In. This stirring spiritual became a favorite selection of the first Black-American jazz bands which proliferated at the beginning of this century in the American South. The song was performed and recorded by many top artists throughout the swing era—and might well be considered America's oldest and best-loved jazz tune.

Whiffenpoof Song. Meade Minnegerode and George S. Pomeroy (Class of 1910) wrote the words to this famous theme song of The Whiffenpoof Society—a male singing group at Yale College. The tune is attributed to Tod B. Galloway. The lyrics are adapted from Rudyard Kipling's poem "Gentlemen Rankers." This terrific college song was popularly revived in the 1930s—and was featured in the 1944 film *Winged Victory.*

Wimoweh. This rhythmic South African Zulu song (retitled "The Lion Sleeps Tonight") became a number one hit for the Tokens (featuring Neil Sedaka) in 1961. Robert John put it back on the charts for 13 weeks in 1972—and it remains today a popular novelty favorite.

Woke Up This Morning (With My Mind on Freedom). This very popular freedom song was originally entitled, "Woke Up This Morning With My Mind Stayed on Jesus." Like other traditional songs of faith, this rousing spiritual was easily adapted as a protest song.

Wondrous Love. The melody of this folk hymn is adapted from another traditional tune, "Captain Kidd." Alex Means, a Methodist minister, wrote the song's words in the early 1800s. "Wondrous Love" appeared in the shape-note hymnals of the period—and was widely performed at religious gatherings (called camp meetings) throughout the country. The simple power and beauty of this folk hymn has made it an enduring American favorite.

Yankee Doodle. The source of this favorite Revolutionary War song has long been a subject of debate. The melody was published in London as early as 1777—and is probably of English or Scottish origin. It has been said that Richard Shackburg, a British army surgeon, wrote the words while stationed in Albany in 1758 (although many alternate verses and parodies are known). During the revolution, the tune was also known as "The Lexington March"—and could be heard at many important battle sites, including Bunker Hill and Lexington.

The Yankee Doodle Boy. Inspired by the revolutionary war favorite "Yankee Doodle," George M. Cohan wrote this showstopper in 1904 for the musical *Little Johnny Jones*. Cohan not only performed this song himself in the title role—he also wrote and directed the show. The song was back on Broadway in 1968 in the musical tribute to his life and work, *George M!* "The Yankee Doodle Boy" has also been featured in several movies, including *Little Johnny Jones* (1929), *Yankee Doodle Dandy* (1942), and *The Seven Little Foys* (1955).

The Yellow Rose of Texas. Also known as "The Song of the Texas Rangers," this traditional song was one of Franklin D. Roosevelt's favorites. Although the song was written in 1858, it enjoyed a popular revival in the 1950s. "The Yellow Rose of Texas" was featured in the film *Night State to Galveston*, starring Gene Autry and Pat Buttram.

You Made Me Love You. This song was written in 1913—and has enjoyed decades of prominent performances and recordings. Melodist James V. Monaco and lyricist Joe McCarthy teamed to create this popular hit—which became a well-known showstopper for both Al Jolson and Judy Garland. "You Made Me Love You" is featured in numerous musical films, including *Broadway Melody of 1938, The Jolson Story, Syncopation,* and *Love Me or Leave Me.* Harry James used it as the theme song for his famous swing orchestra.

You're a Grand Old Flag. This song was first introduced in the 1906 Broadway musical *George Washington, Jr.* by George M. Cohan (who also appeared in the production). The song was an instant success—and has since enjoyed a long career as an American favorite. In 1942, it was featured in the musical film *Yankee Doodle Dandy*, starring James Cagney and Joan Leslie. "You're a Grand Old Flag" was back on Broadway again in 1968 in another great tribute to Cohan's life and work—*George M!*

You're in the Army Now. This traditional marching song of World War I provides a comic warning to the newly enlisted of the drudgery to come. The melody resembles a bugle call—and the trudge of tired boots is all but audible in the heavy march tempo.

INDEX

ABOUT THE AUTHORS

Amy Appleby is an award-winning entertainer and author based in Manhattan. A graduate of Yale University, Amy specializes in music history and popular music education. Her numerous published works include *You Can Play Piano,* You Can Read Music, *You Can Write a Song,* and *You Can Play Harmonica* from Amsco Publications, as well as The *Billboard Book of Songwriting*.

Jerald B. Stone has an extensive background in music and music education. He is musical director of the Light Opera of Manhattan (LOOM) and has enjoyed a long career as a choral conductor, educator, and musical director.

At the age of twenty-two, Mr. Stone became a staff member of the St. Louis Municipal Opera, where he began a career which has included more than one hundred musical productions in New York City, on tour, and in summer stock and educational theatre. Among the stars he has conducted are Pearl Bailey, Leslie Uggams, and Van Johnson.

Mr. Stone has been a coach and voice teacher in his private studio in New York City for thirty years. In addition, he was an adjunct professor at New York University's musical theatre program. He is listed in Who*'s Who in American Education*.